APPEAL

COUNTER THE COUNTERFEIT & BUILD A STRONG FOUNDATION FOR SUCCESS

Books are our best friends, is the adage we have grown up with. However, the pirates of piracy are continuously forging 'our best friends'. Our books and their supplementary online resources are copyrighted, and we don't lend any right-to-copy. Piracy is synonymous to stealing books.

Knowledge comes real, let's not encourage its counterfeit. Therefore, we appeal all our readers to discourage pirated books and **choose authentic ones**.

HOW TO IDENTIFY THE PIRATED BOOKS?

1 Cover and Spine

- Look and feel (new or used book)
- Blurred images on the cover
- Hologram pasted on front
- Defective spine (wrinkles) or air pocket at its bottom
- Unclear ISBN/bar codes
- Missing/non-operational Unique Coupon Code for exclusive access to McGraw Hill Edge

2 Text/Printing/Binding

- Uneven inking of pages
- Poor quality or blurred photographs/images/ charts
- Substandard paper quality and opacity
- Misaligned pages
- Missing pages
- Inferior binding quality

You can further watch this video on How to identify a pirated book

For more information about identifying piracy, visit **https://www.mheducation.co.in/piracy**

To report a pirated book, send 'Hi' on WhatsApp code given on the back cover or write to us at **support.india@mheducation.com**.

Reported pirated books are examined to combat their piracy.

Let's fight the Pirates of Piracy and resolve to go for original!

About the Authors

Sumesh Chahal has been mentoring and guiding students for the most prestigious Civil Services Examination for more than 10 years and has guided many IAS toppers over the years, including All India Ranks-1, 2 & 3. With over 10 years of experience, he specialises in guiding aspirants through the pivotal phase of personality development, the most crucial aspect of the Civil Services Examination. With his profound understanding of the Civil Services Examination, he stands as one of the foremost mentors in this field.

Animesh Pradhan an alumnus of NIT Rourkela, exemplifies dedication and excellence. He has secured an All-India Rank-2 in his very first attempt in the prestigious civil services examination. Animesh has set a benchmark for aspirants across the country. His journey is a testament to perseverance, hard work, and strategic preparation, making him a true role model for future civil servants.

Virupaksh Singh is an accomplished IAS officer and a remarkable achiever, having cracked the civil services examination twice with notable ranks. He secured AIR-49 in CSE 2023 and AIR-392 in CSE 2022. A graduate of the prestigious National Law University (NLU) Delhi, Virupaksh's dedication and resilience have set a high standard for civil services aspirants.

Shubham Jain is an esteemed IPS officer who secured AIR-152 in the CSE 2022. A graduate of the National Law University (NLU) Delhi, Shubham's academic excellence is complemented by his professional experience as an advocate. Before joining the Indian Police Service, he practiced law at the Supreme Court and various appellate fora in Delhi.

Comprehensive Coverage of both Old & New NCERTs from

Class 6th to 12th

NCERT COMPENDIUM

Indian Economy

One Stop Solution for UPSC & STATE-PSCs

Sumesh Chahal

Animesh Pradhan (AIR-2, CSE-2023)

Virupaksh Singh (AIR-49, CSE-2023)

Shubham Jain (AIR-152, CSE-2022)

McGraw Hill Education (India) Private Limited

Published by McGraw Hill Education (India) Private Limited
Registered Office: Anjana Complex No: 5/90 A, Butt Road, St. Thomas Mount, Chennai – 600016, Tamil Nadu, India

NCERT Compendium – Indian Economy

First reprint

Print Edition:
ISBN-13: 978-93-5532-736-9
ISBN-10: 93-5532-736-6

E-Book Edition:
ISBN-13: 978-93-5532-908-0
ISBN-10: 93-5532-908-3

02 03 04 05 06 MAG 28 27 26 25 24

Typeset at 22-B, Ground Floor, Near Karol Bagh Metro Pillar No. 112, Old Rajinder Nagar, New Delhi-110060 and printed and bound in India at Magic International Pvt. Ltd., Plot No. 26E, Sector-31, (Industrial), Site-IV, Greater Noida 201306

Cover Design: Gyanendra Swamy
Cover Image Source: Shutterstock

Visit us at: www.mheducation.co.in
Write to us at: support.india@mheducation.com
CIN: U80302TN2010PTC111532
Toll Free Number: 1800 103 5875

Preface

As authors, having spent several years researching economy and thoroughly investigating UPSC and State-PSC exams, we are proud to introduce **NCERT Compendium-Indian Economy**. This book is carefully designed for aspiring civil servants, offering a thorough understanding of economy for both the preliminary and main examination. This compendium is built on the rich knowledge found in NCERT textbooks from Classes VI to XII, covering the entire economy syllabus for UPSC and State PSC exams. We have closely adhered to the NCERT framework; however, our approach extends beyond just textbook content.

Each chapter is enhanced with analysis, interpretations, and perspectives to encourage deeper understanding rather than just memorisation. This focus on analysis empowers you to develop a deeper understanding of economic concepts, enabling you to answer the questions effectively. Each section of this book ends with carefully crafted MCQs which are meant to prepare you for the Prelims. Furthermore, there are also thought-provoking main examination questions which will make sure that you can frame good answers that are full of insights and are well-structured.

We have no doubt that if utilised properly during your preparation for UPSC CSE or any other State PSC examinations; then this NCERT Compendium- Indian Economy shall serve as a great guide towards achieving success. With dedication alongside having such an all-inclusive study material like this one by your side, there's nothing else left other than being confident enough because success will be yours.

Acknowledgements

The completion of this NCERT Compendium-Indian Economy fills us with immense gratitude. This project wouldn't have been possible without the invaluable contributions of several remarkable individuals. Sincere thanks to the economists and researchers whose insightful perspectives enriched the analysis and interpretations within this book. A special thanks also goes out to the countless UPSC and State PSC aspirants whose unwavering pursuit of knowledge continues to inspire educators like us. A heartfelt appreciation is extended to Shivam Kumar and Vikas Bhankhar for their thorough review and editing.

We are grateful for the support of our parents, family, and friends in our endeavours. We owe our special thanks to the team at McGraw Hill including Lalit Singh, Tanweer Ahmad, Nikhil Wadhera, Raman Vashisth, Suhaib Ali and others for their effort and unstinted cooperation in bringing out this book.

Contents

UNIT 1

Indian Economy on the Eve of Independence

In This Unit

Comprehensive and profound coverage of the following NCERT's chapter:

✓ NCERT Class- 11th (Indian Economic Development), Chapter- 1

Introduction

India was under the British rule for almost two centuries. The foreign rule changed not only political structure of India, but also the Economic structure of India. India, that used to be a vibrant economy prior to arrival of Britishers on its shores was reduced to a colonial economy providing raw materials to booming British industries and market for the finished British goods. India's own economy became stagnant which means that there was little or no growth in the overall sectors of economy. The impact of British rule on Indian economic sectors can be studied as followings:

Low Level of Economic Development under the Colonial Rule

- India was well known in world economy for its agricultural and manufacturing goods.
- Indian **textile (cotton and silk) industry was famous** for its high quality of craftmanship, especially Dhaka was famous for its **Muslins (*Dacca Malmal*).**
- The economic policies pursued by British Government protected the economic interest of Britain over Indians. As a result of this, India was transformed into an exporter of raw material and importer of British manufactured goods.
- Efforts to estimate the **National and Per capita income of India** during colonial rule was done by scholars like Dadabhai Naoroji, William Digby, G. Findlay Shirras, V.K.R.V. Rao and R.C. Desai.
- All these studies estimated that Indian **economic growth rate was less than 2%** and **per capita income growth rate was not more than 0.5%** per year in the 1st half of 20th century.

Agriculture Sector

- Indian economy under colonial rule remained agrarian as close to **85% of Indian population was dependent on agriculture sector.**
- The **agricultural productivity remained stagnant**, due to **British land settlement policies.**
- For example, in **Zamindari system** all the profits incurred from agriculture were taken by British government and Zamindars, leaving poor farmers with no surplus to trade.
- The terms and conditions of revenue settlements were made such that zamindars had **no incentives to invest in the development of agriculture.**
- **Repeated land seizures by Zamindar** officials for overdue rent turned them into ruthless **collectors who heavily exploited poor farmers.**
- There are some evidences of improvement of income **of some farmers because of commercialisation of agriculture**, but this rise in income remained short lived and acted adversely to farmers' plight.
- India's agriculture was **deprived of funding** for terracing, drainage, flood control, and soil desalination despite some advancements in irrigation.
- As the **replacement of food crops with cash crops** made farmers and sharecroppers vulnerable to hunger in case of disasters. It led to rise of cases of Famines in British India.

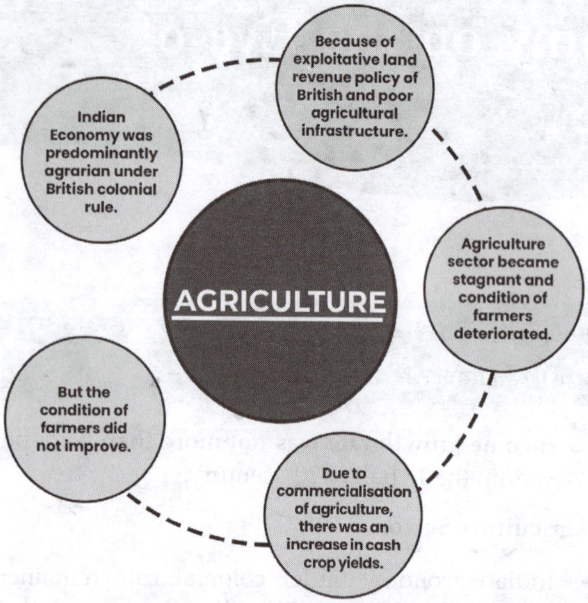

Agriculture Sector

Industrial Sectors

- Indian **indigenous handicraft industries declined** because of un**availability of foreign and domestic market** and also because of **competition from British** made cheap machine products.
- During 2nd half of 19th century, modern industries did come up on the western coast (in Maharashtra, Gujarat) in the form of textile industries and on the eastern coast (Bengal) in the form of **Jute industries**. Also, in 1907 **Tata Iron and Steel Company** (TISCO) started producing **steel**. However, the progress remained slow.
- But India was still dependent on Britain for Capital Goods import, because there was hardly any capital goods industry.
- The **displacement of wholesale indigenous handicraft** industry with few big factories had meagre contribution on India's GDP at that time.
- The **Public sector units** were limited to railways, communication, power generation, ports and some other industries.

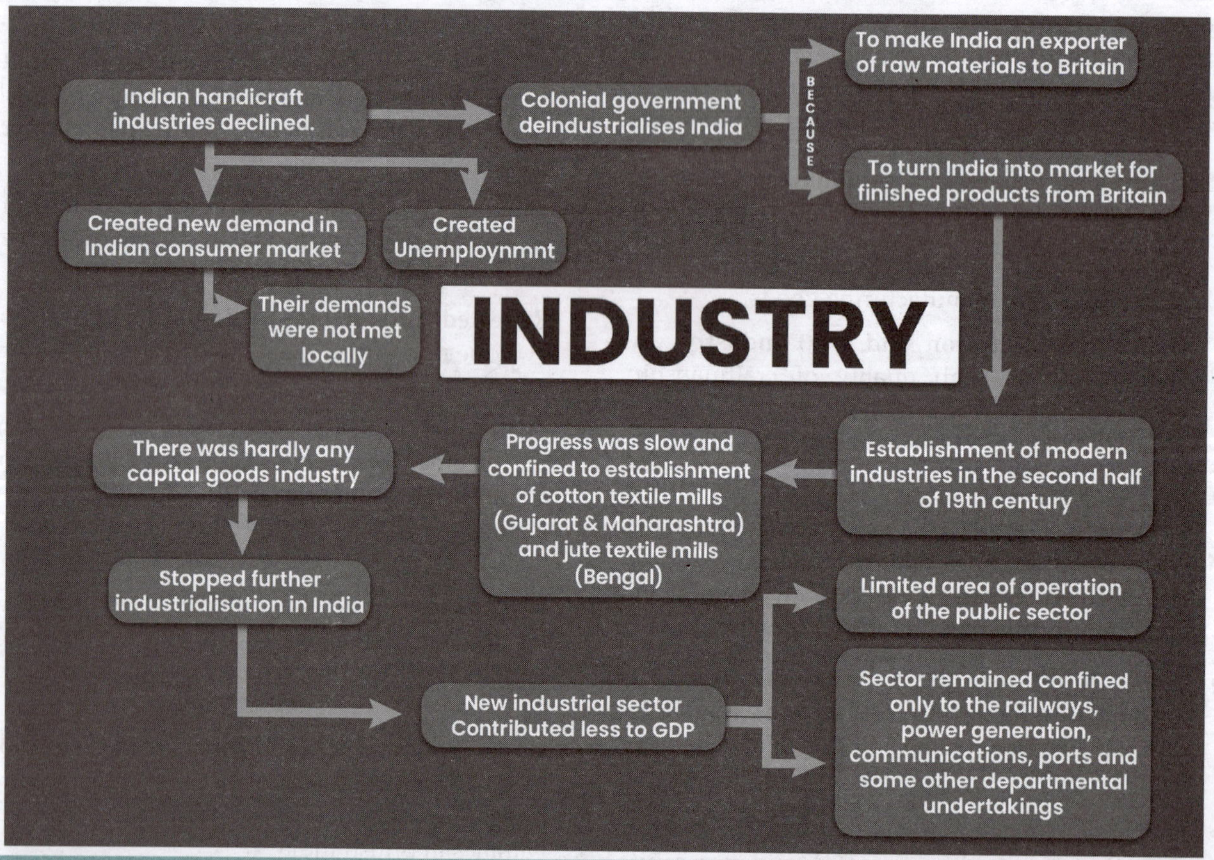

Industry

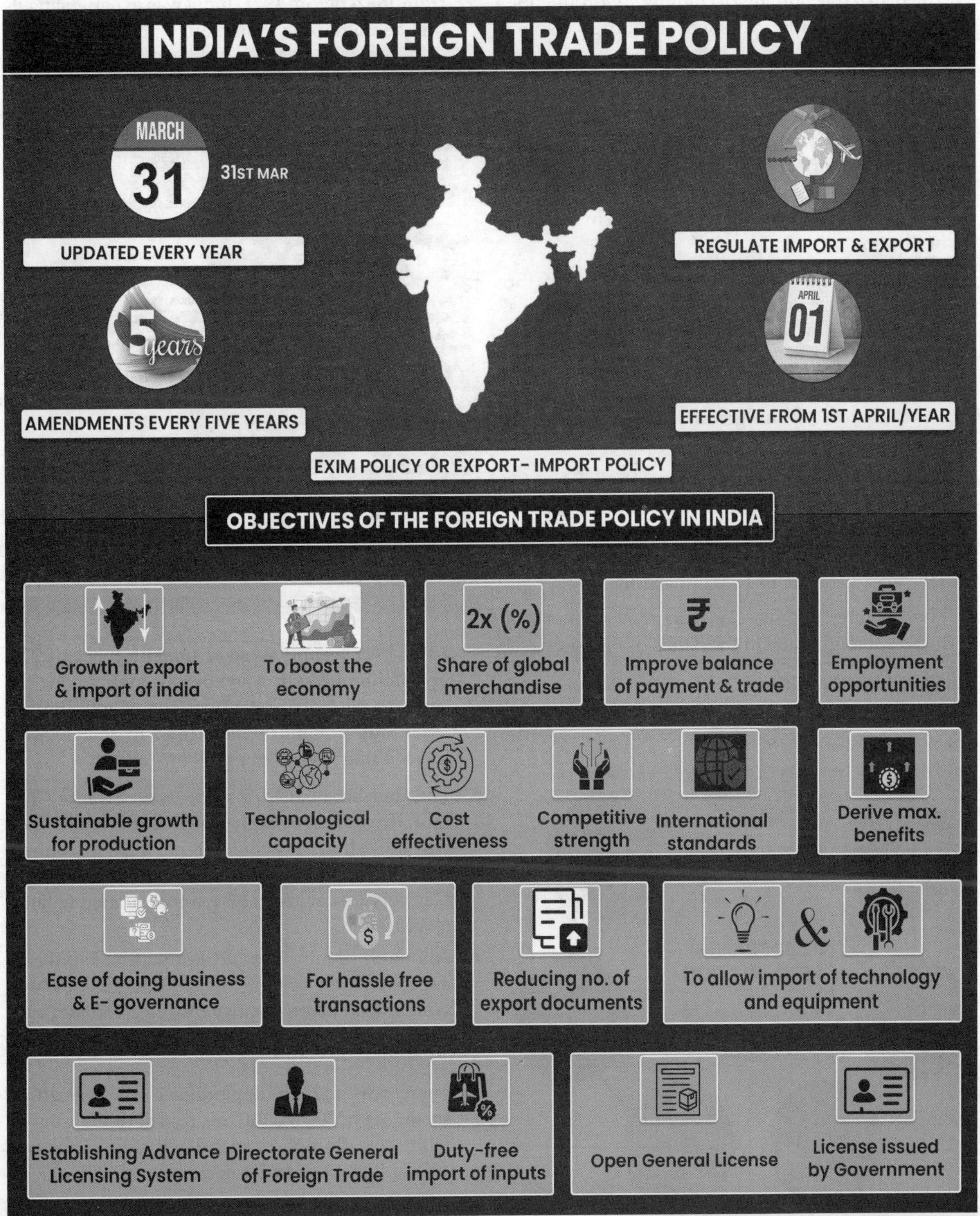

Foreign Trade

- Colonial rule impacted India's foreign trade also. The **restrictive policies** of commodity production, trade and tariff pursued by the colonial government adversely affected the structure, composition and volume of India's foreign trade.
- India became an **exporter of raw materials** like raw silk, cotton, wool, sugar, indigo, jute etc. and an **importer of finished consumer goods** like cotton, silk and woollen clothes and capital goods like light machinery produced in factories of Britain.
- India did trade with countries like Ceylon (Sri Lanka), China, Persia (Iran), but for all practical purposes **India's trade was under British monopoly.**
- India did produce surplus grains, clothes, sugar etc. at the cost of **hunger and deprivation of its population.**
- But **cost of this surplus went to Britain** for instalment payments of loan taken by British government on behalf of India, expenses on war, officers' salaries, rents of warehouses, ports etc. This was the **drain of Indian wealth.**
- The opening of Suez Canal in 1869 further put India's foreign trade in the hands of Britishers.

Demographic Conditions

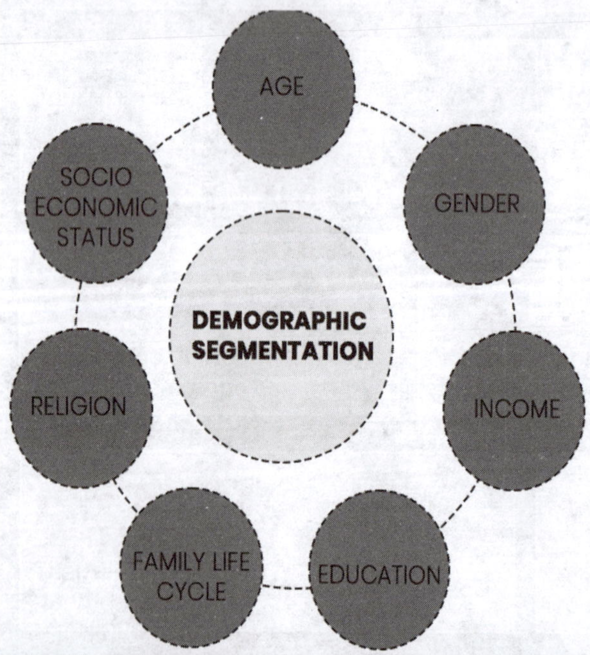

Demographic Segmentation

- British government started collecting census data **from 1882**. Before 1921, India was experiencing its **first demographic transition.**

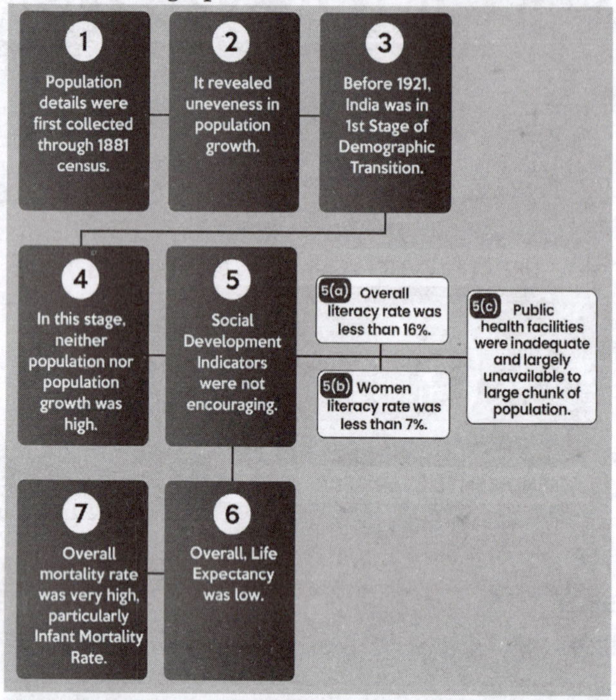

1st Stage of Demographic Transition

- **After 1921 second stage of transition** began. The **population growth was not that high** during the early decades of 20th century. The overall **literacy level was not more than 16%**, in that women literacy rate was not more than 7%.
- The **public health facility was meagre.** The **mortality rate was high**. The infant mortality rate was quite high at about 218 per 1000 in contrast with 35 per 1000 as per NFHS-5. Life expectancy was very low at about 32 years compared to latest 69 years.
- Although there was no estimate of poverty, approximation points out that there was **widespread acute poverty** during colonial rule.

Occupational Structure

- There was a high **dependence on agriculture sector** with **70-75%** of the contribution from it, while contribution of **manufacturing sector was 10%** and that of **service sector was 15-20%.**
- Another striking aspect was the **growing regional variation**. There was decline of dependence on

agriculture sector in Madras Presidency (present day Tamil Nadu, Andhra Pradesh, Kerala and Karnataka), Bombay and Bengal Presidencies with a commensurate increase in the manufacturing and the service sector. While at the same time states such as Orissa, Rajasthan and Punjab saw a rise in dependence on agriculture sector.

Occupational Arrangement

1. Agriculture: 70-75% workforce
2. Manufacturing: 10% workforce
3. Services: 15-20% workforce

Regional Variation

1. Decline in dependence on agriculture and increase in manufacturing & services sector in Madras, Bombay &
2. Increase in share of workforce in agriculture in Odisha, Rajasthan and Punjab.

Occupational Arrangement and Regional Variation

Infrastructure

- **Infrastructure development** like railways, roads, water transport, posts and telegraphs happened during colonial rule. But they mostly **served British interests** at the cost of Indian wealth.
- The roads were **developed to serve the mobilisation of army throughout India**. The absence of all-weather roads in India costed its people dearly during calamities.
- The **development of railway connected parts of India** with each other, people took long journeys through Indian landmass. The first Indian railways started in 1853 between Bombay to Thane for a distance of 34km. This led to breaking of geographical and cultural barriers. It also served for **transportation of finished British goods** to hinterlands and **bringing raw materials** from there.
- British government also undertook development of **inland waterways through digging of canals**, but due to development of railways this proposal was dropped.
- The development of **costly electric telegraph** was done to **maintain law and order** situation in India. The development of **postal service remained inadequate** mostly.

Conclusion

By the time India got its independence, the impact of two centuries of colonial rule was evident on Indian economy. While **agriculture sector was crushed** by inadequate investment and overdependence, the **industrial sectors were asking for more investment** and state's support. The **social sector was marred with problems** of acute poverty, unemployment, illiteracy etc. All these **problems demanded a welfarist approach** from India, which it developed in subsequent years.

Economic Status

- Growth of aggregate real output (real GDP) was less then 2%.
- Growth in per capita output per year was a meagre 0.5%.

Drain of Indian Wealth

Foreign Trade

- Exporter of primary products and importer of finished goods.
- Britain maintain a monopoly control over India's trade.
- Generation of export surplus used to finance wars and British administrative cost.

Status of Infrastructure

- Roads: Mobilise army and drawing out raw materials.
- Railways-break geographical & cultural barriers
- Railways, enhanced commercialisation of agriculture
- Waterways proved uneconomically and were unsatisfactory
- Electric telegraph-maintain law & order
- Postal Service - inadequate

Reasons for Agricultural Stagnation and Low Productivity During British Rule

- Land settlement system
- Revenue settlement
- Low levels of technology / irrigation
- Commerialisation of agriculture
- Lack of investment.

Indian Economy on the Eve of Independence

Poor State of Industrial Sector

- Systematic deindustrialisation
- Destruction of handicraft industries
- Slow growth of modern industries
- Lack of capital goods industries
- Inadequate industrial growth
- Limited role of Public sector

Primary Objective of British Trade Policy

- To reduce India into supplier of raw material for Britain's modern industrial base.
- To reduce India into consumer of finished goods from Britian.

Occupational Structure

- Agriculture Sector-75% of workforce
- Manufacturing Sector-10% of workforce
- Service sector - 15-20% of workforce
- Growing regional variations

Demographic Condition

- Uneven population growth
- Low Literacy rate (16%)
- Inadequate health facilities
- High mortality rate as well as infant mortality rate (218 per thousand)

Indian Economy on the Eve of Independence

TEST YOURSELF

Multiple Choice Questions

Q1. At the time of independence, the Indian economy was:

(a) Underdeveloped economy

(b) Developed economy

(c) Developing economy

(d) None of the above

Q2. In India, before the establishment of the British rule:

(a) Indian handicrafts enjoyed worldwide market

(b) India had an independent economy

(c) Livelihood was mainly based on agriculture

(d) All of the above

Q3. Who made the attempt to calculate India's national income during the British rule?

(a) Mahatma Gandhi

(b) B.R. Ambedkar

(c) Dadabhai Naoroji

(d) Lord Mountbatten

Q4. The main reason for stagnation of agriculture during the British rule was?

(a) Land settlement system

(b) De- industrialisation

(c) Technological deceleration

(d) Lack of irrigation facilities

Q5. Which of the following led to breakdown of handicrafts industry in India?

(a) Land settlement system

(b) De- industrialisation

(c) Technological deceleration

(d) Lack of irrigation facilities

Q6. With reference to India, which of the following is known as the Great Divide year?

(a) 1909 (b) 1921

(c) 1991 (d) 1998

Q7. In which year, the Railways was introduced in India?

(a) 1853 (b) 1854

(c) 1855 (d) 1857

Q8. In India, the colonials dominated jute industry in which area?

(a) Gujarat (b) Bengal

(c) Maharashtra (d) b and c

Q9. Which of the following statements is correct about Muslin?

(a) Muslin is a type of cotton textile which had its origin in Bengal, particularly, places in and around Dhaka.

(b) 'Daccai Muslin' had gained worldwide fame as an exquisite type of cotton textile and the finest variety of muslin was called malmal.

(c) Both 'a' and 'b'

(d) Neither 'a' nor 'b'

Q10. Who among the following notable economists estimated India's per capita income during the Colonial Period?

1. Dadabhai Naoroji 2. William Digby

3. V.K.R.V. Rao 4. R.C. Desai

Select the correct answer using the code given below:

(a) 1 only (b) 3 and 4 only

(c) 1, 2 and 4 only (d) 1, 2, 3 and 4

Q11. Consider the following statements:

1. The structure of India's present-day economy has its roots steeped in history, particularly in the period when India was under British rule.

2. The sole purpose of the British colonial rule in India was to reduce India to being a raw material supplier for Great Britain's own rapidly expanding modern industrial base.

Which of the statements given above is / are correct?

(a) 1 only (b) 2 only

(c) Both 1 and 2 (d) Neither 1 nor 2

Answer Key

Q1.	a	Q2.	d	Q3.	c
Q4.	a	Q5.	b	Q6.	b
Q7.	a	Q8.	b	Q9.	c
Q10.	d	Q11.	c		

Model Questions for Main Examination

Q1. What was the 'Drain of Wealth' during colonial British Raj in India?

Q2. Discuss the conditions of infrastructure and occupational structure during colonial period

UNIT
2

Indian Economy (1950-1990)

In This Unit

Comprehensive and profound coverage of the following NCERT's chapter:

✓ NCERT Class- 11th (Indian Economic Development), Chapter- 2

Introduction

On 15 August 1947, as India became independent it took the future of its economy in its own hands. The biggest challenge before the policy makers of India was that which type of economic model India should follow. India could have not followed the pure capitalist model as prevalent in Western countries due to presence of huge **inequalities and poverty**. At the same time despite being sympathetic to USSR's communist model, India chose not to follow pure communist model. **India decided,** in the **'Industrial Policy Resolution'** of 1948**, that it would follow the mixed model of economy**, where there would be a strong presence of public sector age at the same time private sector and democracy would also be present unlike communist countries. Indian Constitution aspired Indian state to become a **welfarist state.** This is why India went **for planned development** like a socialist economy, by **setting up Planning Commission** in 1950 chaired by the Prime Minister.

Types of Economic Systems

1. **Capitalist Society/Economic System:** The kind of commodities and services which are produced in these societies are determined by **supply and demand** in the market. Only consumer items that can be profitably sold in both domestic and international markets—i.e., **goods that are in demand—will be produced** in a market economy. For instance, bicycles will be created if there is a market for them, just as vehicles will be produced if there is a market for them. More labour-intensive manufacturing techniques will be employed if labour is less expensive than capital, and vice versa. The **distribution of products** generated in a capitalist society **is based on purchasing power**, or the ability to purchase goods and services, rather than what individuals actually need. Although there is a great need for affordable housing for the impoverished, this demand will not be met because the poor lack the means to support it. Jawaharlal Nehru, our first prime minister, was not fond of such a society since it meant that the vast mass of the population would be left behind and unable to raise their standard of living.

2. **Socialist Society/Economic System:** The **government determines** what commodities are produced in a socialist society based on the **demands of the populace.** Consumer preferences are not given much weight age, because it is believed that the government understands what is best for the nation as a whole. Socialist distribution is, in theory, **meant to take into account needs rather than means of production.** For instance, in a socialist country, everyone is **entitled to free healthcare**, unlike in a capitalist one. Since **everything is owned by the state,** there is strictly **no private property** in a socialist society. For instance, socialistic ideals dominate most economic operations in **China and Cuba.**

3. **Mixed Economy:** Most economies are mixed economies, i.e., the **government and the market together answer the three questions of what to produce, how to produce and how to distribute**

what is produced. In a mixed economy, the market will provide whatever goods and services it can produce well, and the government will provide essential goods and services which the market fails to do.

What is a plan?

- A plan delineates the **optimal allocation** of a country's resources.
- It ought to comprise both **overarching aims and particular targets** that must be accomplished within a designated timeframe.
- In India, **five-year plans** were implemented. This was a term we adopted from the former Soviet Union, the forerunner in national planning.
- The objectives specified in our plan documents prior to 2017 delineate not only the tasks to be completed within the five-year plan but also the tasks to be completed over a twenty-year period. This long-range strategy is known as the "**perspective plan.**"
- It is impractical to anticipate that every plan's objectives will be accorded equal weight across all plans. In actuality, there can be a **contradiction between the objectives.** For instance, if contemporary technology eliminates the need for labour, the objective of expanding employment may conflict with the purpose of introducing new technology.
- The planners have a very challenging task—**balancing the aims.**
- In India, we observe that various strategies place varying emphasis on different aims.
- India's five-year plans did not specify the amount of goods and services that must be produced. This is not required nor feasible and the previous Soviet Union attempts to do this were unsuccessful.
- If the plan is limited to the industries in which it has a dominant role—such as irrigation and electricity generation—and leaves the rest up to the market, that will be sufficient.
- **P.C. Mahalanobis** was a statistician and the **Architect of Indian Planning.** He formulated the **Second Five Years Plan** of India. He also founded **the Indian**
- **Statistical Institute** (ISI) based out of Calcutta and started the reputed journal, **Sankhya**, where discourse on statistics would be documented.

The Goals of Five Year Plans

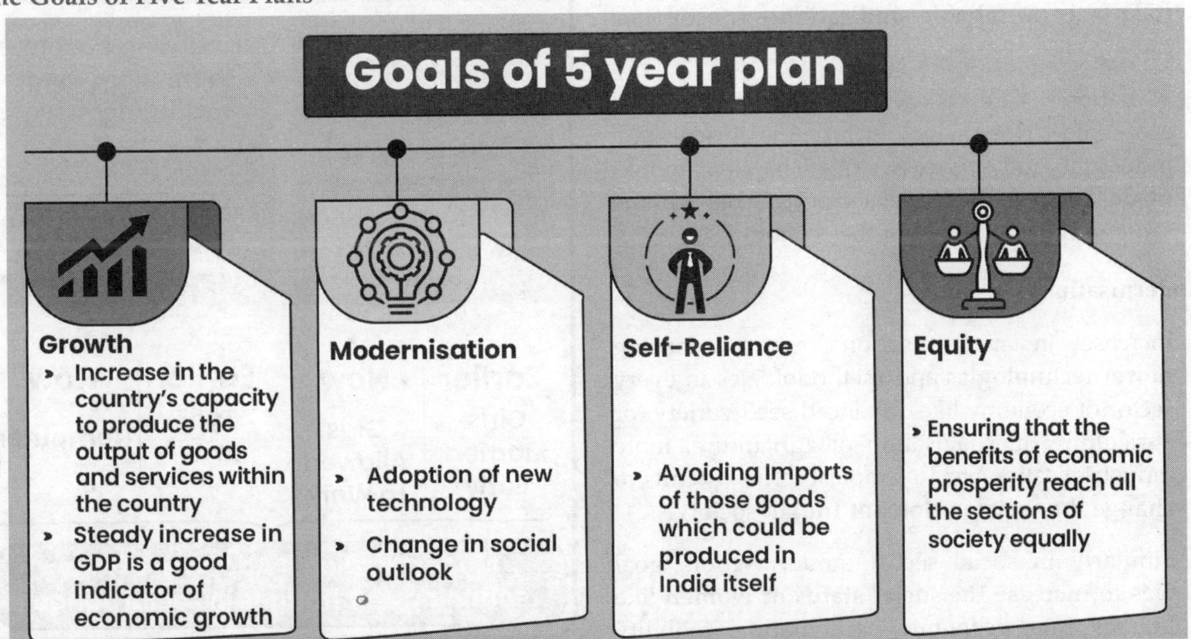

Goals of 5 Year Plans

The goals of the five-year plans are: **growth, modernisation, self-reliance and equity**. Planners had to make sure than the limited resources available at their disposal must be planned in such a way that maximum output could be gained.

Growth

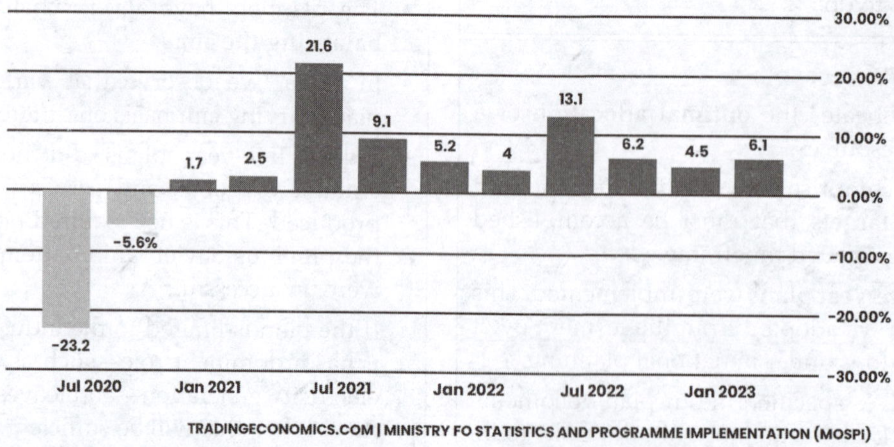

Economic Growth in India from 2020 to 2023

- It alludes to an **expansion in the nation's ability to generate** its own output of goods and services. It suggests an expansion in the quantity of banking and transit services, a larger stock of productive capital, or an improvement in the efficiency of both.
- A consistent **rise in the Gross Domestic Product (GDP) is a reliable indication** of economic growth.
- A nation's GDP is derived from its several economic sectors, which include the agricultural, industrial, and service sectors. The contribution made by each of these sectors makes up the **structural composition** of the economy.

Modernisation

- Increase in modernisation means **adapting newer technologies** and methodologies in every sector of economy like advanced seed variety for agriculture, mechanisation of agriculture, more industrialisation etc. In simplest terms it **tends to change the social outlook of Indian society**.
- Similarly in social sector modernisation, goal was to **increase the social status of women** like literacy rate, economic participation, mobility etc.

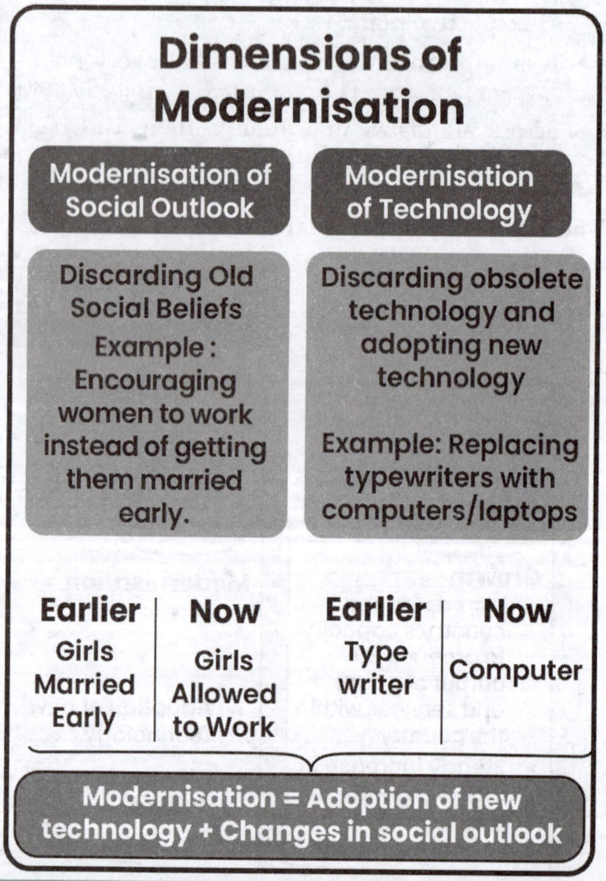

Modernisation

Self-reliance

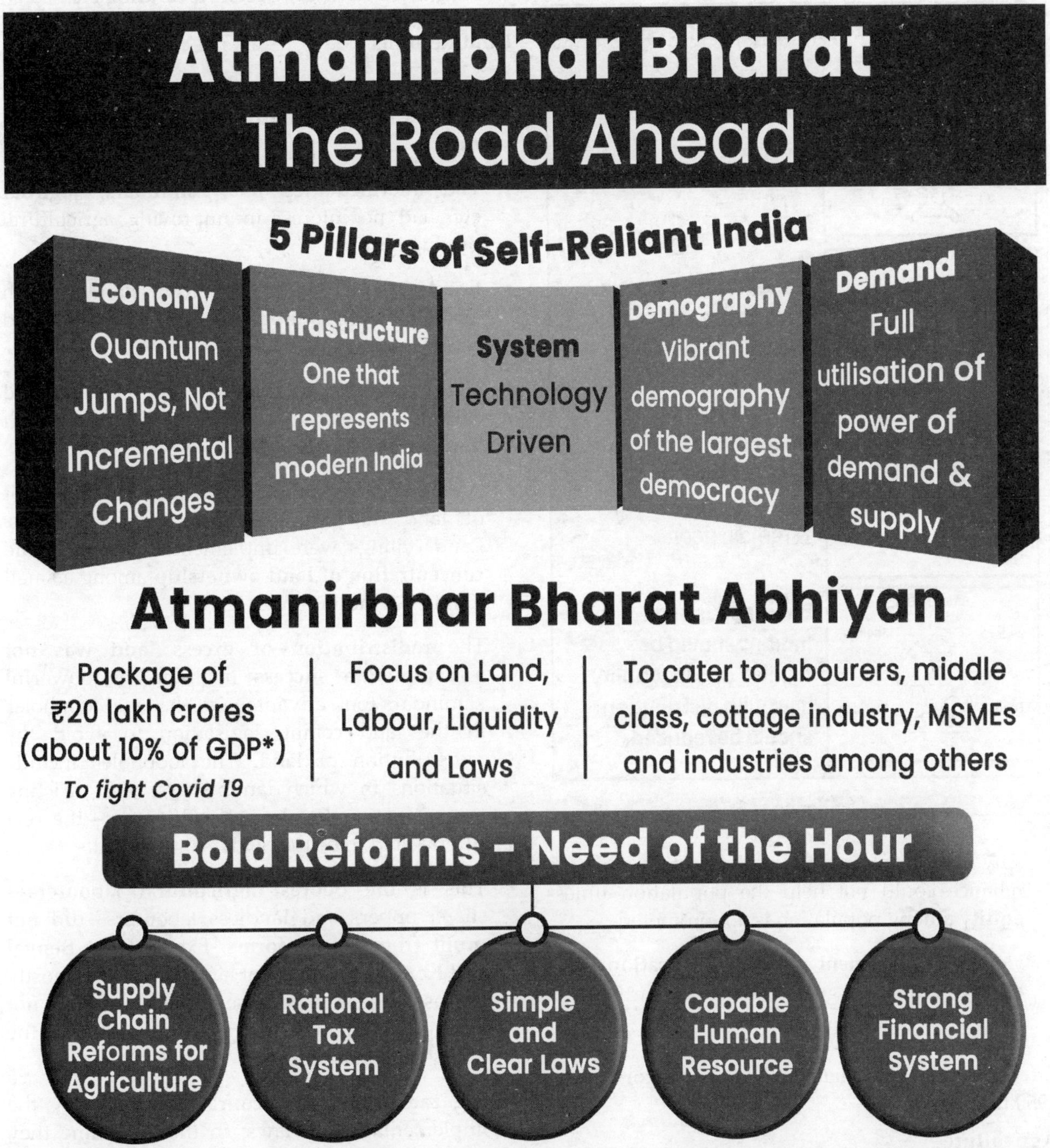

Self-Reliance

- The **first Seven Five-Year Plans** focused on **India becoming self-reliant**. For that import substitution of goods and services which can be produced in India was promoted.
- This was done to save India from foreign influences and to **increase self-respect of Indians.**

Equity

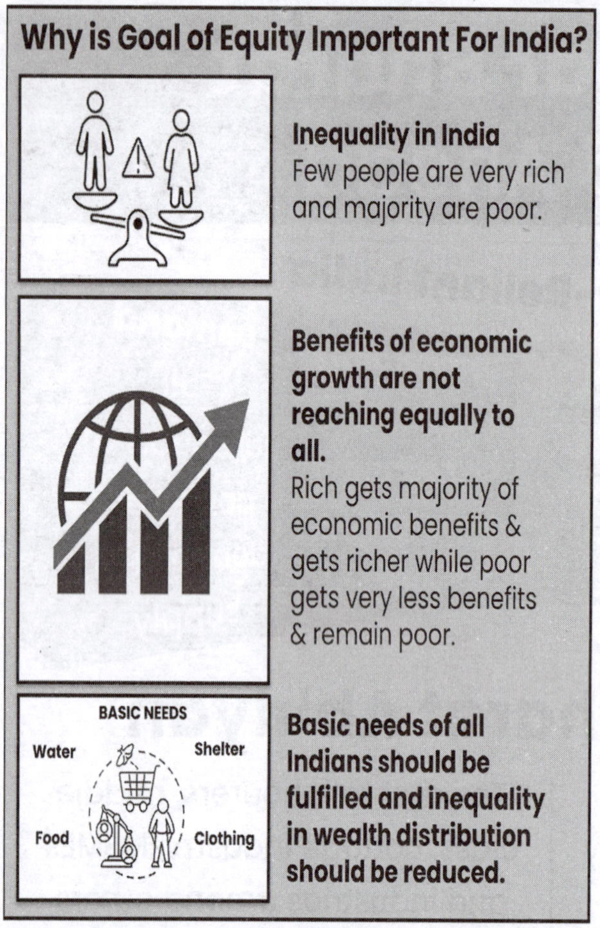

Equity

- Any amount of growth, modernisation and self-reliance could not help the population unless **equity** among population is not promoted.
- Hence **development and modernisation with equity** become the goals of the Five Year Plans in India.

Effect of Five Years Plans on Various Sectors (From 1950 to 1990)

Agriculture

The agriculture sector was most affected among all sectors of economy during colonial period. The low productivity in the agriculture sector forced India to import food from the USA. A large number of people were also dependent on it for their livelihood in the range of 70-75%. Reform in this sector **included land reforms, land ceilings, Green Revolution** etc.

Land Reforms

- At the time of independence, **India inherited a skewed land distribution system from colonial rule.**
- The intermediaries like **zamindars, jagirdar** etc. had no interest in improving agricultural productivity.
- **Equity** also dictated that surplus lands, which are held by big zamindars, must be re-distributed among tenants.
- Hence **abolition of zamindari** followed by **land ceiling laws** were passed by the Parliament and various State Legislatures.
- A land ceiling establishes the maximum amount of land that a single person may possess. Land ceilings were implemented to **lessen the concentration of land ownership** among a small number of individuals.
- The **redistribution of excess land was not a nationwide success** in India, as powerful zamindars took advantage of the legal loopholes in the land ceiling legislation to avoid the redistribution of land. The loopholes include situations in which landowners, after evicting tenants, claimed to be **self-cultivators—the real tillers**—and to be the owners of the land.
- This is **the poorest agricultural labourers**—sharecroppers and landless labourers—**did not profit from land reforms. Except West Bengal and Kerala**, this aspect of land reform was mostly not as successful because these **States did not have governments which were committed** to the policy of land to the tiller.
- **Big zamindars used court cases** to delay the implementation of laws, in the meantime they transferred much of the land to unknown persons and relatives to **evade land redistribution.**
- Regretfully, other States lacked the same dedication, and extreme **disparities in land ownership persist** to this day

Green Revolution

- The low income from agriculture sector and stagnation in productivity from this sector were disrupted by the Green Revolution.
- The Green Revolution involved use **of High Yield Variety (HYV)** seeds which boosted the yield. To take the maximum benefits from HYV seeds high use of **fertilizers, pesticides and irrigation** facilities were needed.
- Hence in its 1st **phase (from mid-1960s to mid-1970s)** the Green Revolution was **limited to more affluent** states like Punjab, Tamil Nadu, Andhra Pradesh etc. and to mostly big farmers cultivating wheat.
- Later in its 2nd **phase (from mid-1970s to mid-1980s),** the Green Revolution **spread to other states.**
- The result of Green Revolution was that it generated **marketed surplus** grains, which led **farmers earn profits**.
- This also **led India to become self-sufficient in grain production** and ended India's dependency on USA and other nations for food (especially USA's PL 480 scheme).
- The high marketed surplus made the **food prices drop**, which in turn helped poor people buy cheap grains. It also helped government to buy grains from farmers to **feed the vulnerable population.**
- **The limitation** of Green Revolution is that it **required more capital** input than conventional method and the HYV plants were more **prone to pest attacks**. This could be **problematic for small farmers,** whose whole investment could vanish if crops were attacked by pests.
- This risk is somehow mitigated by the services rendered by **research institutes established by governments**. Government has also waded in to help small farmers to get full benefits from HYV seeds by providing **cheap loans and subsidies on farm inputs.**

The Debate over Subsidies

- The continuation of subsidies in agriculture after so many years of introduction of Green Revolution is hotly debated in India.
- Some argue that subsidies were needed to overcome the fear among the farmers about the **uncertainty and risk involved in using new technologies.** Once the use of new technology starts reaping benefits, the **subsidies must be withdrawn** slowly. They also argue that the **subsidies are mostly helping fertilizer industry**, big and affluent farmers from rich states.
- On the other hand, some argue that withdrawing subsidies completely cannot be the answer as farming still continues to be a risky business for small and marginal farmers. Hence proposal for small and marginal farmers. Hence **targeted subsidies** must be the way forward rather than withdrawing it completely.

The Service Sector

As countries develop, they undergo a **structural change** in terms of the source of employment for the majority of population where employment in agriculture decreases and they move to the next sector i.e. industry and then the service sector. However, there is still a huge dependence of **workers on agriculture sector** in India (close to 50%). This is because of failure of manufacturing and service sectors to absorb the surplus workforce from agriculture sector. Further, the switch has not been from agriculture to industrial sector, but to the service sector directly. By 1990s, 40% of the Indian population was engaged in delivery of services and this phenomenon has only increased since the liberalisation, privatisation and globalisation reforms of 1991.

Industry and Trade

At the time of independence, **Indian industrial sector was limited to cotton and jute textile** industries and two or more steel plants. However, later the Five Years Plans emphasised **expansion of industrial sector's** contribution in overall GDP.

India's Merchandise Trade (USD billion)

Global Exports ↑ 44.6% y-o-y | ASEAN Exports ↑ 34.4% y-o-y

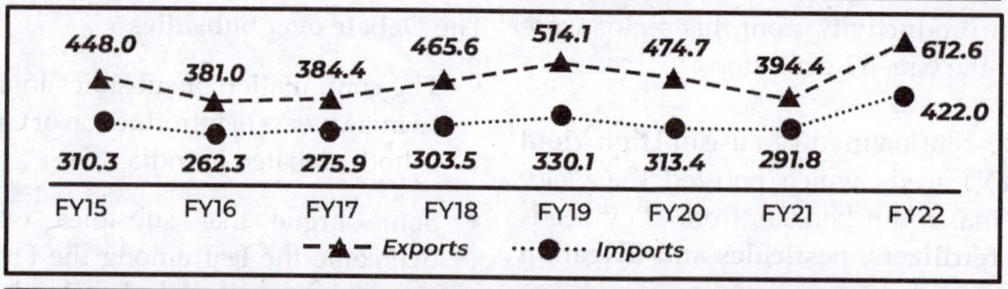

Export-Top 10 commodities	FY22 (USD billion)	% Growth(y-o-y)
Mineral fuels, oils and products	69.6	158.5
Gems and jewelry	39.3	50.1
Nuclear reactors, boilers, machinery	254	34.1
Iron and steel	22.9	88.9
Organic chemicals	22.0	22.8
Vehicles other than railway or tramway	20.2	42.0
Pharmaceutical products	19.8	44.9
Electrical machinery	194	0.1
Cereals	12.9	274
Cotton	10.8	70.7

Top trading partners (FY22) (% of total imports and exports)

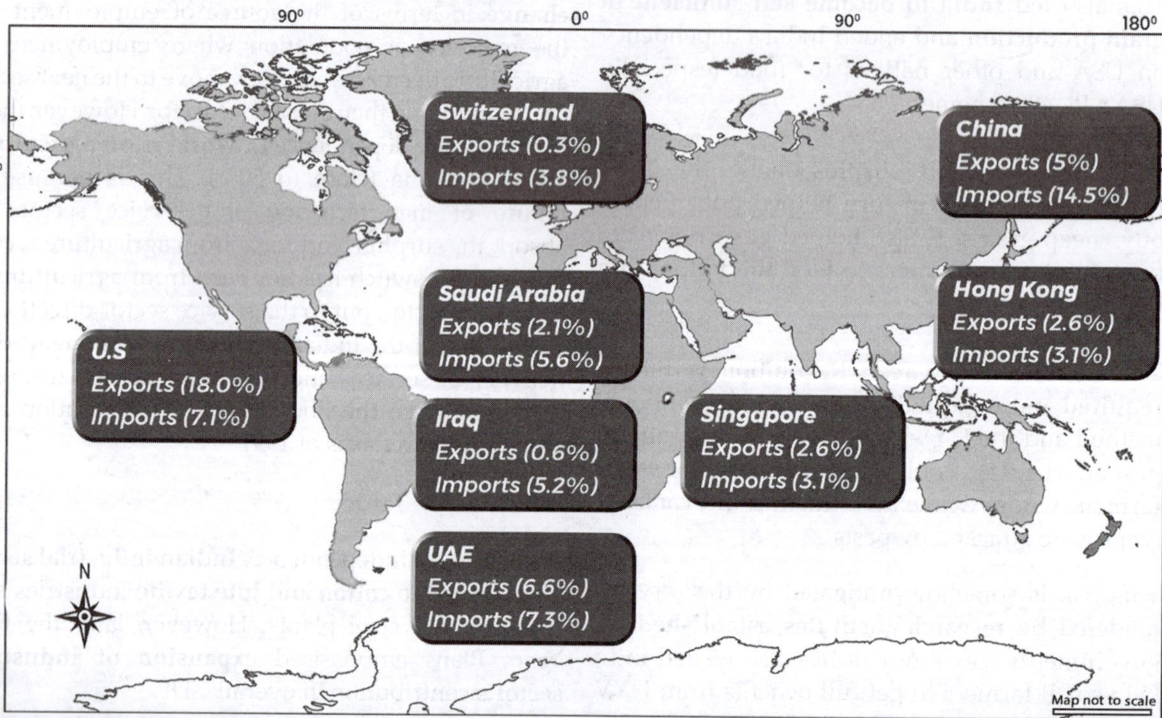

India's Industrial Sector: Some Key Indicators

Public and Private Sectors in Indian Industrial Development

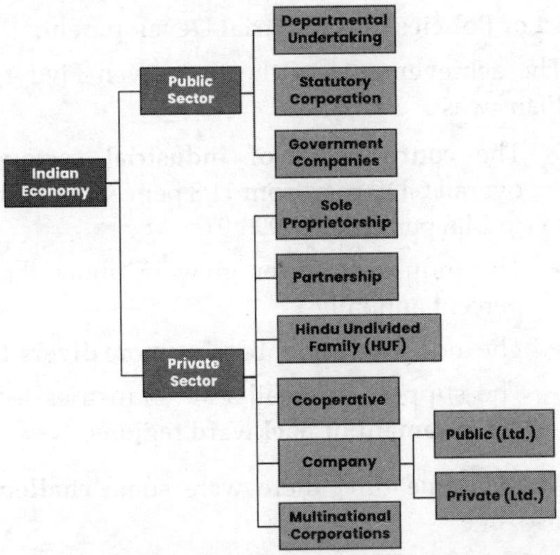

Public and Private Sector

- At the time of independence, the Indian private sector neither had enough capital to start new industries nor did they have enough market for private goods.
- For this reason and also for **equitable development of all regions**, state took upon itself the role to develop the industry sector in India.
- **The 2nd Five-Year Plan** took **special interest in development of industrial** sector, which involved much of public sector complimented with private sectors.

Industrial Policy Resolution 1956 (IPR 1956)

- The IPR 1956 was adopted to give state a commanding role in economy.
- A **socialism** influenced economic model was adopted **in the 2nd Five-Year Plan.**
- Here industries are classified in **three categories:**
  - The first category where industries are **totally controlled by state.**
  - The second category where state took responsibility of starting new unit **supplemented by private sector** later.
  - Third category where the **private sector can start industries.**
- The private sector was not given total freedom, they are required to take **license** to start new industry. This was done to promote industries in backward areas, for which license acquisition was easier and the purpose of **regional equality** is served through this.
- A **license** was also required for existing industry **for expansion or diversification** for current businesses. This was done to control the production of various goods and services as per needs of five-year plans.

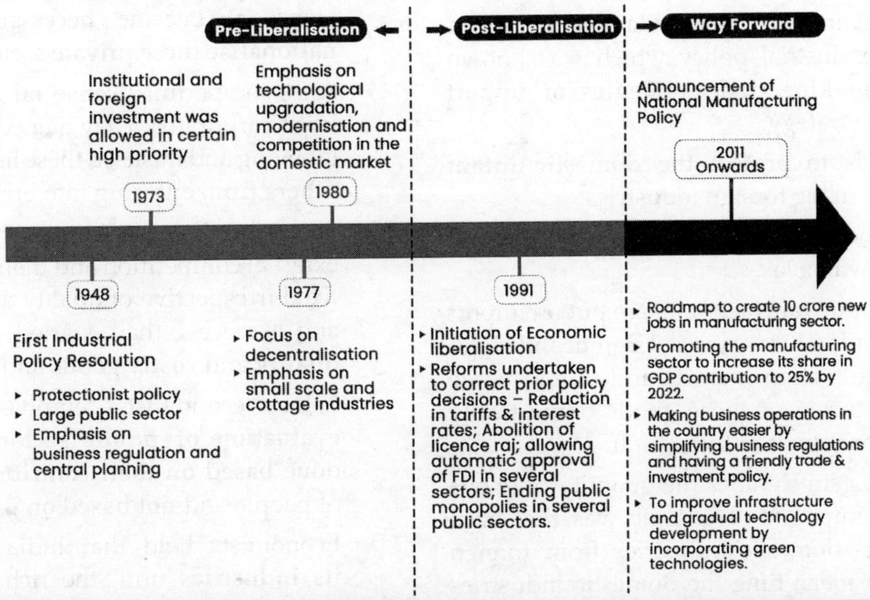

Industrial Policy

Small-Scale Industry

- In 1955, the **Village and Small-Scale Industries Committee**, also called the **Karve Committee**, noted the possibility of **using small-scale industries for promoting rural development.**
- A 'small-scale industry' is defined with reference to the **maximum investment allowed** on the assets of a unit. This limit has changed over a period of time. In 1950 the limit was 5 lakhs, which is up to 1 crore now.
- These industries are **labour intensive industries**. Hence some sectors were exclusively reserved for these industries.
- They were provided **incentives**, lower interest bank loans, low excise duties etc. to **flourish**

Trade Policy: Import Substitution Policy

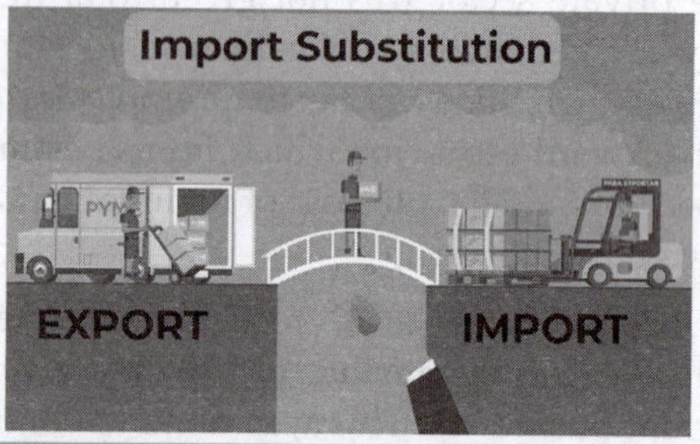

Import and Export

- The industrial policy was closely related with the trade policy.
- The **first seven Five Years Plans** emphasised on type of industrial policy which was known as **inward looking trade strategies or import substitution strategy**.
- The aim was to **protect the domestic infant** industries from big foreign industries.
- This was done with the help of **import duties and quota** tools available.
- The import duties are taxes that are put on import of foreign goods. This was raised significantly high to discourage foreign imports and to encourage the manufacturing of those goods domestically by foreign companies in India itself.
- The quota system signifies the quantity of goods that can be imported. The logic was that once state protects domestic industries from foreign industries in mean time the domestic industries would be able to save themselves on their own.
- There was no serious thought to promote exports till mid-1980s.

Effect of Policies on Industrial Development:

- The **achievements** of the first seven Five Years Plans was:
  - ➢ The **contribution of industrial sectors** in overall GDP **rose** from 11.8 per cent in 1950-51 to 24.6 per cent in 1990-91.
  - ➢ The industrial sector grew by more than 6 percent annually.
  - ➢ The industrial sector became more **diversified**.
  - ➢ The support to small-scale industries led to **development of backward regions**.
- At the same time there were some **challenges** also, like:
  - ➢ The **dominance of public sectors** in the economy, especially over the sectors where the private sector can deliver the same results more efficiently was being questioned by economists.
  - ➢ The state was still involved in some sectors like running hotels etc., where private sector could contribute more.
  - ➢ To counter this argument, it is said that the profit motive of private sector led to closing of sick and loss-making private ventures without considering loss of jobs of their employees. Hence it became necessary for state to **nationalise** these private sectors.
  - ➢ Also, the permit **license raj was misused** by large corporates. They gained license through lobbying and misused these licenses to **prevent others from entering** into business.
  - ➢ Also, since their businesses are protected from external competition and their customers were fixed irrespective of quality and cost of goods and services, they started **producing low quality and costly goods** and services.
  - ➢ Other economists emphasised that the **evaluation of public sector** units must be done **based on their contribution to welfare** of people and **not based on profits**.
  - ➢ Economists held that India should **protect its industries** until the rich and developed nations are doing it.

- These conflicting ideas led to the **economic reforms of 1991**, which changed the industrial as well as trade policy of India.

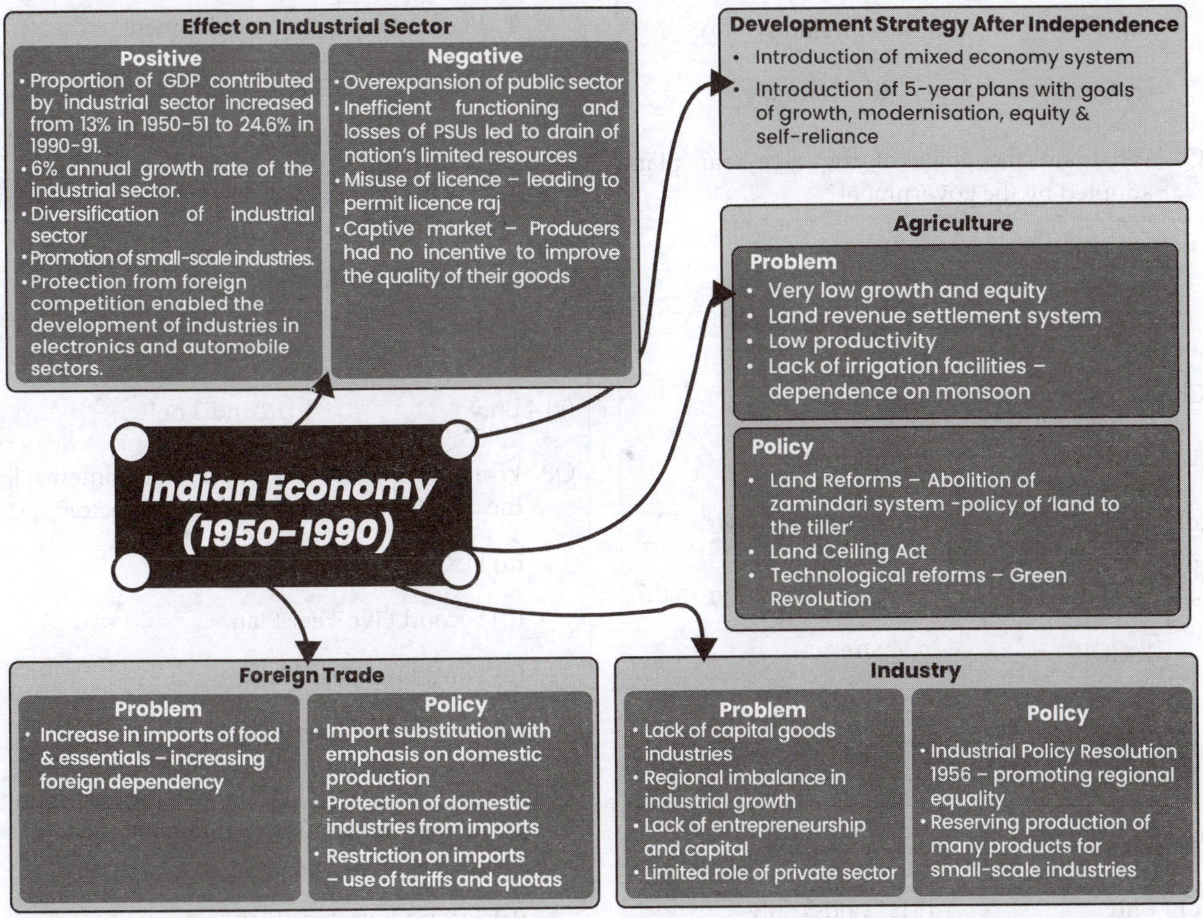

Conclusion

The progress that was made during first seven Five Years Plans was impressive. The colonial economy of India broke the shackle from old zamindari system and increased its productivity through HYV seeds. The expansion of industrial sector is impressive. The excessive state control and inward-looking economy were later criticised by many economists. This led to globalised, liberalised and privatised economy in India after the New Economic Policy (NEP) of 1991.

TEST YOURSELF

Multiple Choice Questions

Q1. What is the main objective for carrying out various economic activities?

(a) Competition (b) Public welfare

(c) Profit (d) All of the above

Q2. Which model of the economy did India decide to follow?

(a) Capitalist economy (b) Mixed economy

(c) Socialist economy (d) None of the above

Q3. The concept of Five-Year plans was borrowed from which country?

(a) USA (b) Ireland

(c) USSR (d) Germany

Q4. What are the goals of the Five-Year plan adopted by the government?

1. Modernisation 2. Growth

3. Self-reliance 4. Equity

Choose from the following options

(a) 1 and 2 (b) 1, 2 and 4

(c) 3 and 4 (d) All of the above

Q5. What is a good indicator of economic growth?

1. GDP 2. GNP

3. NNP 4. NDP

Choose from the following

(a) 1 and 4 only (b) 2 and 4 only

(c) 1 only (d) 1, 2 and 3 only

Q6. During the 1950s and 1960s what was the main economic policy followed by India?

1. Privatisation

2. Market liberalisation

3. Import substitution industrialisation

4. Export-oriented industrialisation

Choose from the following

(a) 3 only (b) 1 and 3 only

(c) 1, 2 and 3 only (d) 2 and 4 only

Q7. What was the major economic policy shift introduced in India in 1991?

1. Planned economic development

2. Import substitution industrialisation

3. Import-oriented industrialisation

4. Liberalisation, privatisation, and globalisation

Choose from the following

(a) 1 only (b) 1 and 4 only

(c) 4 only (d) 2 and 3 only

Q8. Which Five-Year Plan took a special interest in the development of the industrial sector?

(a) First Five-Year Plan

(b) Second Five-Year Plan

(c) Third Five-Year Plan

(d) Fourth Five-Year Plan

Q9. Which Five-Year Plan marked the beginning of planned economic development in India?

(a) First Five-Year Plan

(b) Second Five-Year Plan

(c) Third Five-Year Plan

(d) Fourth Five-Year Plan

Q10. With reference to land reforms in independent India, which one of the following statements is correct? (UPSC-2021)

(a) The ceiling laws were aimed at family holdings and not individual holdings.

(b) The major aim of land reforms was providing agricultural land to all the landless.

(c) It resulted in cultivation of cash crops as a predominant form of cultivation.

(d) Land reforms permitted no exemptions to the ceiling limits.

Q11. With reference to India's Five-Year Plans, which of the following statements is/are correct? (UPSC 2019)

1. From the Second Five-Year Plan, there was a determined thrust towards substitution of basic and capital good industries.

2. The Fourth Five-Year Plan adopted the objective of correcting the earlier trend of increased concentration of wealth and economic power.

3. In the Fifth Five-Year Plan, for the first time, the financial sector was included as an integral part of the Plan.

Select the correct answer using the code given below:

(a) 1 and 2 only (b) 2 only

(c) 3 only (d) 1, 2 and 3

Q12. The main objective of the 12th Five-Year Plan is (UPSC 2014)

(a) Inclusive growth and poverty reduction

(b) Inclusive growth and sustainable growth

(c) Sustainable and inclusive growth to reduce unemployment

(d) Faster, sustainable and more inclusive growth

Q. 13 Which of the following statements is/are correct about the Prasanta Chandra Mahalanobis?

1. He established the Indian Statistical Institute (ISI) in Calcutta.

2. He started a journal, 'Sankhya' which still serves as a respected forum for statisticians to discuss their ideas.

3. India's First Five Year Plan was based on the Mahalanobis Plan.

Select the correct answer using the code given below:

(a) 1 and 2 only (b) 1 and 3 only

(c) 2 and 3 only (d) 1, 2 and 3

Answer Key

Q1.	d	Q2.	b	Q3.	c	Q4.	d
Q5.	c	Q6.	a	Q7.	c	Q8.	b
Q9.	a	Q10.	b	Q11.	a	Q12.	d
Q13.	a						

Model Questions for Main Examination

Q1. Critically examine the impact of Green Revolution and what were its drawbacks?

Q2. Write down the effect of policies on industrial development?

UNIT 3

Liberalisation, Privatisation and Globalisation: An Appraisal

In This Unit

Comprehensive and profound coverage of the following NCERT's chapter:

✓ NCERT Class- 11th (Indian Economic Development), Chapter- 3

Introduction

We have learnt that India adopted a mix of Capitalist and Socialist economic system. This **mixed economy although helped in economic growth but led to an economic crisis** in 1991. India's state led economy and import substituting economy got into serious trouble, where it found itself unable to pay the external debt and import bill of petroleum products. This was known as the **balance of payment (BoP) crisis** of India and led to **New Economic Policy of 1991.**

Background:

- The origin of the financial crisis was in the **financial mismanagement during 1980s.**
- The **tax rates were very high**, because of that **tax evasion was prevalent**. This led to drop in the collection of tax revenue to the government.
- At the same time many developmental policies were started, which needed financial resources.
- These resources were mobilised through **internal borrowing** through RBI and general public and **external borrowing** through international financial institutions.
- The **suboptimal exports** from India and at the same time **rise in import bills** due to rise in crude oil prices were eroding the foreign reserves of India.
- The borrowing and huge fiscal deficits were not used to develop revenue generating operations rather they were used for **revenue expenditures** like giving salaries and pensions etc.

Why Governments Run into Deficit?

The **government raises money from a variety of sources**, including taxes and the operation of public sector businesses, to carry out its general administration and the implementation of various policies.

When **spending exceeds revenue**, the **government borrows** money from banks, citizens of the nation, and foreign financial institutions to make up the difference. When this borrowing happens routinely and persists over a long period of time, a deficit develops.

Since India is a petroleum importing country, it needs to earn foreign exchange (dollars) through exports to be able to purchase petroleum.

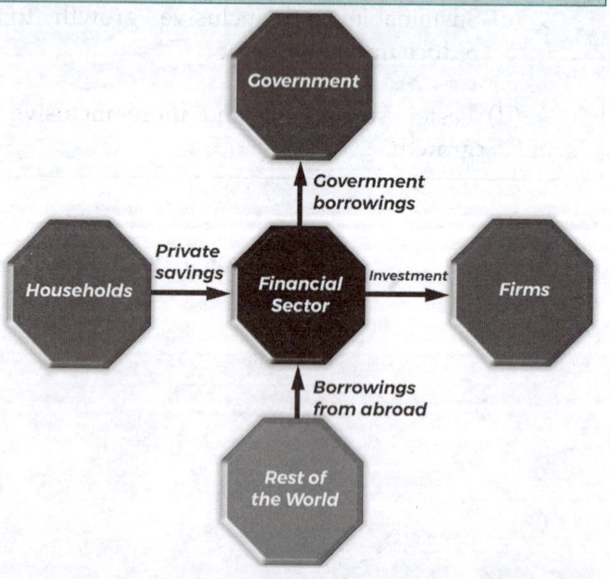

Structure of Financial Sector

- In late 1980s government's expenditure began to exceed its revenue and its import bills started becoming unaffordable.
- Prices of many essential goods rose sharply. Imports grew at a very high rate without matching growth of exports.
- The foreign exchange reserves saw a reduction to a point where they were unable to cover imports for longer than a fortnight.
- Additionally, there wasn't enough foreign currency to cover the interest that had to be given to overseas lenders.
- In India, this circumstance has led to a **"Balance of Payment (BoP)" crisis.**
- Furthermore, no nation or foreign financier was prepared to provide India with a loan.
- India approached the **International Monetary Fund (IMF)** and the International Bank for Reconstruction and Development (IBRD), also referred to as the **World Bank.** A $7 billion loan was given to India to handle the problem.
- **The IMF proposed several conditions,** among them the removal of trade barriers between India and other nations, the reduction of government involvement in various sectors, and the liberalisation and opening up of the Indian economy. After agreeing to those conditions, India introduced the **1991 New Economic Policy (NEP).**
- The NEP's policies can be classified into two groups:
    - ➢ One is **short term policies** for **stabilisation measures** to fight the weaknesses to avert any balance of payment crisis in future and to **bring down inflation.**
    - ➢ Others were **long term policies** for **structural reforms** to improve the efficiency of economy and to increase international competitiveness of India's exports. These reforms fall under three heads: **liberalisation, privatisation and globalisation.**

Liberalisation

It was realised that old laws and regulations were hindering the economic development, investment and export growth in India. A need was felt to reform these restrictive policies. Hence few reforms started in 1980s itself like export-import policy, technology upgradation, fiscal policy and foreign investment. But the reforms initiated in 1991 were more comprehensive and radical in its approach.

WHAT HAS CHANGED IN INDIA'S ECONOMY SINCE 1991

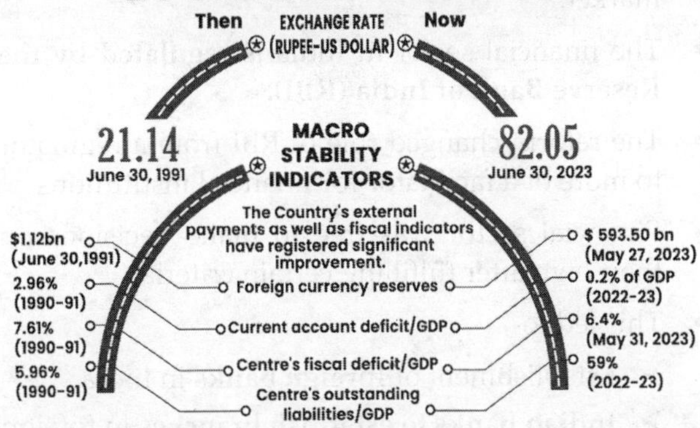

Liberalisation

Industrial Sector Reforms

- The regulation mechanisms were interfering in following four ways:
    - ➢ **Industrial licences** were mandated for industries to start new industries and to expand or diversify the current industry.
    - ➢ **Private sector was restricted** in many sectors.
    - ➢ Some **sectors were reserved for small-scale industries** only.
    - ➢ Controls on **price fixation** and distribution of selected industrial products.
- These restrictions were **deregulated in New Economic Policy as-**
    - ➢ Almost all product categories—including alcohol, cigarettes, dangerous chemicals, industrial explosives, electronics, aerospace, and medications and pharmaceuticals—were **exempt from industrial licencing.**
    - ➢ The only sectors currently kept for the public sector were those involved in the production of **atomic energy** and a few essential **railway transportation** operations.
    - ➢ A large number of products made by small-scale businesses were no longer reserved.

- The market was allowed to set prices in the majority of industries.

Financial Sector Reforms

- Financial sector includes financial institutions, such as commercial banks, investment banks, stock exchange operations and foreign exchange market.
- The financial sector in India is **regulated by the Reserve Bank of India (RBI).**
- The reform changed role of RBI from a regulator to more of a facilitator for financial institutions.
- Financial sector was free to make decisions on their own after fulfilling certain criteria.
- This led to-
  - Establishment of **foreign banks** in India.
  - **Indian banks to establish branches** in foreign countries.
  - **Foreign investment** limits in banks raised around 50 per cent.
  - Banks can expand their branches anywhere in India after fulfilling certain conditions, without asking the RBI every time.
  - This also led to more **liberalised conditions for Foreign Institutional Investors (FIIs)** to invest in Indian stock markets.

Tax Reforms

- Tax reforms are mainly concerned with the government's **fiscal policy**, which include governments' taxation and public expenditure policies.
- The revenue from tax collection consisted of two types of taxes:
  - **Direct taxes** like personal income tax, corporate tax etc. The **rate of direct taxes was reduced**. It was felt that higher taxes were the reason for tax evasion.
  - The **indirect taxes** are levied on commodities. Tax reform in this field involved simplification of various tax regimes through the Goods and Service tax.

Foreign Exchange Reforms

- Before 1991, fixed exchange rate system was followed by the Reserve Bank of India (RBI).
- The 1991 reform first devalued Indian currency to attract investment and raise Indian exports.
- Later, a stage is set to free the determination of value of Indian currency from government control.
- Now Indian currency is valued by market forces.

Trade and Investment Policy Reforms

- Reform in this sector involved **reducing the restriction on foreign imports** and increasing the **international competitiveness** of Indian domestic industries.
- Before 1991, the domestic industries were protected using **quantitative restrictions on imports**, through high tariffs on imports, providing import quotas etc. These regulations were reducing the **efficiencies of domestic industries**.
- The changes to trade policy intended to:

  i. removing quantitative import and export limitations,

  ii. lowering the tariff charges and

  iii. elimination of import licencing requirements. With the exception of businesses deemed hazardous or environmentally sensitive, import licencing was discontinued.
- In April 2001, quantitative limitations on the importation of manufactured consumer items and agricultural products were completely lifted.
- To make Indian goods more competitive in global markets, export tariffs have been eliminated.

Privatisation

- It means giving up control or direction of a business held by the government. There are two ways that government-owned businesses can become private: either they are sold outright or the government removes itself from administration and ownership of the public sector businesses.
- Disinvestment is the process of privatising public sector firms by offering a portion of their ownership to the general public.
- The government stated that the sale was primarily intended to **assist modernisation** and **enhance budgetary discipline**.

- Additionally, it was envisioned that the Public Sector Undertakings' (PSUs) performance might be raised by effectively using private resources and managerial skills.
- The government anticipated that privatisation would give FDI a significant boost.
- Additionally, the government has tried to increase PSU efficiency by granting them **managerial autonomy**. As an illustration, certain PSUs have been given unique status as **Miniratnas, Navratnas, and Maharatnas**.

Globalisation

- It is the result of a number of policies meant to change the world such that there is more **interconnectedness and dependency**.
- It entails the establishment of networks and activities that surpass geographical, social, and economic barriers.
- Globalisation endeavours to create connections so that events occurring far away can have an impact on events occurring in India.
- It is **establishing a borderless world**, uniting the planet. Elements that have made globalisation possible include:
- **Technology**
  - The acceleration of **technological advancement** has been a primary driver of the globalisation movement.
  - The cost and duration of the conveyance of commodities were reduced by rapid **transportation development**.
  - The advancement of **information and communication technologies** (ICTs) has facilitated quick and inexpensive information sharing.
  - Trade across borders is now simpler, less expensive, and more secure thanks to the development of **digital money transfers**.
- Liberalisation of Foreign Trade and Foreign Investment Policy
  - As a result, governments all around the world have **lowered trade barriers**, including tariffs.
  - Following the 1991 reform, India, which had previously imposed hefty import charges on foreign goods, began lowering its tariff rates.
  - **Economic liberalisation** is the process of lowering import taxes and expanding the economy to include greater foreign trade.
  - Following the establishment of the **World Trade Organisation (WTO) in 1995**, this liberalisation gained greater prominence.

Production across Countries

- Historically, the whole process of production has been confined to the borders of the producing nations.
- The producing nations imported only raw materials mostly from colonies and later from less industrially developed nations and exported finished goods. This trend started changing in 1990s and the diversification of production process out from producing nation's boundaries has started.
- **Outsourcing** is the practice of a company hiring regular services from outside sources, primarily from other countries, that were previously provided internally or domestically (e.g., security, computer services, legal advice, and advertising, which are all handled by different departments within the company).
- **Multinational Companies** (MNCs) are a new breed of companies that have formed. These are the businesses that own or manage output across multiple countries.
- MNCs setup their offices or production factories in a country or a region, where they find cheap labours.
- This is the reason for concentration of many western MNCs in cheap labour nations like China, Mexico, South East Asian nations, India etc.
- The whole **diversification of production processes** and outsourcing can **save up to 50-60 per cent of production costs.**

Interlinking Production across Countries

- An MNC starts production in a country if it finds-
  - Factory close to market,
  - Skilled and semi-skilled cheap labour,
  - Availability of other factors of production and
  - Government policies in their interest e.g., working condition of labour, incentives, tax breaks etc.

- After getting all above-mentioned assurances, an MNC would set up its facility. It will buy land, buildings and other assets which is like an investment, known as **Foreign Investment.**
- Sometimes, the production can be started in **joint venture with some local companies.**
- MNCs can bring latest technology and capitals to local companies.
- Local companies can provide them market reach and local expertise.
- For example, joint venture production of motorcycles by Hero-Honda. Here Honda motors infused its technology and capitals in this joint venture, which led to one of the most successful companies in India's two-wheeler segment.
- Another way of investment by MNCs is **directly buying the local companies**. In this way they can expand their reach in the local country. For example, Walmart acquired the Flipkart e-commerce company of India. After this acquisition, Walmart became one of the largest e-commerce companies in India.
- Another way of control of production for MNCs is through **large number of small suppliers.** For e.g., sports goods manufacturing companies like Nike and Adidas get their products from a number of suppliers manufacturing these goods under their brand names.
- In these ways production in these distant locations is getting interlinked.

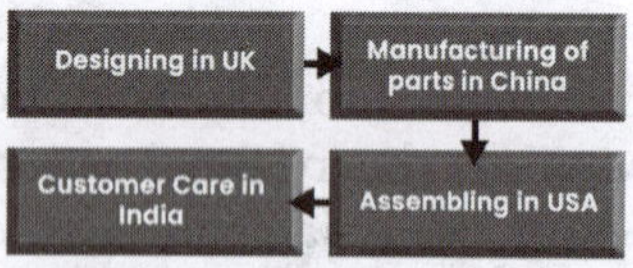

Interlinking Production across Countries

Foreign Trade and Integration of Markets

- Historically, foreign trade had been a major factor in connecting two countries.
- This interconnection became more visible, after the advent of globalisation on world stage.
- Now a product, which is manufactured in one country can be bought in another country.
- Because of opening of borders for trade, lowering of tariffs across borders, **flow of foreign trade has become smooth.**
- Consumers across the world are now getting more options on cheaper prices.
- For example, the handmade blankets were costly in India, which was the reason they were unaffordable for poor people. After introduction of factory made cheap Chinese blankets, the prices of blankets came down in India. Chinese blankets have now replaced the Indian blankets from Indian markets.
- In this way, **foreign trade is connecting the markets** or integrating the markets in different countries.

World Trade Organisation (WTO)

- Established in **1995**, the World Trade Organisation (WTO) **replaced the General Agreement on Trade and Tariffs (GATT).**
- The General Agreement on Tariffs and Trade (GATT) was founded in 1948 by 23 nations as the international trade body responsible for **managing all multilateral trade agreements** by **giving all nations equitable trading opportunities.**
- The WTO is anticipated to develop a trading regime based on rules, prohibiting countries from arbitrarily imposing trade restrictions.
- Its other goals are to safeguard the best possible use of global resources, increase service output and commerce, and **safeguard the environment.**
- The WTO Accords include trade in products and services. It aims to promote bilateral and multilateral trade by **removing tariff and non-tariff barriers** and giving all member countries **greater market access.**
- **India is a member of WTO.** Some scholars raise concern about futility of WTO, where developing countries are forced to open their market, cutting their subsidies on agricultural products, while developed countries escape the opening of their markets through non-tariff barriers and they are still giving huge subsidies to their farmers, which are hurting small and poor farmers in developing nations.

Impact of Globalisation in India

- Firstly, **MNCs have increased their investments in India** over the past 15 years, which means investing in India has been beneficial for them.

➢ MNCs have been interested in industries such as cell phones, automobiles, electronics, soft drinks, fast food or services such as banking in urban areas.

➢ These products have a large number of well-off buyers.

➢ In these industries and services, **new jobs have been created**.

➢ Also, **local companies supplying raw materials**, etc. to these industries have prospered.

- Secondly, several of the top **Indian companies** have been able to **benefit from the increased competition.**

➢ They have invested in **newer technology** and production methods and raised their production standards.

➢ Some have gained from **successful collaborations with foreign** companies.

➢ Moreover, globalisation has enabled some large **Indian companies** to emerge as **multinationals themselves.**

➢ Tata Motors (automobiles), Infosys (IT), Ranbaxy (medicines), Asian Paints (paints), Sundaram Fasteners (nuts and bolts) are some **Indian companies** which are **spreading their operations worldwide**.

- Globalisation has also **created new opportunities for companies providing services**, particularly those involving IT.
- However, for a large number of **small producers and workers, globalisation has posed major challenges.**
- **Competition and Uncertain Employment:** The demands of competitiveness and globalisation have significantly altered workers' life. These days, the majority of firms choose to hire employees "flexibly" due to increased competition. This implies that **employment security has vanished** for workers.

Impact of Globalisation in India

The Struggle to Make Globalisation Fairer

- The above points show that globalisation has **not benefited** everyone equally.
- Those who are already well off have benefited from globalisation.
- **Consumers** of consumer goods like mobile phone, electronics etc. benefitted as they got more options and **cheaper products**. The **small-scale manufacturers lost their market** because of competition from global giants.
- The skilled workers gained more opportunities due to globalisation. The **unskilled and unorganised workers lost the job certainty** and are forced to work on flexible jobs and on low wages.
- The **developed countries benefited** more from globalisation, as they got more open and broad market for their finished goods. Weak and **developing nations lost** as they did not get the reciprocity from the developed nations.
- Hence, people across the world are aspiring for a more balanced and fairer globalisation, which benefits all.
- In the past, massive campaigns by people and civil societies have led to change in rules and regulations related to globalisation in favour of developing nations **like Doha Development Agenda** etc.

Assessment of Indian Economy Post 1991 Reforms

Sector	1980-91	1992-2001	2002-07	2007-12	2012-13	2013-14	2014-15	2021-22
Agriculture	3.6	3.3	2.3	3.2	1.5	4.2	-0.2	3
Industry	7.1	6.5	9.4	7.4	3.6	5	2.8	11.7
Services	6.7	8.2	7.8	10	8.1	7.8	10.6	7.8
Total	5.6	6.4	7.8	8.2	5.6	6.6	7.2	9.7

Sectoral and Total GDP Growth Rates

Growth Rate

- Globalisation certainly contributed to a **marginal increase in the growth rate** of our economy as measured by gross domestic product (GDP).
- Average annual growth over the past three decades has been 5.8% per annum, slightly higher than 5.6% in the decade before 1991.
- But even this **growth has been uneven**, with the rate sliding to only 5% in the last decade.
- Clearly, our **growth acceleration was not sustained**, despite a pick-up in the pace of reforms.
- However, on a long-term comparison, the economy did better than its 4.1% average of the first 40 years of independence.
- But then, **growth rates are deceptive.** In any case, our first four decades should be compared with the pre-1947 phase, and on that score, we saw a massive growth improvement.

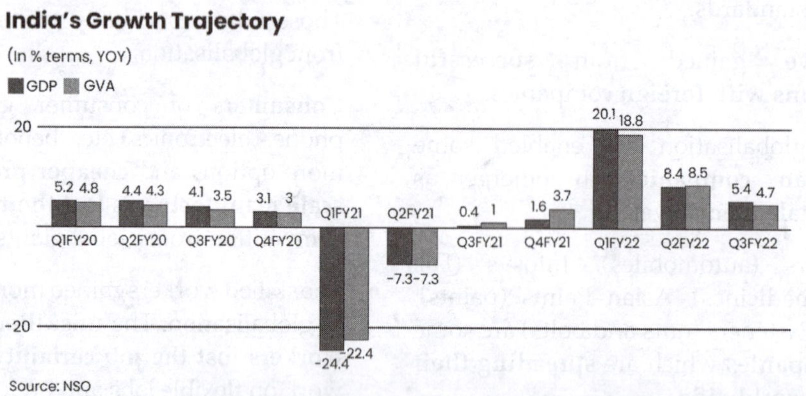

India's Growth Trajectory (in terms of %, Year on Year comparison)

Widening inequalities

- 30 years on, the situation for most of our population remains unchanged.
- The reforms created a class of rich entrepreneurs and a small but vocal middle class in urban areas, but it also contributed to widening **inequality**, which has worsened after 1991 and is now at its worst levels since 1947 in almost all dimensions.
- The **widening of disparities** is not limited to gaps across households in income or consumption, but also **between urban and rural areas, between laggard states and developed** ones.
- Disparities have increased even further in terms of **access to health and education** and several other human development indicators.
- On most of these, be it education, health, women's workforce participation and hunger, we remain at the bottom of any global chart of comparison. The logic of reforms meant that **expenditure on welfare and investment in human development were not a policy priority.**

Employment

- The situation is no different on employment, with our latest data suggesting an absolute decline on this count and a **historic rise in unemployment** rates.

- Today, a **declining share of wages in manufacturing** and for the economy as a whole means **sluggish growth in worker incomes**.
- Rising **informalisation and contractualisation** of the country's workforce has been a factor in the worsening of most workers' working conditions.
- The past decade has seen almost **stagnant real wages** for a majority of casual workers.

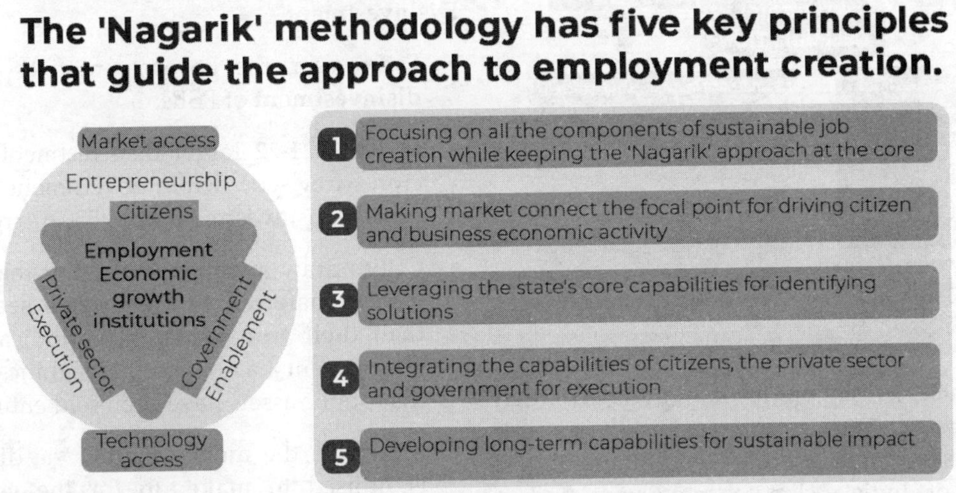

'Nagrik Methodology' for Employment Creation

Agricultural Reforms

- Agriculture has not benefited from reforms; in fact, **growth has slowed in this sector**.
- Public **spending in the agriculture sector has decreased** since 1991, particularly in the area of infrastructure e.g. roads, irrigation, electricity, market connections, and research—all of which were essential for the Green Revolution.
- Moreover, the partial **elimination of the fertiliser subsidy** has increased production costs, which has negatively impacted small and marginal farmers.
- **Numerous legislative changes** have affected this industry, including the removal of quantitative constraints on the import of agricultural products, the reduction of import levies on agricultural items, and the establishment of a low minimum support price.
- Due to **rising worldwide competition**, Indian farmers have suffered.
- Furthermore, production for the local market has shifted to **production for the export market**, with a **concentration on cash crops** rather than food grains, as a result of export-oriented governmental measures in agriculture. This drives up the cost of food grains.

Reforms in Industry

- Additionally, there has been a **downturn in industrial growth**.
- This is a result of the **declining market for industrial goods** for a number of reasons, including cheaper imports and insufficient infrastructure spending.
- Because of globalisation, developing nations must expose their economies to increased capital and products flows from industrialised nations, making their sectors more **susceptible to imports**.
- **Cheaper imports** have thus supplanted the market for homegrown products.
- **Imports are posing a threat to domestic** manufacturing.
- Due to insufficient investment, the **infrastructure facilities**, such as power supply, have **remained inadequate**.
- Thus, globalisation is frequently perceived as fostering the free flow of goods and services from other nations, which has a negative impact on domestic industries and job prospects in emerging nations.

- Moreover, **large non-tariff barriers** prevent developing nations like India from accessing the markets of wealthy nations.

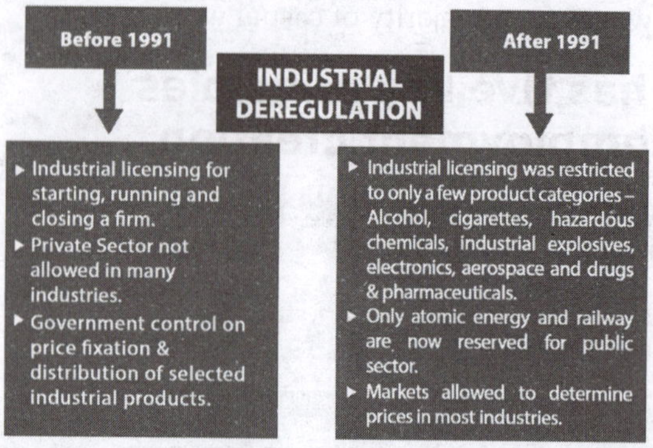

Reforms in Industry

- For instance, whisky produced in India is of high quality. Some, such as Amrut Distilleries, sell their whisky brands to the UK and other nations. Because of India's climate, producers find it difficult to scale up and comply with the three-year maturing period requirement, which causes spirits to evaporate. After a three-year maturing process, approximately 95% of the product is retained in Scotland and only 65% in India. Moreover, increased transportation and storage expenses may make manufacturing unprofitable.

Disinvestment

- Every year, the government fixes a **target for disinvestment** of PSEs.
- In **FY 2021-22** target disinvestment was 78,000 crores (revised), while government was able to achieve disinvestment of 13,530.67 crores.
- Critics draw attention to the fact that PSE assets were **transferred to the private sector for less than their true value.** This indicates that the government has suffered a significant loss and that public assets have been sold entirely.
- Moreover, the **money gained** via disinvestment is utilised **to make up for the government's lack of revenue rather than being employed to expand PSEs** and construct the nation's social infrastructure.

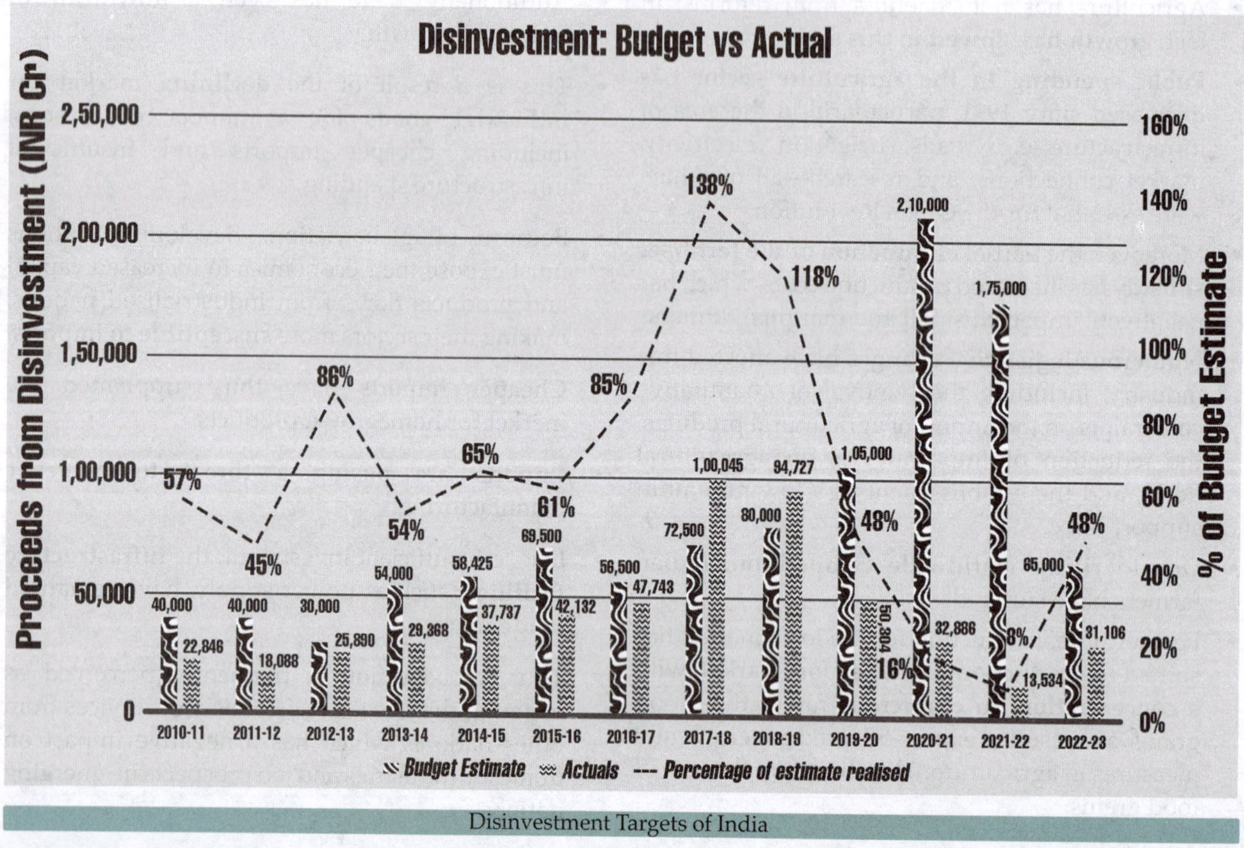

Disinvestment Targets of India

Reforms and Fiscal Policies

- Economic changes have **limited the expansion of governmental spending**, particularly in the social sectors.
- The government's tax revenue has not increased as a result of the tax reductions implemented throughout the reform period, which were intended to enhance revenue and reduce tax evasion.
- Furthermore, the reform attempts concerning tariff reduction **have curtailed the possibility of earning revenue from customs duties**.
- **Tax incentives are given to foreign** investors in order to draw in foreign capital, which further limits the potential to increase tax revenues. This has an **adverse effect on spending on welfare** and development.

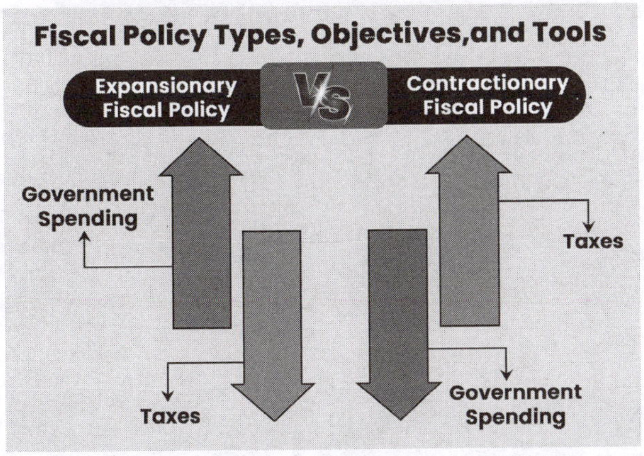

Fiscal Policies

Conclusion

- **Globalisation**, facilitated by policies of liberalisation and privatisation, has had both **favourable and unfavourable outcomes** for India and other nations.
- Some academics contend that globalisation presents opportunities for improved access to international markets, advanced technology, and the potential for developing nations' large businesses to become into significant actors in the international arena.
- Conversely, detractors contend that industrialised nations use globalisation as a tactic to open up new markets elsewhere.
- They claim that it has **jeopardised the identity and well-being of citizens of developing nations.**
- Moreover, it has been noted that market-driven globalisation has **increased the gaps in wealth** across different countries and groups of people.
- When viewed in the context of India, some studies have claimed that the crisis that broke out in the early 1990s was essentially the result of **ingrained inequality in Indian society**, and that the government's economic reform measures, which included a package of externally recommended policies, were implemented in response to the crisis and **made the inequality even worse**.
- Moreover, **only high-income groups have benefited** from the increase in income and quality of consumption, and the **growth has only been concentrated in a few key areas** of the services sector, such as trade, real estate, entertainment, finance, telecommunication, information technology, and travel and hospitality services, as opposed to vital industries like agriculture and industry, which support millions of people nationwide.

TEST YOURSELF

Multiple Choice Questions

Q1. With reference to the Indian economy after the 1991 economic liberalisation, consider the following statements: (UPSC- 2020)

1. Worker productivity (Rs. per worker at 2004 — 05 prices) increased in urban areas while it decreased in rural areas.
2. The percentage share of rural areas in the workforce steadily increased.
3. In rural areas, the growth in non-farm economy increased.
4. The growth rate in rural employment decreased.

Which of the statements given above is / are correct?

(a) 1 and 2 only (b) 3 and 4 only

(c) 3 only (d) 1, 2 and 4 only

Q2. Which of the following has/have occurred in India after its liberalisation of economic policies in 1991? (UPSC - 2017)

1. Share of agriculture in GDP increased enormously.
2. Share of India's exports in world trade increased.
3. FDI inflows increased.
4. India's foreign exchange reserves increased enormously.

Select the correct answer using the codes given below:

(a) 1 and 4 only (b) 2, 3 and 4 only

(c) 2 and 3 only (d) 1, 2 and 3

Answer Key	
Q1.	b
Q2.	b

Model Questions for Main Examination

Q1. Write about the impact of liberalisation on the Indian economy in 1991?

Q2. Elaborate LPG reforms and what were the disadvantages faced by the Indian economy post the LPG policies?

UNIT 4

Poverty

In This Unit

Comprehensive and profound coverage of the following NCERT's chapter:

✓ NCERT Class- 11th (Indian Economic Development), Chapter- 4

Introduction

- Since independence poverty has been a major challenge for India. To fulfil the **objective of a welfarist state as given in the Indian Constitution**, India needs to **address the extreme poverty** prevalent in the country.
- **"This achievement (Independence) is but a step, an opening of opportunity, to the great triumphs and achievements that await us... the ending of poverty and ignorance and disease and inequality of opportunity," Jawaharlal Nehru** had stated in a 1947 speech to the Constituent Assembly.
- **Poverty** is not only problematic for India; it **is a global problem**. World is facing the threat of extreme poverty. At the same time, the way to define poverty and the ways to tackle poverty etc. are riddled with their own problems.

Who are the Poor?

- Because poverty is multifaceted, social scientists examine it using a range of metrics. Usually, the metrics employed are associated with **income and consumption levels**.
- A significant portion of the impoverished population **lacks even access to clean drinking water, less-polluting cooking fuels, electricity**, and other necessities.
- Extreme gender inequality has been shown to exist in terms of involvement in school, gainful employment, and family decision-making. Lesser care is given to poor women when they become mothers. There is a lower chance that their offspring will live or be born healthy.
- The **impoverished are classified** by economists **according to their assets and type of employment.** They claim that the majority of the **rural poor** are employed as tenant cultivators with tiny land holdings, **landless workers** engaged in a range of non-agricultural jobs, or landless agricultural labourers.
- The **urban poor** are mostly made up of labourers who work various part-time occupations, self-employed people who sell a range of goods on roadside kiosks, and rural poor people who have moved to urban regions in search of alternative jobs and means of subsistence.

Poverty Explained

The circumstances of poverty are summarised by two academics **Shaheen Rafi Khan and Damian Killen** as below:

- **Hunger** is poverty.
- Being ill and **unable to see a doctor** is poverty.
- Being **unable to attend school** and lacking reading comprehension are signs of poverty.
- To be poor is **not to have a job**.
- Fear about the future and **eating only once a day** are signs of poverty.
- The loss of a kid due to **disease caused by contaminated water** is poverty.
- Being poor means **not having freedom, representation**, or authority.

How are Poor People Identified?

- **Dadabhai Naoroji** was the first person to raise the idea of **a poverty line in pre-independence India.**
- There have been multiple attempts to devise a system to determine the number of impoverished people in India since the country's independence.
- For example, a **Study Group** was **founded in 1962 by the Planning Commission**, which has now been replaced by **the NITI Aayog**. The **"Task Force on Projections of Minimum Needs and Effective Consumption Demand"** was another organisation established in 1979. Later, **"Expert Groups"** were established for the same reason in 1989 and 2005.
- In addition to the Planning Commission, numerous **lone economists** have also tried to create a system for identification of poor.
- To define poverty, individuals are classified into two groups: the **impoverished** and the **non-poor, with** a poverty line dividing the two.
- But there are other **types of poverty**: **absolute poverty, very poor,** and the **poor itself.**
- The **non-poor** also come in several varieties: the **rich, the very rich, the absolute rich, the middle class, and the upper middle class.**

IDENTIFICATION OF POOR

Pre-Independence	Post-Independence
Dadabhai Naoroji was the first to discuss poverty in pre-independent India.	• In 1962, Planning Commission established a study group for identifying the poor. • Task Force on Projections of Minimum Needs & Effective Consumption Demand (1977-79) was set up by Planning Commission. • Lakdawala Expert Group (1989) and Tendulkar Committee (2005) were set up for poverty estimation.

Identification of Poor

Categorizing Poverty

- Poverty can be classified in a variety of ways.
- The term **"chronic poor"** refers to a group of people who are impoverished all the time as well as those who are poor most of the time but occasionally have a little extra money (such as casual labourers).
- The **sometimes poor**, who are usually wealthy but may experience a streak of bad luck, and the **churning poor**, who alternately enter and exit poverty on a regular basis like small farmers and seasonal workers are two examples of this. We refer to them as the **impermanent poor.**
- And then there are the **non-poor**, the people who are never in poverty.

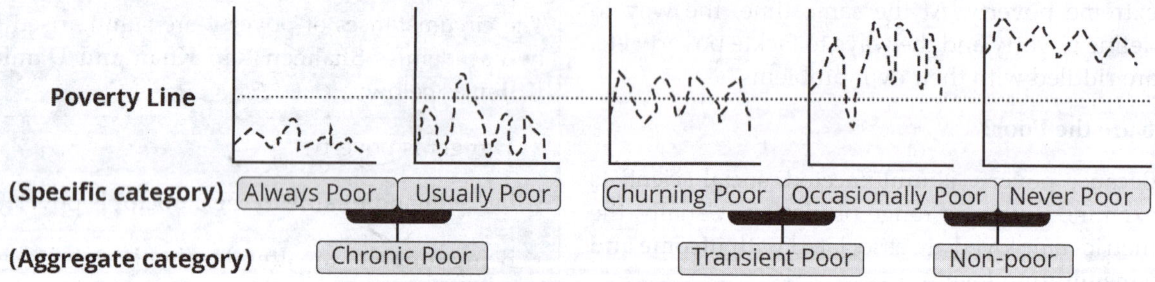

The Chronic Poor, Transient Poor and Non-poor

Types of Poverty

The Poverty Line

- One way to determine poverty line is by monetary value (per capita expenditure) of minimum calories intake that was estimated at 2400 calories per person for rural household and 2100 calories for urban household.
- In 2011-12, based on this, poverty line for rural area was defined as **Rs 816 per person a month and Rs 1000 for urban region.**
- There are various limitations of such a monetary poverty line:
  - ➢ It clubs all the poor together and **does not classify who is poorest** among them.

- It takes into account expenditure on food and a few select items as proxy for income, which is challenged by many economists.
- It **ignores socioeconomic elements** including discrimination, lack of civil and political liberties, ill health, lack of access to resources, and illiteracy that cause and prolong poverty.
- Many economists contend that **governments modify** the items included in consumption baskets, the methods used to calculate the poverty line, and other factors to skew **and obscure poverty statistics.**

- Besides monthly calories intake, other factors can also be considered to estimate poverty line. For example, the **accessibility to basic education, health care, drinking water and sanitation.**
- Owing to a number of shortcomings in the official definition of poverty, researchers have looked for alternatives. For example, the renowned Nobel Laureate Amartya Sen created the **Sen Index.** Other techniques include the **Squared Poverty Gap** and **Poverty Gap Index.**
- Using **sample surveys, the poverty line is estimated** on a regular basis (often **every five years)** by the **National Sample Survey Organisation** (NSSO) of India.
- However, many international agencies, such as **the World Bank, employ a uniform criteria** for the poverty line when comparing developing nations which is a minimum availability of **$1.90 per person per day.**

Poverty Estimates

	Poverty ratio (%)			Number of poor (In millions)		
Year	Rural	Urban	Total	**Rural**	**Urban**	**Combined**
1993-94	50	32	45	329	75	404
2004-05	42	26	37	326	81	407
2009-10	34	21	30	278	76	355
2011-12	26	14	22	217	53	270

India's Poverty Estimates Using the **Tendulkar Methodology from 1993 to 2012**

- From the above-mentioned table, it is clear that **poverty in absolute and in percentage term has decreased** from 1993-94 to 2011-12, as per **Tendulkar methodology estimates.**
- In 2011–12, the percentage of those living below the poverty line decreased even more, reaching almost 22%.
- In the coming years, the percentage of individuals living in poverty could drop to less than 20% if the current trend continues.
- The **number of impoverished decreased** from 407 million in 2004–05 to 270 million in 2011–12, with an **average yearly fall of 2.2 percentage points between 2004–05 and 2011–12.** This was despite the fact that the percentage of people living in poverty had decreased in the preceding two decades (1973–1993).

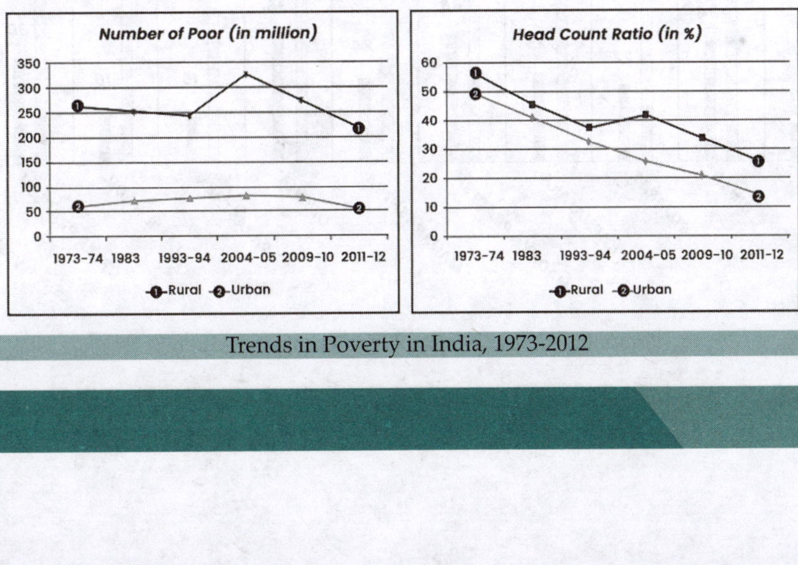

Trends in Poverty in India, 1973-2012

- While the **total number of impoverished people in rural areas decreased** in the 1990s, the **number of impoverished people in urban areas somewhat grew**.
- The **poverty rate** in both rural and urban areas has been **steadily declining**. The accompanying chart shows that while the share of the poor and their number have decreased between 1973 and 2012, the direction of this fall is not encouraging.
- Compared to the total number of impoverished people in the nation, the ratio is decreasing far more slowly.
- We will also observe that there has been a **decrease in the absolute number of poor** people living in rural and urban areas, yet the **ratio of poverty has increased** between 2011–12.

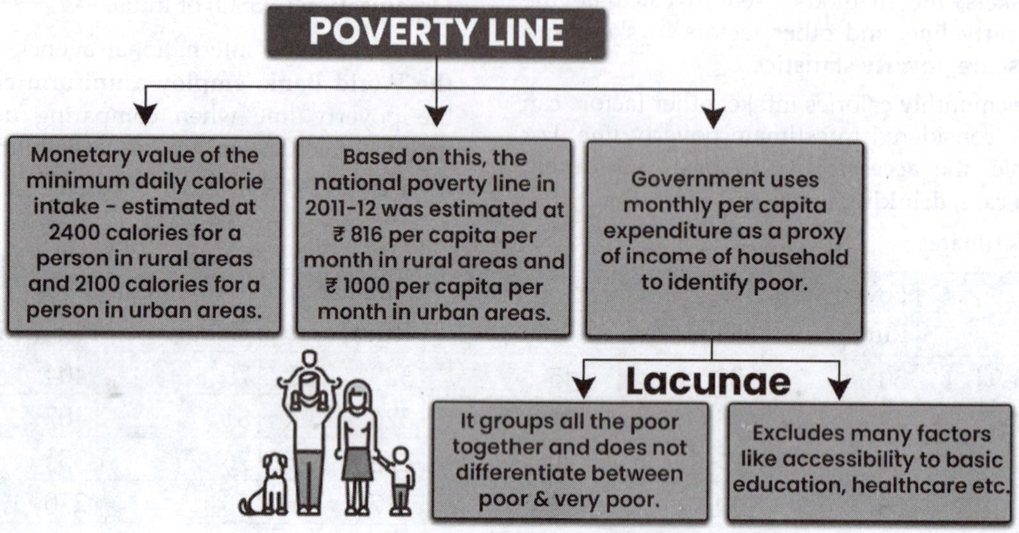

Poverty line

Interstate Disparities in Poverty

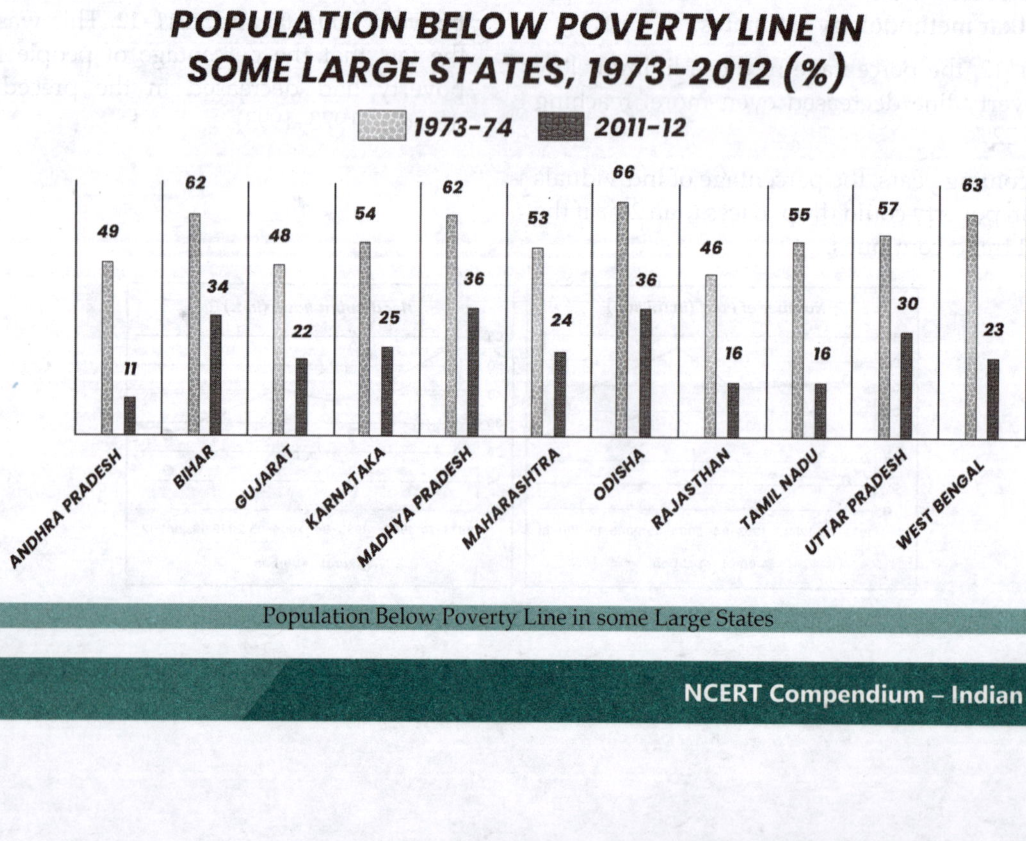

Population Below Poverty Line in some Large States

- The graph above shows that in 1973–74, a sizable portion of the poor lived in six states: Tamil Nadu, Uttar Pradesh, Bihar, Madhya Pradesh, West Bengal, and Odisha.
- Many Indian states saw significant reductions in poverty between 1973 and 2012.
- Nonetheless, the four states of Odisha, Madhya Pradesh, Bihar, and Uttar Pradesh have poverty rates that are still significantly higher than the national average.
- Compared to other states, Andhra Pradesh, Rajasthan, West Bengal, and Tamil Nadu have significantly lower rates of poverty.

Poverty among Vulnerable Groups

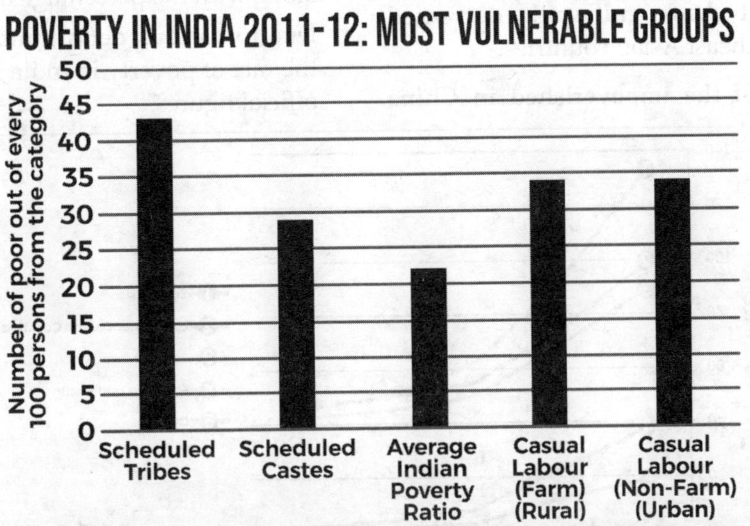

Poverty Graph in India (2011-2012)

- In India, the percentage of the population living in poverty varies across different social and economic classes.
- **Scheduled Caste and Scheduled Tribe** households are the most susceptible social groupings to poverty.
- Similarly, homes with **casual work in cities** and households with **agricultural labour in rural** areas are the most susceptible economic groups.
- The percentage of the poor in each of these groups is displayed on the graph.
- Despite the fact that the average number of Indians living below the poverty line is 22, 43 out of 100 members of Scheduled Tribes are unable to meet their basic necessities.
- Corresponding to this, 34% of **urban casual workers** fall below the poverty level.
- Approximately 34% of casual labourers work as **farmers in rural areas**, and 29% of Scheduled Castes are impoverished as well.
- The severity of the issue is highlighted by the **dual disadvantage** of belonging to a **landless casual wage worker** home among the **socially disadvantaged** scheduled caste or scheduled tribal population.
- According to some recent studies, all three of these groups—**scheduled castes, rural agricultural labourers, and urban casual labour households**—saw a decrease in poverty in the 1990s, with the exception of scheduled tribe homes.
- In addition to these socioeconomic divisions, **income inequality** also exists inside families.
- Everyone suffers in impoverished households, but some suffer more than others.
- Occasionally, **women, the elderly, and female infants** are not given equal access to family resources.

Global Poverty Scenario

- The percentage of individuals in various nations experiencing extreme economic poverty, which the World Bank defines as subsisting on less than \$1.90 per day, decreased from 36% in 1990 to 5% in 2015.

- **Global poverty has significantly decreased,** although **there are still significant regional variations.**
- Due to **enormous expenditures in human resource development** and rapid economic expansion, **poverty has significantly decreased** in China and Southeast Asian countries.
- The **proportion of the impoverished in China has decreased** from 88.3% in 1981 to 14.7% in 2008 to 0.6% in 2019.
- The **South Asian countries** (India, Pakistan, Sri Lanka, Nepal, Bangladesh, Bhutan) have likewise **experienced a sharp fall,** going from 34% in 2005 to 15.2% in 2014.
- The **number of the poor has drastically decreased** from 510.4 million in 2005 to 274.5 million in 2013, along with the percentage of the poor declining.
- Due to **various definitions of the poverty line,** the rate of poverty in India is also higher than the official figures.

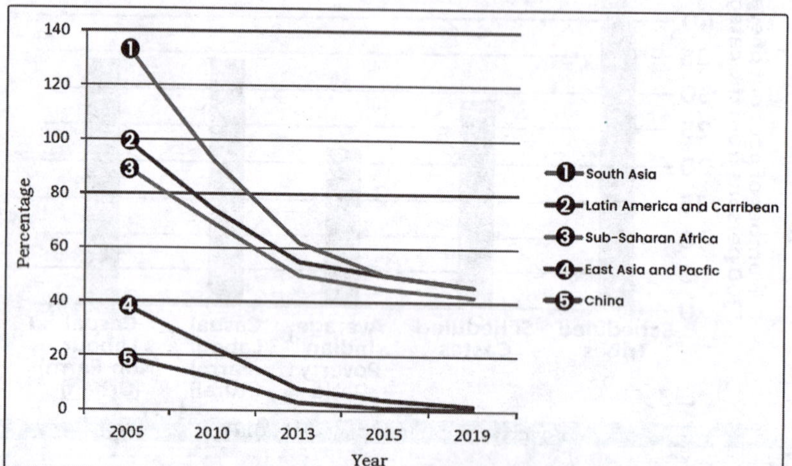

Share of people living on \$1.90 a day, 2005-2019

Global Poverty Scenario

- In actuality, **poverty in Sub-Saharan Africa decreased,** falling from 51 percent in 2005 to 40.2% in 2018 (see graph above).
- The **percentage of people living in poverty in Latin America has likewise decreased,** from 10% in 2005 to 4% in 2018 (see graph above).
- In several of the former socialist nations, such as **Russia,** where it was formerly officially non-existent, **poverty has also returned.**
- The percentage of the population in each country that falls below the international poverty line, which is defined as having less than \$1.90 per day, is displayed in the table below.

Country	% Of population below \$1.90 a day (2011 PPP)
Nigeria	39.1 (2018)
Bangladesh	14.5 (2016)
India	22.5 (2011)
Pakistan	4.0 (2015)
China	0.5 (2016)
Brazil	4.4 (2018)
Indonesia	3.6 (2018)
Sri Lanka	0.9 (2016)

Proportion of People Living under Poverty

- The United Nations Sustainable Development Goals propose ending poverty of all types by 2030 (Goal 1).

Causes of Poverty

- Poverty can be caused as a result of
  - i. social, economic and political inequality
  - ii. social exclusion
  - iii. unemployment

iv. indebtedness

v. unequal distribution of wealth

vi. illiteracy.

- Poverty is also explained by general, economy-wide problems, such as
  i. low capital formation
  ii. lack of infrastructure
  iii. lack of demand
  iv. pressure of population
  v. lack of social/ welfare nets.
- **Aggregate poverty** is just the sum of individual poverty. There are **historical reasons** for large number of poor people in India. The two centuries of **British Colonial rule has led to impoverishment** of millions of Indians. High dependence on **subsistence agriculture, deindustrialisation, stagnation of agriculture productivity, lack of manufacturing and exploitative land settlement systems** etc. have pushed millions of Indians into extreme poverty.
- A large section of rural poor in India are **small farmers.** They have **fragmented lands** and no capital for livestock rearing. They practise subsistence farming and are dependent on monsoonal rains and government's input subsidies. For them, **agriculture is a medium of survival. It does not generate much surplus** income.
- Most of the members of **Schedule Caste and Schedule Tribes** do not get proper employment due to absence of competent skills. Hence, they fall back into poverty.
- A large section of urban poor are the poor rural people, who have migrated to urban area in the search of jobs. **These poor are not absorbed into workforce**. Most of them are either informally employed or temporarily employed.
- Therefore, the **nature of job and poverty are intimately associated.** Poverty is reinforced by underemployment, unemployment, and the sporadic and irregular nature of employment in both rural and urban settings. These factors push people to become **indebted**. One of the main things contributing to poverty is debt.
- Lower income groups experience more hardship and suffering as a result of a **sharp increase in the price of food grains** and other necessities at a rate that is higher than that of luxury products.
- The continuation of poverty in India is partly a result of the **unequal distribution of wealth and income.**

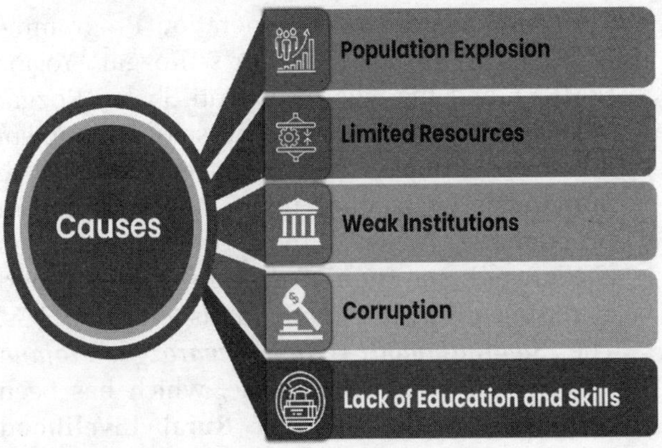

Causes of Poverty

Programmes and Policies Aimed at Reducing Poverty

- The **Indian Constitution** and Five-Year Plans declare **social justice to be the main goal** of the government's development policies.
- The **government's approach to poverty reduction** has three dimensions:
  - ➢ First approach is **growth-oriented approach,**
  - ➢ Second approach is work and **employment generation** approach,
  - ➢ Third approach is targeted **delivery of minimum basic amenities** to the people.
- The **first approach** is clearly seen in 1950s and 1960s, here the five-year plans were focused on economic growth to **address the poverty.** The rural region and agriculture sector had concentration of poor. The **land reforms and Green Revolution** were brought to deal with the prevalence of poverty in rural region. Similarly, **redistribution of lands** had made tillers the owners of land and land to landless farmers provided them a medium to survive the poverty.

- The **second approach** was initiated from Third Five Years Plan (1961-66) and progressively enlarged after that.
- The most noted program initiated in the 1970s was the **Food for Work**. Building on that, most of the Five Years Plans later focused on **self-employment** of people for poverty alleviation.
- The Rural Employment Generation Programme (REGP), the Prime Minister's Rozgar Yojana (PMRY), and the Swarna Jayanti Shahri Rozgar Yojana (SJSRY) are a few of self-employment initiatives. Initially finances were provided to individuals or families under self-employment programmes. Now the beneficiaries are encouraged to **form Self-help Groups** and government would provide funds to these SHGs. The *Swarnajayanti Gram Swarozgar Yojana (SGSY)* was one such scheme, which has been **restructured into National Rural Livelihood Mission (NRLM).**
- Governments are also providing **wage employment programmes**. In this sector the **Mahatma Gandhi National Rural Employment Guarantee Act (MGNREGA)** is significant, which provides **100 days guaranteed wage** employment to **semi-skilled and unskilled** workers in **rural region.**
- The **third approach** initiation can be **traced from the Fifth Five Years Plan**. Policy makers realised that event if poor are provided employment, they would not be able to buy all essential services and goods. Hence this approach supplements the ability of poor to gain all essential goods and services.
- This help can be given in field of health, food, nutrition, education, drinking water, sanitation, housing, communication and electricity etc.
- In this respect, schemes such as **National Health Mission, Pradhan Mantri Gram Sadak Yojana, Public Distribution Schemes, Mid-day meal Scheme, National Social Assistance Program and recently Pradhan Mantri Jan Dhan Yojana, and Pradhan Mantri Jan Arogya Yojana.**

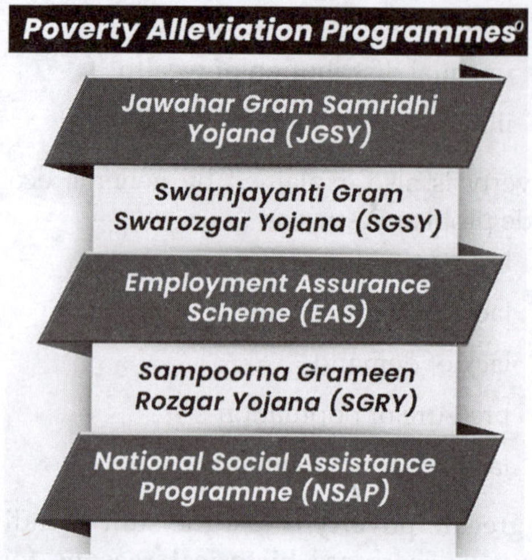

Poverty Alleviation Programmes

Programmes to Reduce Poverty: A Critical Evaluation

- The **percentage of absolute poor in some states is now significantly lower** than the national average, indicating that efforts to reduce poverty have paid off for the first time since independence.
- In many parts of India, **hunger, malnourishment, illiteracy, and a lack of basic facilities persist** despite the implementation of different measures aimed at alleviating poverty.
- Over the past 70 years, the approach to reducing poverty has changed gradually, but there hasn't been a significant shift in it. Nomenclature changes, programme integrations, and mutations are all possible. Nevertheless, **none brought about any significant alteration in the ownership of assets, the industrial process, or the provision of basic services to the poor.**
- During the evaluation of these projects, academics identify three primary areas of concern that impede their successful execution.
- The **non-poor have usurped the advantages of direct poverty alleviation** efforts because of the unequal distribution of land and other assets.
- There are **insufficient resources allotted for these projects** in relation to the extent of poverty.
- Furthermore, the implementation of these schemes is primarily dependent on bank and government authorities. **Resources are wasted**

and spent inefficiently because these officials lack motivation, are poorly trained, are prone to corruption, and are susceptible to pressure from a range of local elites.

- Additionally, **local level institutions are not involved** in the implementation of the plan.
- Additionally, the **bulk of vulnerable individuals** who live at or near the poverty level have **not been adequately addressed by government** initiatives.
- It also shows that **poverty cannot be eradicated by rapid growth** alone.
- Any programme cannot be implemented successfully without the poor's active participation. Only until the impoverished actively participate in the process of growth will poverty be effectively erased. A **social mobilisation approach** that empowers and encourages the participation of the poor makes this possible.
- Additionally, this will aid in the **creation of job opportunities**, which could result in higher income, skill levels, health, and literacy rates.
- It is also important to **pinpoint locations that are impoverished** and provide infrastructure there, including training facilities, schools, roads, electricity, communication, and IT services.

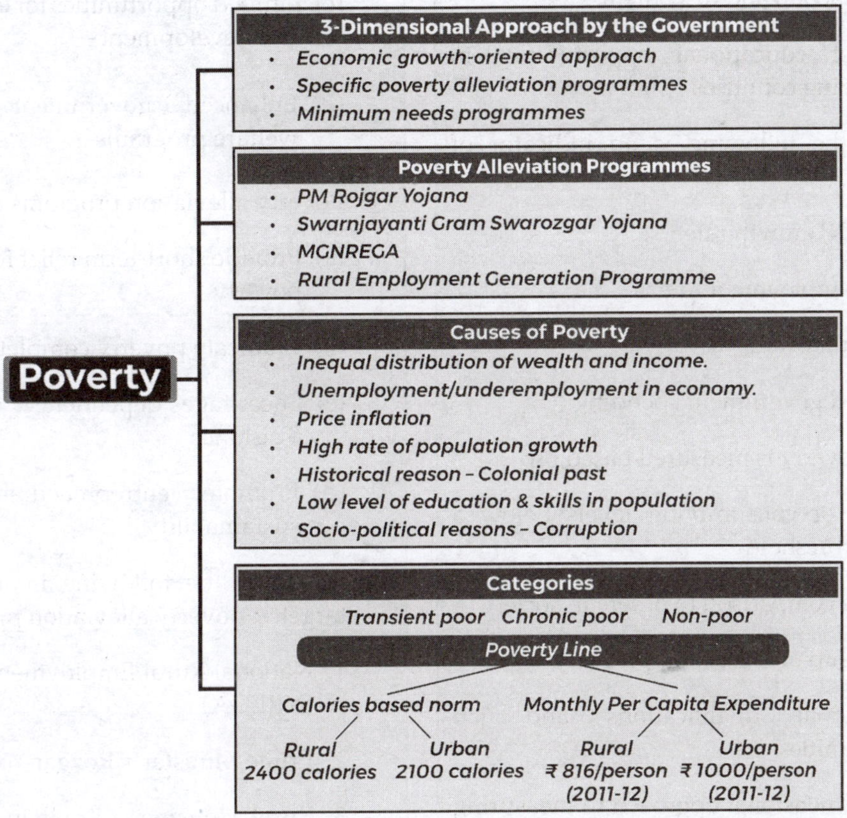

Conclusion

Being a **welfarist state**, it is **enshrined in our Constitution** that the state must ensure the **protection of dignity** of each and every citizen of India. Poverty is the biggest threat to live a dignified life. Since independence many government schemes have tried to deal with the problem of poverty. They have achieved some success as the absolute number and percentage of poor people has decreased since independence. But the peer-to-peer comparison of India's performance to other developing countries shows that India's performance could have been better. The **benefits of poverty alleviation programmes are not distributed equally** among all citizens, because of that there are disparities among citizens in terms of social, political and economic development.

The international experience of poverty alleviation efforts shows that the effort of governments must be supplemented with **involvement of civil societies and people themselves.** This is the way forward to achieve the **Sustainable Development Goal 1 i.e., No Poverty.**

TEST YOURSELF

Multiple Choice Questions

Q1. What is poverty?

(a) Lack of basic necessities and resources required for a decent standard of living

(b) Unequal distribution of wealth in society

(c) A state of mind characterised by dissatisfaction and discontent

(d) Lack of educational opportunities in developing countries

Q2. Which of the following is an indicator of poverty?

(a) High GDP growth rate

(b) Low unemployment rate

(c) Low literacy rate

(d) Increased government spending

Q3. Absolute poverty is measured based on:

(a) Income or consumption levels below a certain threshold

(b) Relative comparison to others in society

(c) Ownership of assets and property

(d) Educational qualifications and job opportunities

Q4. The multidimensional approach to measuring poverty takes into account:

(a) Only income and consumption levels

(b) The average standard of living in the country

(c) Economic indicators such as GDP per capita

(d) Social indicators such as education and health

Q5. Which of the following is a consequence of poverty?

(a) Improved healthcare and access to education

(b) Increased social mobility and reduced inequality

(c) Limited opportunities for economic growth and development

(d) Enhanced government support and welfare programs

Q6. Poverty alleviation programs aim to:

(a) Provide short-term relief for individuals in poverty

(b) Eradicate poverty completely from society

(c) Encourage dependency on government assistance

(d) Promote entrepreneurship and self-sustainability

Q7. Which of the following is an example of a targeted poverty alleviation program in India?

1. National Rural Employment Guarantee Act (NREGA)
2. Prime Minister's Rozgar Yojana (PMRY)
3. Rural Housing – Pradhan Mantri Gramin Awaas Yojana (PMGAY),
4. Swarna Jayanti Shahri Rozgar Yojana (SJSRY).

Choose from the following

(a) All of the above (b) 1 only

(c) 2 and 3 only (d) 1, 2 and 3 only

Q8. Who was the first in pre-independent India to talk about the poverty line?

(a) Mahatma Gandhi (b) B.R. Ambedkar

(c) Dadabhai naoroji (d) Lala Lajpat Rai

Q9. Poverty can be caused as a result of

1. Unemployment
2. Social, economic and political inequality
3. Indebtedness
4. Unequal distribution of wealth

Choose from the following

(a) a and b (b) b and c

(c) All of the above (d) a and d

Q10. Which of the following statements is/are correct about Poverty Reduction in India?

(a) Economic growth widens opportunities and provides the resources needed to invest in human development, which in turn reduces poverty.

(b) The growth in the agriculture sector has an indirect bearing on poverty in India

(c) Both (a) and (b)

(d) Neither (a) nor (b)

Q11. Which of the following statements is/are Incorrect about Poverty Line in India?

(a) While determining the poverty line in India, a minimum level of food requirement is considered.

(b) The present formula for food requirement while estimating the poverty line is based on the desired calorie requirement.

(c) The accepted average calorie requirement in India is 2100 calories per person per day in rural areas and 2400 calories per person per day in urban areas.

(d) In India, for the year 2011–12, the poverty line for a person was fixed at Rs 816 per month for rural areas and Rs 1000 for urban areas.

Q12. In a given year in India, official poverty lines are higher in some States than in others because (2019)

(a) Poverty rates vary from State to State

(b) Price levels vary from State to State

(c) Gross State Product varies from State to State

(d) Quality of public distribution varies from State to State

Answer Key

Q1.	a	Q2.	c	Q3.	a
Q4.	d	Q5.	c	Q6.	b
Q7.	a	Q8.	c	Q9.	c
Q10.	a	Q11.	c	Q12.	b

Model Questions for Main Examination

Q1. Discuss the differences between rural and urban poverty?

Q2. Define poverty and write about the difference between absolute and relative poverty?

UNIT 5
Human Capital Formation in India

In This Unit

Comprehensive and profound coverage of the following NCERT's chapter:

✓ NCERT Class- 11th (Indian Economic Development), Chapter- 5

Introduction

Like any other factor of production in economics, **Human capital** also plays an important role. The population, which is historically considered as liability for a nation to feed is now increasingly considered as an asset for nation's growth. After the advent of globalisation at world's stage it had become evident that countries, which have invested in development of human capital have garnered more out of globalisation than others. **Investment in human capital through education, training, medical care** yields a return just like investment in physical capital. This is vindicated in India's success of Green Revolution and Information Technology boom. Green Revolution saw the investment in agricultural and IT Boom saw investment in technology as well as investment in technical education in India.

What is Human Capital?

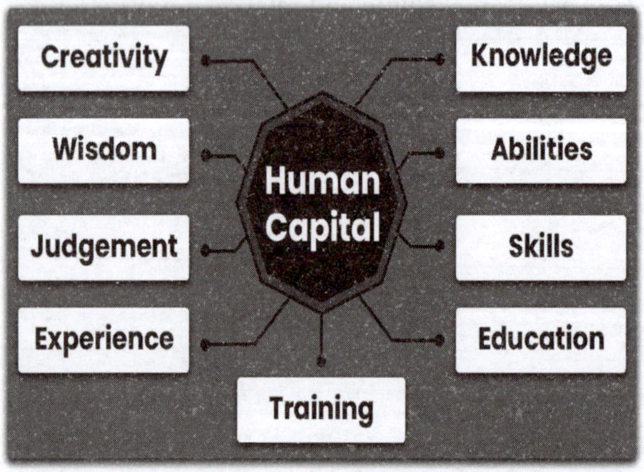

Human Capital

Any **raw material can be converted into high yielding products through value addition** like iron ore can be converted into steels, which further can be converted into specialised steels, which in turn can be used to make automobiles, ships etc. In a similar way human resources can also be converted into high yielding assets through investments into health, education, skill development, nutrition, sanitation etc. This **high-quality Human Capital** can give high **productivity in economy** through their **enhanced capabilities, skills and knowledge**. This means that we need investment in human capital to produce more human capital out of human resources.

Sources of Human Capital

Education spending is regarded as one of the **primary sources of human capital**. Additional sources of human capital accumulation include: 1) health investments; 2) on-the-job training; 3) migration; and 4) information.

- **Education**: An educated human resource is better equipped to give high return on same level of inputs, in an economy. An **increase in literacy level** of a region/state/country **impacts the growth rate** of that region/state/country. The **UNDP's Human Development Report** puts much emphasis on investment in education for raising quality of human resource.
- **Health**: A workforce that is in good health is more capable of boosting economic growth than one that is ill. One may consider **funding for maternity and child health** to be funding for the development of human capital. The several types

of health expenditures include **vaccinations** for preventive medicine, medical interventions for **curative medicine** during disease, **health literacy** promotion in the community, and **the supply of clean drinking water** and hygienic conditions. Spending on health care directly contributes to the availability of a **healthy labour force**, which is how human capital is formed.

- **On-the-job-training**: Firms spend on-the-job-training to raise the qualities and knowledge sets of their workforce, which can increase the productivity of a firm's labour force in future. The **cost of training,** education, loss of worktime during training can be **recovered from the benefits of enhanced skill sets** of the trained work force in future.
- **Migration**: People **migrate from rural to urban**, from **developing countries to developed countries in the search of higher salaries**, career growth etc. The rise in migration costs like transportation costs, living standard costs, psychic costs of migration can be fetched from **raise in the salaries** and better opportunities from migrated region. Therefore, spending on migration contributes to the creation of human capital.
- **Acquisition of Information**: Individuals pay money to obtain knowledge about the job market as well as other sectors, such as health and education. People want to know, for instance, how much different jobs pay, whether or not educational institutions offer employable skills, and how much such talents will cost. Decisions about **investments in human capital as well as the effective use of the acquired human capital stock** require this knowledge. Another source of human capital production is the money spent on learning about the labour market and other marketplaces.

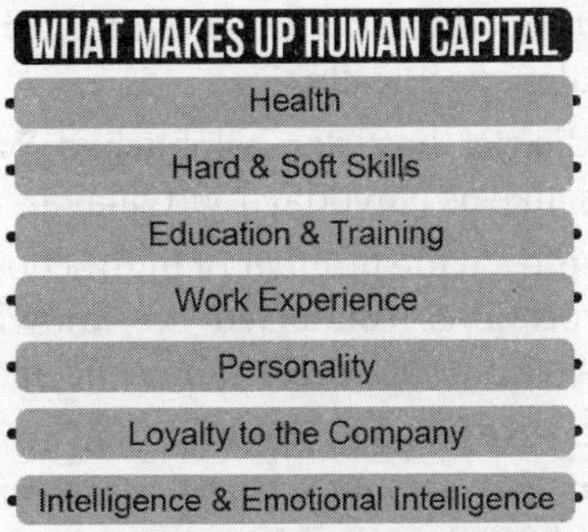

Human Capital Formation

Human and Material Capital

- Both types of capital formation are results of **deliberate investment choices.**
- One bases their decision about investing in tangible capital on their level of understanding in this area.
- The entrepreneur is equipped with the information to determine the projected rates of return for various investments and thereafter makes a logical decision regarding which investment to make.
- Physical capital development is primarily an economic and technological process, but ownership of that capital is the result of the owner's deliberate decision.
- A significant portion of developing one's human capital occurs when they are unable to determine whether doing so would maximise their revenue.
- Parents and society provide children with many forms of schooling and health care services.
- Decisions on **investments in human capital are influenced by peers, instructors, and society** even at the tertiary level, or college level.
- Furthermore, the development of human capital at this stage is reliant on the human capital that has already been established at the school level.
- Human capital formation is a **result of both social processes and the deliberate choices** made by the individuals who hold it.
- We are aware that the owner of a physical capital, such as a bus, does not always need to be present at the location where it is used; but, when the bus is being used to carry persons and materials, the bus-driver, who is qualified to operate the vehicle, needs to be present.
- **Physical capital is easily traded** and sold on the market, just like any other commodity. **Human capital is an intangible asset** that is naturally ingrained in its possessor's body and intellect.

- Only the services rendered by human capital are sold in the market; therefore, the owner of the human capital must be present in the location of production.
- Human capital is inseparable from its owner, although physical capital can be separated from it.
- The **mobility of the two types of capital varies** throughout space. All **physical capital is transferable** across nations, with the exception of some fictitious trade barriers.
- Because **nationality and culture impose restrictions on travel**, human capital is not fully transportable across borders.
- Because of this, physical capital formation can still be built through imports, even though the development of human capital requires careful policy formulation in line with the needs of the economy and society as well as individual and governmental spending.
- While **both types of capital experience depreciation** over time, the rate of depreciation varies. Continuous use of machine leads to depreciation and change of technology makes a machine obsolete. When it comes to human capital, depreciation occurs with age but can be substantially mitigated by ongoing investments in health, education, and other areas.
- In addition, unlike physical capital, this **investment helps human capital adapt to technological change.**
- The gains that come from human capital are not the same as those that come from physical capital. **Human capital is advantageous to society** as a whole in addition to its owner. We refer to this as an **external advantage.** An educated individual can actively participate in a democratic process and advance a country's socioeconomic standing. A healthy individual prevents the spread of infectious diseases and epidemics by practicing good personal hygiene and sanitation.
- Unlike **physical capital**, which **exclusively generates private rewards**, human capital generates both private and social benefits.
- In other words, people who pay for the goods and services created by a capital good reap the rewards.

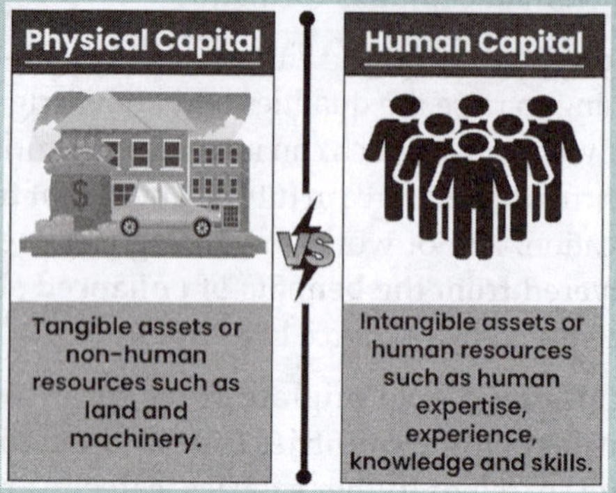

Physical Capital vs Human Capital

Quality of Population

It usually depends on literacy rate, health of a person and skill formation acquired by the people of the country.

Education

- An investment in education of human resource bears fruit in the form of **increased productivity of human resource in future.**
- It opens **new horizon** for people, provides new aspiration and develops values of life.
- Education also plays a role in the development of society.
- It raises the level of cultural diversity, the national income, and the effectiveness of government.
- Universal access, retention, and quality in elementary education are provided, with a focus on females specifically.
- Every district has also established **pace-setting schools**, like as Navodaya Vidyalaya.
- To provide a wide number of high school students with vocations connected to knowledge and abilities, vocational streams have been developed.
- From Rs 151 crore in the first plan to Rs 3766.90 crore in the eleventh plan, **more money was allocated to education.**

- According to a budgetary estimate, the share of **GDP spent on education increased** from 0.64% in 1951–1952 to 3.3% in 2013–14.
- The percentage of people who are literate has risen from 18% in 1951 to 74% in 2010–11.

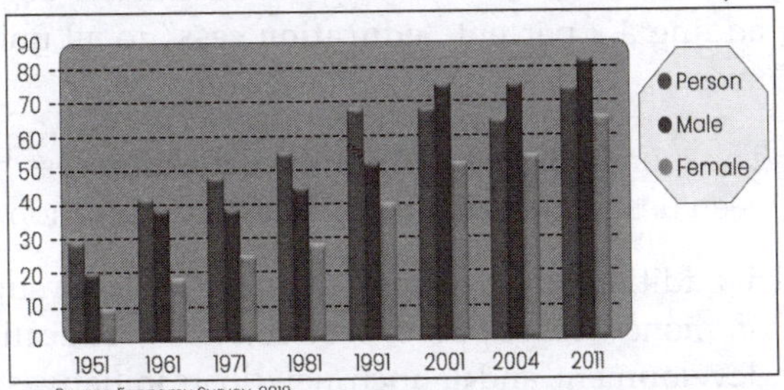

Source Economy Survey, 2012.

Literacy Rates in India

- In addition to being a right, literacy is also necessary for citizens to carry out their responsibilities and fully exercise their rights.
- But there is a noticeable gap in several demographic groups.
- **Male literacy is approximately 16.6% higher** than female literacy, and it is **16.1% higher in urban than in rural** areas.
- 2011 saw a range of literacy rates, from 62% in Bihar to 94% in Kerala.
- There were around 7.68 lakh primary schools in the country in 2004–05. Regrettably, this enormous expansion of schools has been countered by the poor quality of instruction and high dropout rates.
- A significant step towards guaranteeing that every kid between the ages of six and fourteen receives a basic education by 2010 is the **Sarva Siksha Abhiyan.**
- In order to boost primary school enrolment, **back-to-school camps and bridge courses** have also been introduced.
- The purpose of the **mid-day meal programme** is to enhance children's nutritional health and promote their attendance and retention.
- These measures have the potential to increase India's literate population. The eleventh plan aimed to raise the percentage of **adults in the 18–23 age range enrolled in higher education** to 15% by 2011–12 and 21% by the twelfth plan.
- Increasing access, quality, vocationalisation, acceptance of state-specific curriculum modifications, and networking on information technology use are the main objectives of the plan.
- The strategy also emphasises the **convergence of formal, non-formal, distant, and IT education institutions,** as well as distant education.
- There has been a **noticeable increase in the number of universities** and other higher education institutions in specialised fields over the last 50 years.

Year	Number of Colleges	Number of Universities	Students	Teachers
1950-51	750	30	2,63,000	24,000
1990-91	7,346	177	49,25,000	2,72,000
1996-97	9,703	214	67,55,000	3,21,000
1998-99	11,089	238	74,17,000	3,42,000
2007-08	18,064	378	14,00,000	4,92,000
2011-12	31,324	611	-	-
2012-13	37,204	723	28,00,000	-
2020-21	43,796	1113	20,207,338	15,12,000

Growth in Education Sector from 1951 to 2011-12.

- Let's examine the table to observe the growth in the number of institutions and colleges, student enrolment, and teacher recruitment from 1951 to 2011–12.
- States' per capita public spending on primary education in 2014–15 varied greatly; in Himachal Pradesh, it was as high as Rs 34,651, while in Bihar, it was as low as Rs 4,088.
- This causes variations in state-by-state educational possibilities and accomplishments.
- When comparing the current amount of education spending to the suggested level set by several committees, it becomes clear that it is insufficient.
- Approximately half a century ago, the **Education Commission (1964–1966) suggested allocating at**

least 6% of GDP to education in order to achieve a discernible growth in educational attainment.

- The **Tapas Majumdar Committee**, which was established by the Indian government in 1998, calculated that it would cost about Rs 1.37 lakh crore over ten years (1998–1999 to 2006–07) to enrol all Indian children between the ages of six and fourteen in school.
- The current level of education expenditure, little over 4 percent of GDP, has fallen well short of the targeted goal, which is approximately 6 percent of GDP.
- Ideally, six percent must be attained; this has been acknowledged as a necessity for the upcoming years.
- **The Right of Education Act** was passed by the Indian government in 2009, establishing **free education as a basic right for all children aged 6 to 14.**
- Additionally, the Indian government has begun adding a 2 percent "**education cess**" to all union taxes.
- The money collected from the education cess has been designated to fund elementary education.
- In addition, the government approves large sums of money to support postsecondary education development and launch new loan initiatives to entice students to pursue higher education.

Sl.No	Particulars	1990	2000	2015
1.	Adult Literacy Rate (per cent of people aged 15+)			
	1.1 Male	61.9	68.4	81
	1.2 Female	37.9	45.4	63
2.	Primary completion rate (per cent of relevant age group)			
	2.1 Male	78	85	94
	2.2 Female	61	69	99
3.	Youth literacy rate (per cent of people aged 15+ to 24)			
	3.1 Male	76.6	79.7	92
	3.2 Female	54.2	64.8	87

Educational Attainment in India from 1990 to 2015

Future Prospects in Education Sector

- **Striving for Education for All:** Although India has reached a decent level of literacy level after 75 years of independence, yet education for all is a distant dream for India.
- **Gender Equity-Better Than Before**
  - ➢ There has been progress towards gender parity as seen by the shrinking gaps in literacy rates between males and females.
  - ➢ There is an urgent need to **advance women's education** in India for a number of reasons, including raising women's economic and social standing and having a **positive effect on fertility rates and maternal and child health**.
  - ➢ As a result, even while the literacy rates are rising, we still have a long way to go before reaching 100% adult literacy.
- Higher Education-a few Takers
  - ➢ The **steepness of the Indian education pyramid** indicates that less and **fewer people are obtaining higher education.**
  - ➢ Moreover, young people with education have the **highest unemployment rate**.
  - ➢ According to NSSO data, the unemployment rate for young boys in rural areas who completed their education and above in 2011–12 was 19%.
  - ➢ At sixteen percent, the jobless rate was comparatively lower for their urban counterparts.
  - ➢ **Young rural female graduates** were the most badly hit, with over **30% of them unemployed.**
  - ➢ In comparison, only 3–6% of young people with only an elementary education in both rural and urban areas were unemployed.
  - ➢ Therefore, in order to ensure that students at these institutions acquire employable skills,

the government should both enhance funding for higher education and raise the bar for these institutions.

Health

- Having good health is essential to achieving one's goals in life.
- From now on, the nation's top focus has been to improve the population's health.
- Additionally, the goal of our national strategy is to increase access to family welfare, health care, and nutrition services, with a particular emphasis on the impoverished population.
- India has created the manpower needed at the **basic, secondary, and tertiary levels** in the government and commercial sectors over the past 50 years, in addition to building up a **sizable health infrastructure**.
- In many parts of India, even these most basic amenities are lacking.
- Only 751 medical colleges and 323 dental colleges exist nationwide.
- The states with the highest number of colleges are Andhra Pradesh, Karnataka, Maharashtra, and Tamil Nadu.

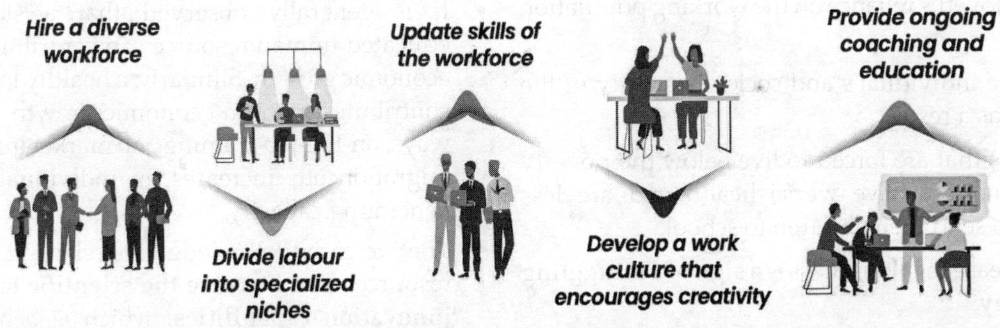

Ways to Boost Human Capital

Unemployment

- Unemployment is said to exist when people who are willing to work at the going wages cannot find jobs.
- The **workforce** population includes people from **15 years to 59 years**.
- In case of India, we have unemployment in rural and urban areas.
- However, the nature of unemployment differs in rural and urban areas.
- In case of **rural areas**, there is **seasonal and disguised unemployment**.
- **Urban areas** have mostly **educated unemployment**.
- **Seasonal unemployment** happens when people are not able to find jobs during some months of the year. People dependent upon agriculture usually face such kind of problem. There are certain busy seasons when sowing, harvesting, weeding and threshing is done. Certain months do not provide much work to the people dependent on agriculture.
- In case of **disguised unemployment** people appear to be employed. They have agricultural plot where they find work. This usually happens among family members engaged in agricultural activity. The field requires the service of five people and the three extra people are disguised unemployed.
- In **metropolitan places, educated unemployment** has become a widespread occurrence. Numerous young people with degrees in matriculation, graduation, and post-graduation are unable to obtain employment. According to a study, post-graduate and graduate unemployment has increased more quickly than that of matriculating students.
- There is a **paradoxical labour situation** when there is a scarcity of labour in certain categories and an excess of labour in others.
- On the one hand, there is a lack of technical skills necessary for economic growth, and on the

other, there is **unemployment among technically competent** individuals.

- A lack of work results in the **waste of human resources.** Individuals who are beneficial to the economy eventually become liabilities.
- The youth have a sense of helplessness and despondency. Individuals struggle to make ends meet and maintain their families.
- The incapacity of educated individuals who are willing to work to secure profitable employment suggests significant social waste. **Economic overload** typically increases unemployment. The unemployed's reliance on the working population grows.
- Both the individual's and society's quality of life suffers as a result.
- Families that are forced to live below the poverty line generally have worse health and are less likely to send their children to school.
- An increase in **joblessness** is a **sign of a struggling economy**.
- As a result, unemployment negatively affects an economy's ability to grow overall.
- Moreover, the resource that may have been used profitably is wasted.
- People are inherently looked as a liability to the economy if they are not a resource.
- Poor people cannot afford to sit idle. **They tend to engage in any activity irrespective of its earning potential.** Their earning keeps them on a bare subsistence level.
- Additionally, **self-employment** in the primary sector is a defining feature of the employment structure. Even though not everyone is truly needed, the entire family pitches in. Therefore, there is **covered-up unemployment in the agricultural industry**.
- However, this **does not lessen the family's poverty** because over time, surplus labour from every household tends to leave the area in search of employment.
- Job situation in various sectors is varied. The industry that uses the most workers is agriculture. The **population's reliance on agriculture has decreased** recently, in part due to the previously mentioned hidden unemployment.
- A portion of the excess manpower in the agricultural sector has been transferred to the secondary or tertiary sectors.
- **Small-scale manufacturing** is the most labour-intensive in the secondary sector.
- Regarding the tertiary sector, a number of **new services**, such as information technology and biotechnology, are currently emerging.

Human Capital and Economic Growth

- It is generally observed that a skilled and educated human resource can contribute more in economic growth. Similarly, a healthy labour force contributes more in economic growth. In similar ways, on-the-job-training, job market information, migration etc. increases an individual's income generating capacity.
- The increased knowledge and skill set of human resources also **increase the scientific temper and innovation capabilities,** which is beneficial for the growth of country itself.
- There is conflicting empirical data to support the theory that growing human capital leads to economic expansion. This can be the result of measuring issues. For instance, a country's genuine health status may not be reflected by health services assessed in monetary terms, life expectancy, and death rates, or by education measured in years of schooling, teacher-pupil ratios, and enrolment rates.
- Using the aforementioned variables, a study of real per capita income growth and improvements in the health and education sectors in both rich and developing nations reveals that there is **convergence in human capital measures but no evidence of convergence in real per capita income.**
- Stated differently, developing nations have had a faster growth in human capital, but not as quickly as per capita real income growth.
- There are grounds for thinking that **human capital and economic growth are causally related** in both directions. In other words, more income leads to the development of high human capital, and vice

versa—that is, income growth is caused by high human capital.

Case Study: India

- India recognised the importance of human capital in economic growth long ago.
- The **Seventh Five Year Plan** says, **"Human resources development (read human capital) has necessarily to be assigned a key role in any development strategy, particularly in a country with a large population.** Trained and educated on sound lines, a large population can itself become an asset in accelerating economic growth and in ensuring social change in desired directions."
- It is difficult to establish a relation of cause and effect from the growth of human capital (education and health) to economic growth but we can see in following Table that these sectors have grown simultaneously.

Particulars		1951	1981	1991	2001	2014-15
Real Per Capita Income (in Rs)		7,651	12,174	15,748	23,095	72,900
Crude Death Rate (Per 1,000 Population)		25.1	12.5	9.8	8.1	6.7
Infant Mortality Rate		146	110	80	63	37
Life Expectancy at Birth (in Years)	Male	37.2	54.1	59.7	63.9	67
	Female	36.2	54.7	60.9	66.9	70
Literacy Rate (%)		16.67	43.57	52.21	65.20	76

Indicators of Development in Education and Health Sectors

- Growth in each sector probably has reinforced the growth of every other sector.
- Two independent reports on the Indian economy, sometime back have identified that India would grow faster due to its strength in human capital formation.
- **Deutsche Bank,** a German bank, in its report on "Global Growth Centres" stated that **India is set to emerge as a top four major growth centre** and that **human capital is the most important factor of production** in today's economies. Increases in human capital are crucial to achieving increases in GDP.
- **World Bank,** in its report, **'India and the Knowledge Economy — Leveraging Strengths and Opportunities'**, states that India should make a transition to the knowledge economy and if it uses its knowledge as much as Ireland does (it is judged that Ireland uses its knowledge economy very effectively), then the **per capita income** of India will increase from a little over US $1000 in 2002 to US $ 3000 in 2020.
- It further states that the Indian economy has all the key ingredients for making this transition, such as, a **critical mass of skilled workers, a well-functioning democracy and a diversified science and technology infrastructure.**
- Consequently, the two assessments highlight the fact that India's economy will expand at a faster rate if it continues to build its human capital.

Human Development and Capital

- Although the two terms have a similar sound, they are clearly different from one another.
- **Human capital views health and education** as ways to **boost labour output**.
- The foundation of human development is the belief that health and education are essential to human well-being since these attributes alone allow people to make other decisions that they value, such as being able to read, write, and live long, healthy lives.
- **Human capital views people as a means to an end**, with increased production being the goal.
- According to this perspective, any expenditure on health and education is wasted if it doesn't increase the output of products and services.
- From the perspective of **human development, individuals are ends in and of themselves.**
- Even in the event that investments in health and education do not boost labour productivity, human welfare should nonetheless be elevated.

- Therefore, regardless of how they affect labour productivity, basic health and education are vital in and of themselves.
- According to this perspective, everyone has the right to get a minimum level of education and healthcare; in other words, everyone has the right to be literate and lead a healthy life.

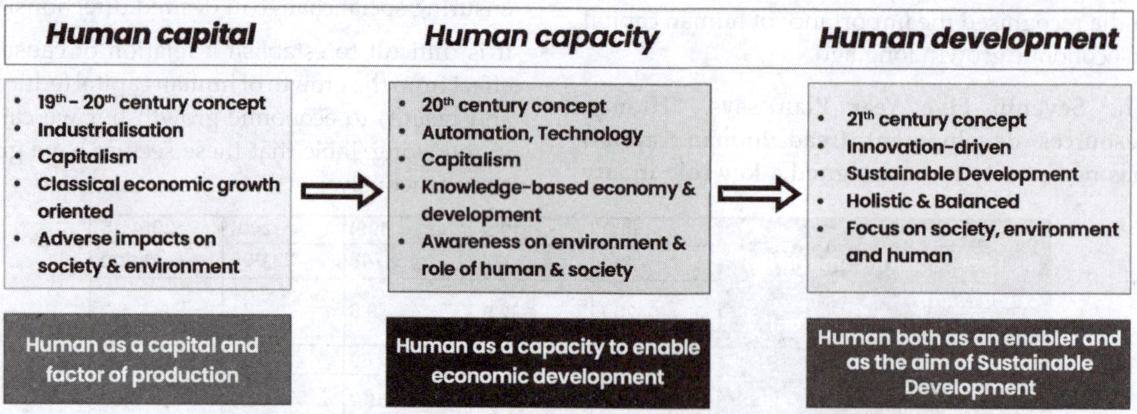

Human Capital v/s Human Capacity v/s Human Development

State of Human Capital Formation in India

- Human capital formation in India involves the investment in all of the sources of human capitals i.e., **education, health, on-the-job-training, migration and job information etc.**
- Being a federal country, the investments for health and education sectors are done by the **Union, state and local area governments.** Even the **private sectors also pitch in for investment in health and education sectors** where the Government agencies act as regulators and investigators to prevent the exploitation of poor population by private sectors due to lack of information.
- Institutions in the education sector are supported in India by departments of education, union and state ministries of education, and various agencies such as the University Grants Commission (**UGC**), All India Council of Technical Education (**AICTE**), and National Council of Educational Research and Training (**NCERT**).
- Similar to this, institutions that fall within the health sector are supported by departments of health, ministries of health at the federal and state levels, and numerous organisations like the Indian Council for Medical Research (**ICMR**).
- Developing nations such as India, where millions of people live in poverty, are unable to pay for increased health and educational expenses.
- Hence governments must shoulder a large portion of investment in education and health to make them affordable for poor people.

Conclusion

The economic and social benefits that formation of human capital bring is enormous to an economy. For that reason, it is imperative for a country to invest in human capital formation, especially in education and health. For India, which is the most populous nation, a high-quality human resource would be an asset and a poor-quality human resource would be a drag and liability for the country. For that reason, an **enhanced budgetary outlay** for these sectors and a **better emphasis on human capital formations** become need of the hour for the country.

TEST YOURSELF

Multiple Choice Questions

Q1. What are the main sources of human capital?

1. Investment in health
2. Investment in education
3. On-job training
4. Acquisition of information

Choose from the following

(a) 1 only (b) 1 and 4 only

(c) all of the above (d) 2, 3 and 4 only

Q2. What is the meaning of human capital formation?

(a) The process of creating physical infrastructure

(b) The process of enhancing human skills and capabilities

(c) The process of increasing financial investments

(d) The process of improving technological advancements

Q3. Which of the following is NOT a component of human capital?

(a) Education (b) Health

(c) Infrastructure (d) Skills

Q4. What is the primary objective of human capital formation in India?

(a) Increasing the GDP growth rate

(b) Improving the standard of living

(c) Expanding the agricultural sector

(d) Reducing income inequality

Q5. Which government ministry is primarily responsible for human capital development in India?

(a) Ministry of Finance

(b) Ministry of Education

(c) Ministry of Agriculture

(d) Ministry of Commerce

Q6. What role does education play in human capital formation?

(a) It provides individuals with skills and knowledge.

(b) It improves physical infrastructure.

(c) It increases financial investments.

(d) It enhances technological advancements.

Q7. What is the role of healthcare in human capital formation?

(a) It improves literacy rates.

(b) It enhances agricultural productivity.

(c) It reduces poverty rates.

(d) It improves the health and productivity of individuals.

Q8. Which sector of the economy benefits the most from human capital formation?

(a) Manufacturing (b) Services

(c) Agriculture (d) Construction

Q9. What is the relationship between human capital formation and economic growth?

(a) Human capital formation has no impact on economic growth.

(b) Economic growth leads to human capital formation.

(c) Human capital formation leads to economic growth.

(d) Economic growth and human capital formation are independent of each other.

Q10. What are the challenges to human capital formation in India?

(a) Lack of infrastructure development

(b) Insufficient investment in education and healthcare

(c) Inadequate skill development programs

(d) All of the above

Q11. What measures can be taken to promote human capital formation in India?

(a) Increasing government spending on education and healthcare

(b) Enhancing vocational training programs

(c) Encouraging private sector participation in skill development

(d) All of the above

Q12. Which of the following statements is/are correct about the Quality of the Population?

1. The quality of the population depends upon the literacy rate, health of a person indicated by life expectancy and skill formation acquired by the people of the country.
2. The quality of the population has no role in the growth rate of the country.

Select the correct answer using the code given below:

(a) 1 only (b) 2 only

(c) Both 1 and 2 (d) Neither 1 nor 2

Q13. Which of the following statements is/are incorrect for the Worker-population ratio?

1. The Worker-population ratio is an indicator that is used for analysing the employment situation in the country.
2. This ratio is useful in knowing the proportion of the population that is actively contributing to the production of goods and services of a country.
3. In India, the worker-population ratio is higher in urban areas than in rural area.

Select the correct answer using the codes given below:

(a) 1 and 2 only (b) 1 and 3 only

(c) 3 only (d) 1, 2 and 3

Q14. Consider the following statements: (UPSC-2018)

Human capital formation as a concept is better explained in terms of a process which enables

1. Individuals of a country to accumulate more capital.
2. Increasing the knowledge, skill levels and capacities of the people of the country.
3. Accumulation of tangible wealth.
4. Accumulation of intangible wealth

Which of the statements given above is/are correct?

(a) 1 and 2 only (b) 2 only

(c) 2 and 4 only (d) 1, 3 and 4 only

Answer Key

Q1.	c	Q2.	b	Q3.	c	Q4.	b
Q5.	b	Q6.	a	Q7.	d	Q8.	b
Q9.	c	Q10.	d	Q11.	d	Q12.	a
Q13.	c	Q14.	c				

Model Questions for Main Examination

Q1. How does investment in human capital contributes to growth in economy?

Q2. Discuss the impact of expenditure on 'on- job training' on human capital formation?

UNIT 6 Rural Development

In This Unit

Comprehensive and profound coverage of the following NCERT's chapter:

✓ NCERT Class- 11th (Indian Economic Development), Chapter- 6

Introduction

Poverty is one of the main challenges to Indian economy. Role of rural areas is most significant, as a large chunk of the population lives in villages and most of them live in **absolute poverty.** Hence any **fight to eradicate poverty** cannot be effective without a **simultaneous emphasis on rural development.** As most of the rural population is associated with agriculture and allied sectors, a growth in these sectors is paramount for any rural development.

Rural Development: What is it?

- The word "rural development" means **taking action to advance the regions of the village economy that are lagging behind overall**. It is a broad concept.
- Among the many challenges faced in rural India, these are the ones that require new development initiatives:
  - **Human resource development,** comprising health, addressing both public health and sanitation.
  - **Literacy,** particularly female literacy, education, and skill development
  - **Land reforms.**
  - The growth of each location's **productive resources.**
  - The development of **infrastructure**, such as those related to lending, marketing, irrigation, energy, and transportation, including building village roads and feeder roads to adjacent highways, facilities for agricultural research and extension, and the transmission of information.
  - Particular actions to **reduce poverty** and significantly **improve the living circumstances** of the population's poorer segments, with a focus on facilitating access to chances for **gainful work.**
- Hence all those who are engaged in farm and non-farm activities in rural area must be provided various means to increase their productivity.
- It has been established that after 1947 and more prominently after 1991 the **share of agriculture sector in the overall GDP has gone down.** On the other hand, the **share of workforce** dependent on agriculture sector **has not come down** as much.
- The **growth of agriculture sector has deaccelerated** to about 3 per cent per annum during 1991-2012. Academics pinpoint the primary cause of this loss as the **reduction in state investment** in agriculture since 1991.
- All this led to **distress in agriculture** sector, which itself led to distress in rural economy.

Credit and Marketing in Rural Areas

Credit

- Growth of rural economy is primarily dependent on the **infusion of capital.**
- Farmers need credit from credit sources for purchase of inputs like **seeds, fertilizers etc.**, as there is a gestation period for the crops to be harvested and sold in market.
- This credit was provided by moneylenders and traders in early days.

- They used to exploit small and marginal farmers. And they were mostly outside the control of banking regulations.
- A major change came in the form of **nationalisation of banks in 1969.**
- **National banks for Agriculture and Rural Development (NABARD)** was set up in 1982 **as an apex body to mobilise and regulate the finances to rural economy.**
- The Green Revolution brought a significant change in the field of infusion of credit in rural economy.
- Today, a variety of multi-agency institutions comprise the institutional framework of rural banking, including **commercial banks, cooperatives, regional rural banks (RRBs), and land development banks.**
- They are anticipated to provide **sufficient credit at more affordable prices.**
- Because the conventional credit distribution mechanism has not only proven inadequate but has also not been properly incorporated into the overall rural social and community development, Self-Help Groups, or SHGs, have recently formed to fill the vacuum in the formal credit system.
- A significant number of low-income rural households were automatically excluded from the lending network due to the requirement for some form of collateral.
- The **SHGs** encourage **frugal living** in tiny doses by requiring a minimum payment from each member. The members in need **receive credit from the pooled funds**, which they must repay in tiny instalments at fair interest rates. By the end of March 2003, it was reported that **over seven lakh SHGs** were linked to loans. These types of lending arrangements are commonly known as **micro-credit initiatives**.
- SHGs have contributed to **women's empowerment**.
- It is believed that the majority of the borrowings are for personal consumption.

SOURCES OF RURAL CREDIT

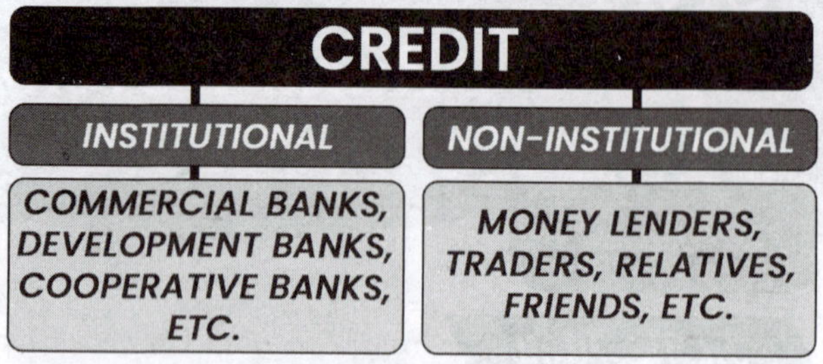

Sources of Rural Credit

> **The Poor Women's Bank**
>
> Kudumbashree' is a women-oriented community-based poverty reduction programme being implemented in Kerala. In 1995, a thrift and credit society was started as a small savings bank for poor women with the objective to encourage savings. The thrift and credit society mobilised Rs 1 crore as thrift savings. These societies have been acclaimed as the largest informal banks in Asia in terms of participation and savings mobilised.

Rural Banking-a Critical Appraisal

- Particularly following the **Green Revolution**, the **rapid expansion of the banking** system **benefited rural farm** and non-farm productivity, income, and employment by enabling farmers to access a range of loans and credit facilities to satisfy their production demands.
- Famines have become a thing of the past; our current state of **food security is demonstrated by the large buffer** reserves of cereals.
- All is not well, though, with our banking system.
- Other formal institutions, maybe with the exception of commercial banks, have not succeeded in fostering a culture of deposit mobilisation, lending to creditworthy customers, and successful loan recovery. **Loan default rates** in agriculture have consistently been **high**.
- As a result, following reforms, the development and promotion of the rural banking sector has suffered.
- It is recommended that **banks shift from being lenders** alone to **developing relationship** banking with the borrowers in order to ameliorate the situation.
- It is imperative to improve the instillation of thrift and smart financial resource management among farmers as well.

Agricultural Marketing System

- The process of assembling, storing, processing, transporting, packing, grading, and distributing various agricultural commodities across the nation is known as **agricultural marketing.**
- **Before independence**, farmers experienced inaccurate weighing and account manipulation while selling their crops to dealers. Farmers were frequently forced to sell at cheap prices because they **lacked the necessary knowledge of market prices.** Additionally, they **lacked enough storage** facilities to hold onto their produce in order to sell it at a higher price in the future. As a result, **government involvement was required** to control private dealers' operations.
- There are **four such measures that were initiated to improve the marketing aspect.**
- **The first step** was **regulation of markets** to create orderly and transparent marketing conditions. By and large, this policy benefited farmers as well as consumers.
- However, there is still a need to develop about 27,000 rural periodic markets as regulated market places to realise the full potential of rural markets.
- **Second** component is **provision of physical infrastructure** facilities like roads, railways, warehouses, godowns, cold storages and processing units.
- The current infrastructure facilities are quite inadequate to meet the growing demand and need to be improved.
- **Cooperative marketing**, in realizing fair prices for farmers' products, is the **third aspect of government initiative.**
- The **success of milk cooperatives** in transforming the social and economic landscape of Gujarat and some other parts of the country is testimony to the role of cooperatives.
- However, cooperatives have received a setback during the recent past due to inadequate coverage of farmer members, lack of appropriate link between marketing and processing cooperatives and inefficient financial management.
- The **fourth element** is the **policy instruments** like (i) assurance of minimum support prices (**MSP**) for agricultural products (ii) maintenance of **buffer stocks** of wheat and rice by **Food Corporation of India** and (iii) distribution of food grains and sugar through the Public Distribution System (**PDS).**
- These instruments are aimed at **protecting the income of the farmers** and providing **foodgrains** at a **subsidised rate to the poor**.
- However, despite government intervention, private trade by moneylenders, rural political elites, big merchants and rich farmers predominates agricultural markets.

Agricultural Marketing System

- The **need for government intervention** is **imminent** particularly when a large share of agricultural products, is handled by the private sector.
- Agricultural marketing has come a long way with the intervention of the government in various forms.
- Some scholars argue that **commercialisation of agriculture offers tremendous scope** for **farmers to earn higher incomes** provided the government intervention is restricted.

Emerging Alternate Marketing Channels

- It's been shown that **farmers make more money when they sell their produce directly** to customers.
- **Rythu Bazars** (vegetable and fruit markets in Andhra Pradesh and Telangana), **Hadaspar Mandi** (Pune), **Apni Mandi (**Punjab, Haryana, and Rajasthan), and **Uzhavar Sandies** (farmers markets in Tamil Nadu) are a few instances of these channels.
- Further, several **national and multinational fast-food** chains are increasingly entering into **contracts/ alliances with farmers** to encourage them to cultivate farm products (vegetables, fruits, etc.) of the desired quality by providing them with not only seeds and other inputs but also assured procurement of the produce at pre-decided prices.
- It is argued that such arrangements will help in reducing the price risks of farmers and would also **expand the market for farm products.**

Diversification into Productive Activities

- Diversification includes two aspects - one relates to **change in cropping pattern** and the other relates to a **shift of workforce** from agriculture to other allied activities (livestock, poultry, fisheries etc.) and non-agriculture sector.
- The need for diversification arises from the fact that there is greater risk in depending exclusively on farming for livelihood.
- Diversification towards new areas is necessary not only to reduce the risk from agriculture sector but also to provide productive sustainable livelihood options to rural people.
- Diversification helps farmers in lean seasons to get employed into some productive work and supplements the main income from farm sectors.
- The diversification becomes necessary in rainfed agriculture region, where there is a vulnerability for small farmers of the crop failures.
- As the agriculture has become overcrowded, the diversification in other allied sector might reduce the pressure on agriculture sector and reduce the disguised unemployment problem.
- Some of the **sub-sectors of agriculture like agro-processing industries**, food processing industries, leather industries, tourism etc. are **growing** more dynamically than farm sector. These sectors have potential but they lack infrastructure and investments.
- These **subsectors employ women** workforce in large quantity.

Tamil Nadu Women in Agriculture (TANWA)

Tamil Nadu Women in Agriculture (TANWA) is a project initiated in Tamil Nadu to train women in latest agricultural techniques. It induces women to actively participate in raising agricultural productivity and family income. At a Farm Women's Group in Thiruchirapalli, run by Anthoniammal, trained women are successfully making and selling vermicompost and earning money from this venture. Many other Farm Women's Groups are creating savings in their group by functioning like mini banks through a micro-credit system. With the accumulated savings, they promote small-scale household activities like mushroom cultivation, soap manufacture, doll making or other income - generating activities.

Animal Husbandry

- In India, the farming community uses the mixed crop-livestock farming system **cattle, goats, fowl are the widely held species.**
- Livestock production provides increased stability in income, food security, transport, fuel and nutrition for the family without disrupting other food-producing activities.
- Today, livestock sector alone provides alternate livelihood options to over 70 million small and marginal farmers including landless labourers.
- A significant number of **women also find employment** in the livestock sector.
- **Figure on 'Poultry and Livestock in India'** shows that poultry accounts for the largest share with 58 per cent.

Distribution of Poultry and Livestock in India, 2012

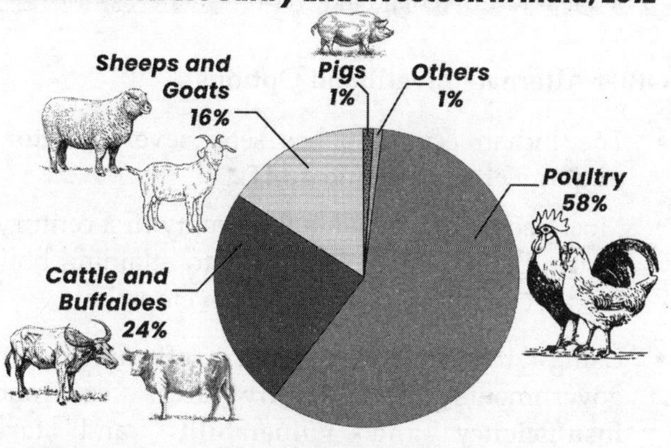

Distribution of Poultry and Livestock in India, 2012

- The lowest level is occupied by other animals such as camels, asses, horses, ponies, and mules. In 2012, India had over 300 million animals, of which 108 million were buffaloes.
- Over the past thirty years, the **Indian dairy industry** has demonstrated remarkable performance. Between 1951 and 2014, the country's milk production climbed by a factor of more than eight.
- The fundamental reason for this is the effective execution of **"Operation Flood"** where farmers can pool their milk output based on different quality categories, process the milk in cooperatives, and sell it to cities. Under this arrangement, farmers are guaranteed a just price and revenue from selling their milk to cities. Many states have looked to Gujarat as a model for the effective implementation of milk cooperatives.
- **By-products** such as meat, eggs, wool, and others are also **becoming a significant source of income** and diversification.

Fisheries

- Fisheries development in India has advanced significantly with a **steady rise in budgetary allotment** and the introduction of new technologies in aquaculture and fisheries.
- Currently, the marine sector (sea and oceans) provides **36% of the overall value of fish output**, with inland sources accounting for roughly 64% of the total.
- Currently, the entire **fish production contributes 0.8% of the GDP.**
- India's top fish-producing states include Tamil Nadu, West Bengal, Andhra Pradesh, Kerala, Gujarat, and Maharashtra.
- Many households who employ **fishers are impoverished.** The fishing community is currently facing numerous challenges, including **widespread underemployment, poor per capita incomes, limited labour mobility** to other industries, and a high percentage of **illiteracy and indebtedness.**
- Despite not actively participating in fishing, women make up over 60% of the workforce in export marketing and 40% in internal marketing.
- Increasing financing options for fisherwomen via cooperatives and SHGs is necessary to help them fulfil the working capital needs for marketing.

Horticulture

- Blessed with a varying climate and soil conditions, India has adopted growing of diverse horticultural crops such as fruits, vegetables, tuber crops, flowers, medicinal and aromatic plants, spices and plantation crops.
- These crops play a vital role in providing **food and nutrition**, besides addressing employment concerns.

- Horticulture sector contributes nearly one-third of the value of agriculture output and six per cent of Gross Domestic Product of India.
- India has emerged as a **world leader** in producing a variety of fruits like **mangoes, bananas, coconuts, cashew nuts and a number of spices and is the second largest producer of fruits and vegetables.**
- Economic condition of many farmers engaged in horticulture has improved and it has become a means of improving livelihood for many unprivileged classes.
- Flower harvesting, nursery maintenance, hybrid seed production and tissue culture, propagation of fruits and flowers and food processing are highly remunerative employment options for women in rural areas.
- Though, in terms of numbers, our **livestock population is quite impressive** but its **productivity is quite low** as compared to other countries.
- It requires improved technology and promotion of good breeds of animals to enhance productivity.
- Improved veterinary care and credit facilities to small and marginal farmers and landless labourers would enhance sustainable livelihood options through livestock production.
- Production of fisheries has already increased substantially.
- However, problems related to over- fishing and pollution need to be regulated and controlled.
- Welfare programmes for the fishing community have to be reoriented in a manner which can provide long-term gains and sustenance of livelihoods.
- Horticulture has emerged as a successful sustainable livelihood option and needs to be encouraged significantly.
- Enhancing its role requires **investment in infrastructure** like electricity, cold storage systems, marketing linkages, small-scale processing units and technology improvement and dissemination.

Steps to Turnaround Indian Horticulture Sector.

Other Alternate Livelihood Options

- The Indian economy has seen **several sectors undergo change thanks to IT**.
- Most people agree that in the twenty-first century, IT can be extremely important to attaining both food security and sustainable development.
- Using relevant data and software tools, governments can **identify areas of food insufficiency and vulnerability** and take appropriate measures to prevent or lessen the likelihood of a disaster.
- It benefits the agriculture industry as well since it may spread knowledge about new technology and their uses, as well as on costs, weather patterns, soil types, and other factors that affect crop growth.
- Even if IT cannot bring about change on its own, it can be a useful instrument in unlocking society's creative potential and knowledge.
- Additionally, it has the ability to provide jobs in rural areas.
- Several regions of India are the sites of IT experiments related to rural development.

Sustainable Development and Organic Farming

- Recently people have become aware about the harmful effects of chemical fertilizers, pesticides on human health and environment.
- Because of that a chemical free cultivation process is gaining currency around world, which is **organic farming.**
- In short, organic agriculture is a whole system of farming that **restores, maintains and enhances the ecological balance.**
- There is an **increasing demand** for organically grown food to enhance food safety throughout the world.

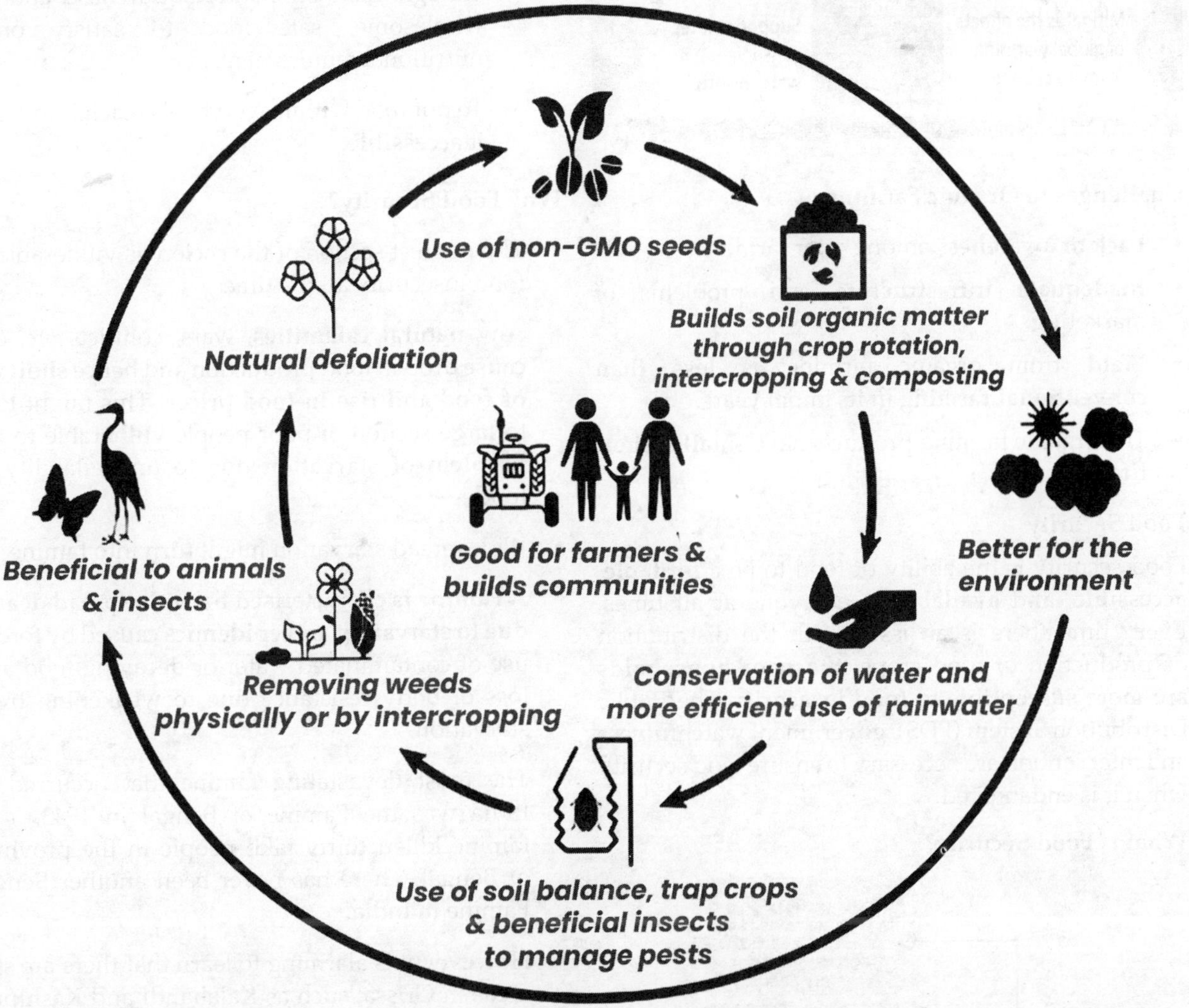

Process of Organic Farming

Benefits of Organic Farming

- It offers a means to **substitute costlier agricultural inputs** with locally produced organic inputs that are cheaper.
- Since the market for crops farmed organically is growing, it makes **money through exports.**
- Foods grown organically are **more nutritious** than crops farmed conventionally, according to studies.
- It is more **labour intensive**, hence can provide employment to large number of people.
- Finally, the product is chemical free hence **eco-friendlier and more sustainable.**

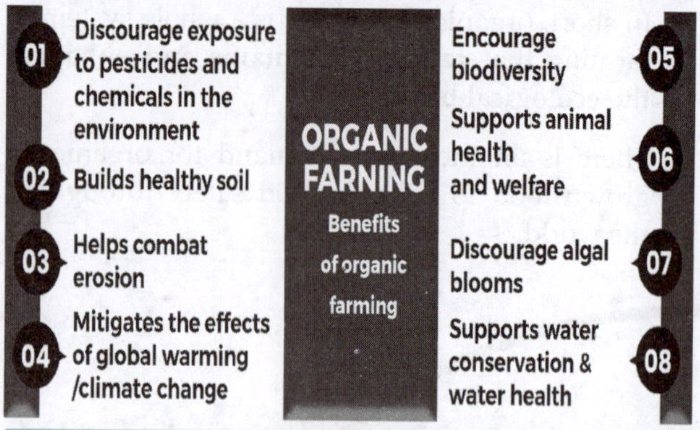

Benefits of Organic Farming

Challenges to Organic Farming

- **Lack of awareness** among poor farmers.
- **Inadequate infrastructure** and problems of marketing.
- **Yield** from organic farming is **less than conventional farming** in its initial years.
- The organic farming products have **smaller shelf life.**

Food Security

Food security is the ability of food to be **affordable, accessible, and available** to everyone at all times. Every time there is an issue with the distribution or production of food crops, **the poor households are more susceptible to food insecurity.** The Public Distribution System (PDS), government watchfulness and intervention are necessary to ensure food security when it is endangered.

What is Food Security?

Food Security

- The following are the components of food security:
  - **Food availability,** which includes food produced domestically, food imports, and food kept in government granaries from the previous year.
  - Being able to **afford** food means having enough cash on hand to purchase enough wholesome, safe food to satisfy one's nutritional requirements.
  - To put food within everyone's reach is to make it **accessible.**

Why Food Security?

- The poorest section of the society is vulnerable to food insecurity all the time.
- Any **natural calamities**, wars, conflicts etc. can cause drop in food production and hence **shortage of food and rise in food prices**. This might lead to large section of poor people vulnerable to the **problem of starvation** due to unavailability of food.
- Widespread starvation might turn into famine.
- A **Famine is characterised by wide spread deaths due to starvation and epidemics** caused by forced use of contaminated water or decaying food and loss of body resistance due to weakening from starvation.
- The most devastating famine that occurred in India was the Famine of Bengal in 1943. This famine killed thirty lakh people in the province of Bengal. There has never been another Bengal Famine in India.
- However, it is alarming to learn that there are still areas in Orissa, such as Kalahandi and Kashipur, where **famine-like conditions have persisted** for a long time and where reports of hunger fatalities have occurred.
- In recent years, reports of starvation deaths have also been made from numerous other distant places, including the Palamau district in Jharkhand and the Baran district in Rajasthan.
- In order to guarantee food at all times, a nation must have food security.

Who are Food-Insecure?

- While many individuals in India experience food and nutrition insecurity, those who are landless and rely on little or no land, traditional craftspeople, those who provide traditional services, small-scale self-employed workers, and the impoverished, including beggars, are the groups most negatively impacted.
- The unorganised sector and the jobless population in urban areas.
- Individuals from economically and socially disadvantaged groups landless people, Schedule Casts, Scheduled Tribes and some Other Backward Classes (OBCs).
- Individuals affected by natural calamities.
- Women in the poor families.
- Unborn child in poor families, girl child in poor families.
- Those who lack access to food are disproportionately numerous in some parts of the nation, including tribal and isolated communities, states with high rates of poverty and economic regression, and areas that are more vulnerable to natural disasters.
- The majority of the nation's food insecure citizens are actually found in the states of Uttar Pradesh (both the eastern and south-eastern regions), Bihar, Jharkhand, Orissa, West Bengal, Chhattisgarh, and portions of Madhya Pradesh and Maharashtra.

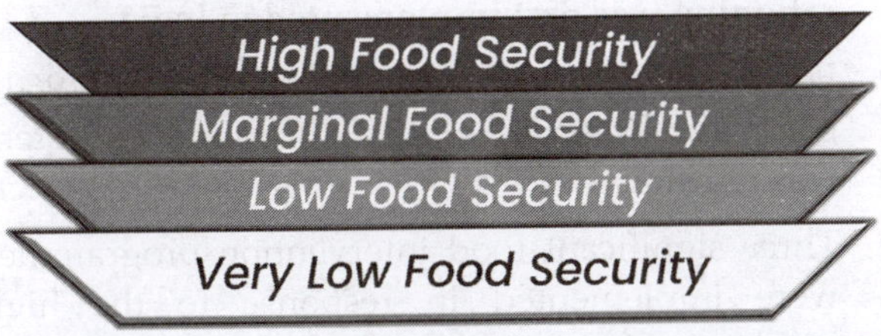

Food Insecurity

Hunger

- Hunger is another aspect indicating food insecurity. Hunger is not just an **expression of poverty**; it **brings about poverty.**
- The attainment of food security therefore involves eliminating current hunger and reducing the risks of future hunger.
- **Hunger has chronic and seasonal dimensions.**
- **Chronic hunger** is a consequence of diets persistently inadequate in terms of quantity and/or quality.
- Poor people suffer from chronic hunger because of their very low income and in turn inability to buy food even for survival.
- **Seasonal hunger** is related to cycles of food growing and harvesting.
- This is prevalent in rural areas because of the seasonal nature of agricultural activities and in urban areas because of the casual labour, e.g., there is less work for casual construction labour during the rainy season.
- This type of hunger exists when a person is unable to get work for the entire year.

Percentage of Households with 'Hunger' in India

Year	Type of Hunger		
	Seasonal	Chronic	Total
Rural			
1983	16.2	2.3	18.5
1993-94	4.2	0.9	5.1
1999-2000	2.6	0.7	3.3
Urban			
1983	5.6	0.8	6.4
1993-94	1.1	0.5	1.6
1999-2000	0.6	0.5	0.9

- The accompanying table indicates a drop in the percentage of both chronic and seasonal hunger in India.
- Since gaining independence, India has strived towards foodgrain self-sufficiency.
- Following independence, Indian policymakers implemented all necessary measures to attain food grain self-sufficiency.
- India implemented a **new agricultural policy** that gave rise to the **"Green Revolution,"** particularly in the production of rice and wheat. Nonetheless, the rise in foodgrains was out of proportion.

- In Uttar Pradesh and Punjab, where foodgrain output peaked in 2012–13 at 78.9 million tonnes, the fastest growth rates have been attained.
- Production of foodgrain in Uttarakhand, Jharkhand, Assam, Tamil Nadu has dropped.
- Conversely, the rice yields in West Bengal and Uttar Pradesh saw notable rises in 2012–13.

Food Security in India

- Since the advent of the Green Revolution in the early- 1970s, the **country has avoided famine** even during adverse weather conditions.
- India has **become self-sufficient** in foodgrains during the last thirty years because of a variety of crops grown all over the country.
- The availability of foodgrains even in adverse weather conditions or otherwise at the country level has further been ensured with a carefully designed food security system by the government.
- This system has two components: **(a) buffer stock and (b) public distribution system.**

Production of foodgrains in india

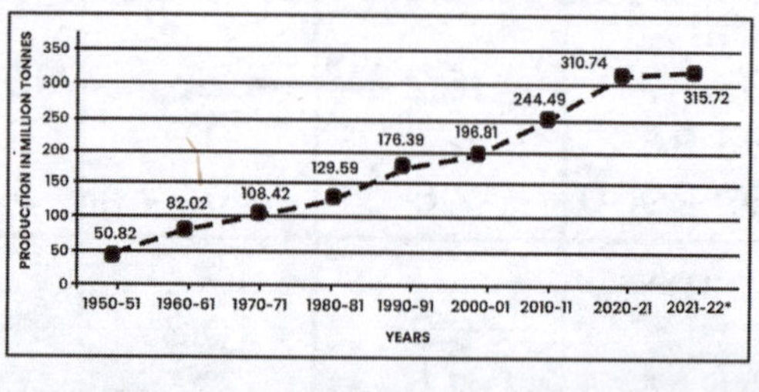

Production of Foodgrains in India

What is Buffer stock?

- Buffer Stock is the foodgrain stock that the **government purchases through Food Corporation of India (FCI),** specifically rice and wheat.
- When there is an excess of wheat and rice in a state, the farmers sell them to the FCI.
- A **predetermined** price is given to the farmers in exchange for their produce which is the **Minimum Support Price.**
- Every year, the **government announces the MSP prior to the planting season** in order to encourage farmers to increase the yield of these crops.
- Granaries are used to store the foodgrains that are purchased.
- Foodgrains are distributed at a price lower than the market price, commonly known as the **Issue Price,** to the weaker strata of society and in deficit areas.
- This additionally addresses the issue of food scarcity in inclement weather or during times of disaster.

What is the Public Distribution System?

- The food that the FCI purchases is given to the less fortunate members of society via ration stores that are subject to government regulations. This is the **Public Distribution System.**
- Nowadays, you may find ration shops in most towns, cities, villages, and communities.
- Nationwide, there are over 5.5 lakh ration stores.
- Ration stores, also called **Fair Price stores,** maintain supplies of food grains, sugar, and cooking kerosene oil.
- Customers purchase these goods for less than what the market would bear.
- Any family that has a ration card* can get monthly ration from the ration shop nearby.

(*Ration cards come in three varieties: (a) Antyodaya cards for the extremely poor; (b) BPL cards for people living in poverty; and (c) APL cards for everyone else.)

- In the midst of the Bengal famine in the **1940s, rationing was first implemented** in India.
- Following a severe food shortage in the 1960s, before the Green Revolution, the rationing system was reinstated.
- Three significant food intervention programmes were implemented in response to the high incidence of poverty levels, as reported by the NSSO in the mid-1970s: the Public Distribution System (**PDS**) for food grains, which had been in place earlier but was strengthened thereafter; **Integrated Child Development Services** (ICDS), which was implemented on an experimental basis in 1975; and **Food-for-Work**** (FFW), which was implemented in 1977–1978.

(**The **National Food Security Act 2013** enables people to live with dignity by providing food and nutritional security at reasonable prices. **75% of people living in rural areas and 50% of those living in urban areas** are considered eligible families under this act for food security.)

- With increasing programme administration experience, a number of new initiatives have been introduced throughout time, and some have undergone structural changes.
- Currently, there are a number of **Poverty Alleviation Programmes (PAPs),** primarily in rural regions that explicitly include food assistance.
- Although certain programmes, like **midday meals and PDS,** are solely focused on promoting food security, the majority of PAPs also work to improve food security.
- Employment projects have a significant impact on food security by raising the poor people's income.

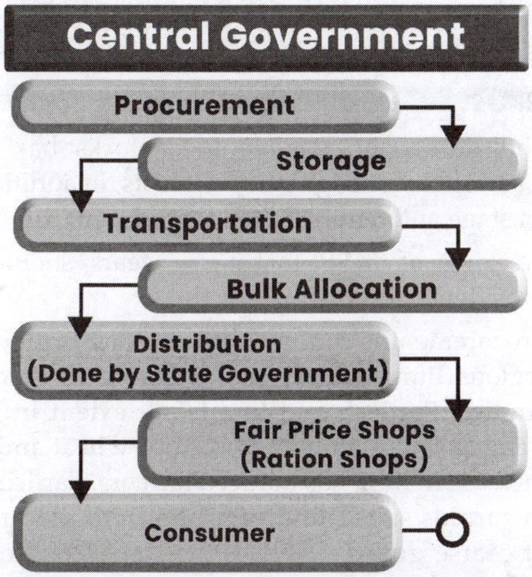

Public Distribution System

Current Status of Public Distribution System

- The Public Distribution System (PDS) represents the primary measure implemented by the Government of India (GoI) to guarantee food security.
- Initially, PDS was available to everybody, with no distinction made between those in poverty and those who were not.
- The PDS policy has **undergone revisions** over time to improve its efficiency and focus.
- In 1,700 blocks around the nation, the **Revamped Public Distribution System (RPDS)** was implemented in 1992. The goal was to introduce **remote and underdeveloped** areas to the advantages of PDS.
- **Targeted Public Distribution System (TPDS)** was implemented in June 1997 as part of a redoubled effort to implement the idea of **focusing on the "poor in all areas."**
- **For the first time, a policy of differentiating prices for the poor and the non-poor was implemented**. Additionally, two unique programmes were introduced in 2000: the **Annapurna Scheme (APS)** and the **Antyodaya Anna Yojana (AAY),** with the **"poorest of the poor" and "indigent senior citizens" as their respective target populations**.
- **Antyodaya Anna Yojana (AAY):** AAY was launched in December 2000. Under the scheme one crore of the poorest among the BPL families covered under the targeted public distribution system were identified. Poor families were identified by the respective state rural development departments through a Below Poverty Line (BPL) survey. Twenty-five kilograms of foodgrains were made available to each eligible family at a highly subsidised rate of Rs 2 per kg for wheat and Rs 3 per kg for rice. This quantity has been enhanced from 25 to 35 kgs with effect from April 2002. The scheme has been further expanded twice by additional 50 lakh BPL families in June 2003 and in August 2004. With this increase, 2 crore families have been covered under the AAY.
- The functioning of these two schemes was linked with the existing network of the PDS.
- The PDS system has proved to be the **most effective system to avert the problem of starvation** and famines in India.
- It has **led to transfer of grains** from surplus region to deficit region.
- It has **helped farmers to raise their income** through sale of grains.

Some Important Features of PDS

Name of scheme	Year of Introduction	Coverage target group	Latest volume	issue price (₹ per kg.)
PDS	UpTo 1992	Universal	-	W-2.34 R-2.89
RPDS	1992	Backward blocks	20 kg of food grains	W-2.80 R-3.77
TPDS	1997	Poor and non-poor BPL APL	35 kg of food grains	BPL-W- 4.15 R-5.65 APL-W-6.10 R-8.30
AAY	2000	poorest of the poor	35 kg of food grains	W-2.00 R-3.00
APS	2000	Indigent senior citizens	10 kg of food grains	Free
National Food Security Act (NFSA)	2013	Priority households	5kg per person per month	W-2.00 R-3.00 Coarse-1.00 grains

Important Features of PDS

- One of the problems with the PDS system is that while the FCI's godowns are flowing with grains, **mismanagement of storage** system has led to **wastage of many tonnes** of grains annually.

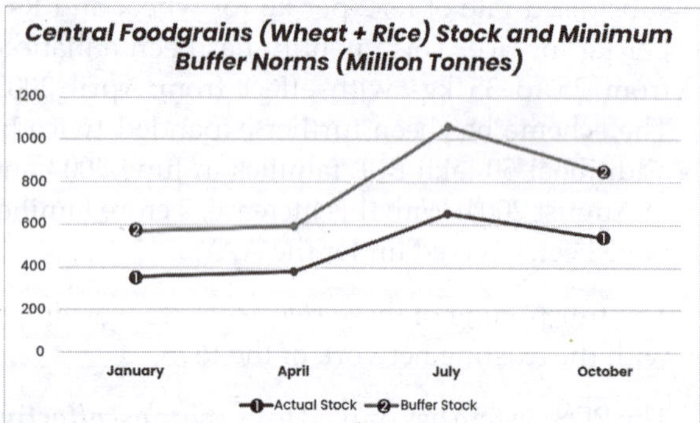

Central Foodgrains (Wheat + Rice)

Problems with Current Stocking Norms and Rationing System

- There is a general consensus that **high level of buffer stocks** of foodgrains is very **undesirable and can be wasteful.**
- The storage of massive food stocks has been responsible for **high carrying costs,** in addition to wastage and **deterioration in grain quality.**
- Freezing of **MSP** for a few years should be considered seriously.
- Procurement is concentrated in a few prosperous regions (**Punjab, Haryana, Western Uttar Pradesh, Andhra Pradesh and to a lesser extent in West Bengal)** and mainly of two crops **wheat and rice** increase in MSP has induced farmers, particularly in surplus states, to divert land from production of coarse grains, which is the staple food of the poor, to the production of rice and wheat.
- The intensive utilisation of water in the cultivation of rice has also led to environmental degradation and fall in the water level, threatening the sustainability of the agricultural development in these states.
- As per NSSO, report, in rural India, the per person per month consumption of rice has declined from 6.38 Kg. in 2004-05 to 5.98 Kg in 2011-12.
- In urban India, the **per person per month consumption of rice, too has declined** from 4.71 Kg in 2004-05 to 4.19 Kg in 2011-12.

- Per **Capita consumption of PDS rice has doubled** in rural India and increased by 66% in urban India since 2004-05.
- The per **Capita consumption of PDS wheat has doubled** since 2004-05 in both rural and urban India.
- **PDS dealers are sometimes found resorting to malpractices** like **diverting the grains** to open market to get better margin, **selling poor quality grains at ration shops**, irregular opening of the shops, etc.
- It is common to find that ration shops regularly have **unsold stocks of poor-quality grains** left. This has proved to be a big problem. When ration shops are unable to sell, a massive stock of foodgrains piles up with the FCI. In recent years, there is another factor that has led to the decline of the PDS.
- Earlier every family, poor and non-poor had a ration card with a fixed quota of items such as **rice, wheat, sugar etc.** These were sold at the same low price to every family. The **three types of cards** and the range of prices that you see today did not exist. A large number of families could buy foodgrains from the ration shops subject to a fixed quota. These included **low-income families whose incomes were marginally higher than the below poverty line families.**
- Now, with **TPDS** of three different prices, any family above the poverty line gets very little discount at the ration shop.
- The price for APL family is almost as high as open market price, so there is **little incentive for them to buy these items** from the ration shop.

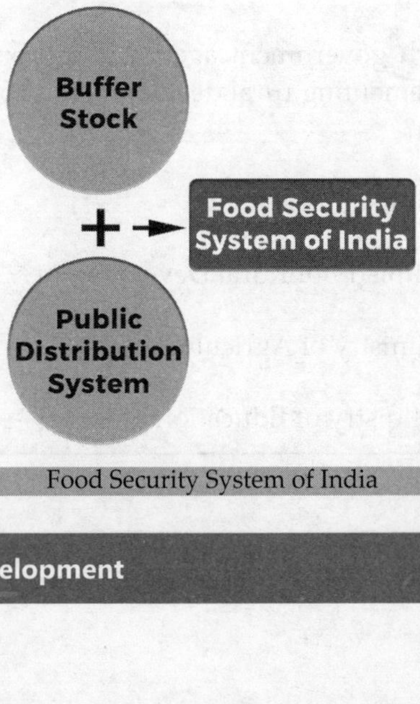

Food Security System of India

Role of Cooperatives in Food Security

- The **cooperatives** are also playing an important role in food security in India especially in the southern and western parts of the country.
- The cooperative societies set up shops to sell low priced goods to poor people.
- For example, out of all fair price shops running in Tamil Nadu, around 94 per cent are being run by cooperatives.
- In Delhi, Mother Dairy is making strides in provision of milk and vegetables to the consumers at controlled rate decided by Government of Delhi.
- **Amul** is another **success story of cooperatives in milk and milk products from Gujarat**. It has brought about the White Revolution in the country.
- These are a few examples of many more cooperatives running in different parts of the country ensuring food security of different sections of society.
- Similarly, in **Maharashtra, Academy of Development Science (ADS)** has facilitated a network of NGOs for setting up grain banks in different regions. ADS organises training and **capacity building programmes on food security for NGOs.**

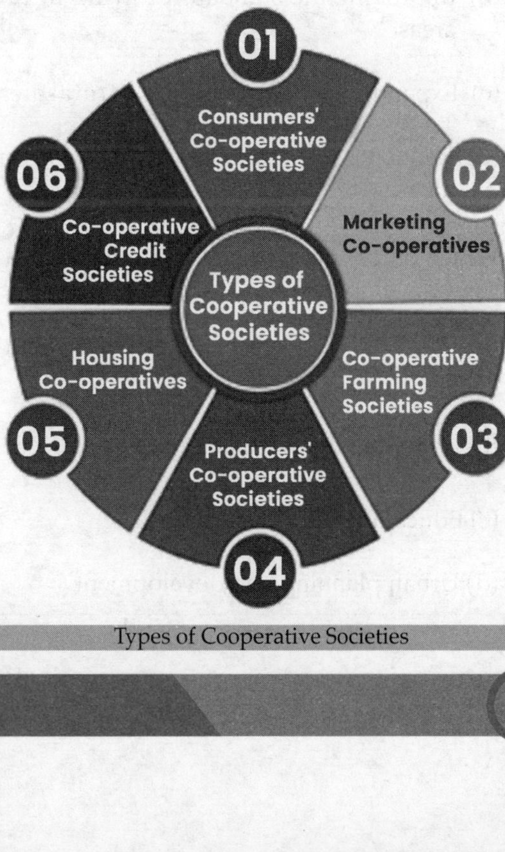

Types of Cooperative Societies

- **Grain Banks** are now slowly taking shape in different parts of **Maharashtra.**
- ADS efforts to set up Grain Banks, to facilitate replication through other NGOs and to influence the Government's policy on food security are thus paying rich dividends.
- The ADS Grain Bank programme is acknowledged as a successful and innovative food security intervention.

Conclusion

Without a good rural development programme, there can be no successful programme aimed at reducing poverty. Despite this, the rural economy is becoming more diverse thanks to the dairy, poultry, and other related industries. Their lack of investment is causing them troubles. The **lack of both public and private investment** and infrastructure is a problem for the rural economy.

These days, protecting the environment and promoting human welfare are inextricably linked. Because of this, **organic farming has enormous potential**. It is necessary to inform small and low-income farmers and provide them with a **support system** to make up for the production decline in the first few years.

The **food security** has become a **major part of poverty alleviation** program. The PDS system, on the success of Green Revolution, has helped India to shed the image of a nation marred with famines and starvation. The current stocking norms are facing many challenges. The MSP and marketing of farm products are also facing challenges. The **current PDS system** has served its purpose well, now there is **need to reform** the limitation of the system to handle the rising food subsidy bills and destruction of environment from chemicals.

TEST YOURSELF

Multiple Choice Questions

Q1. What is the main objective of rural development?

(a) Promoting urbanisation

(b) Improving the standard of living in rural areas

(c) Expanding industrialisation in rural areas

(d) Reducing the population density in rural areas

Q2. Which of the following is NOT a focus area of rural development?

(a) Agriculture and allied activities

(b) Infrastructure development

(c) Education and healthcare

(d) Urban planning and development

Q3. What is the role of Self-Help Groups (SHGs) in rural development?

(a) Providing microfinance and promoting entrepreneurship

(b) Constructing infrastructure projects in rural areas

(c) Improving educational facilities in rural schools

(d) Promoting urban migration among rural population

Q4. Which government agency is responsible for implementing rural development programs in India?

(a) Ministry of Finance

(b) Ministry of Rural Development

(c) Ministry of Agriculture

(d) Ministry of Education

Q5. What is the significance of rural electrification in rural development?

(a) It promotes access to modern energy sources and enhances productivity.

(b) It reduces the need for agricultural practices in rural areas.

(c) It increases the dependency on traditional sources of energy.

(d) It encourages urbanisation and migration from rural areas.

Q6. Which of the following is an example of a rural development scheme in India?

(a) Pradhan Mantri Jan Dhan Yojana

(b) Make in India

(c) Smart Cities Mission

(d) Swachh Bharat Abhiyan

Q7. What is the role of rural infrastructure development in rural development?

(a) It provides access to basic amenities and services.

(b) It promotes urbanisation and industrialisation.

(c) It increases agricultural subsidies and incentives.

(d) It encourages migration to urban areas.

Q8. What is the significance of rural employment generation in rural development?

(a) It reduces unemployment rates in urban areas.

(b) It provides income opportunities and reduces poverty in rural areas.

(c) It promotes foreign direct investment in rural sectors.

(d) It encourages the growth of the urban informal sector.

Q9. Which of the following is NOT a potential challenge to rural development in India?

(a) Lack of access to quality education and healthcare

(b) Insufficient infrastructure development

(c) High agricultural productivity and surplus production

(d) Limited access to credit and financial services

Q10. What measures can be taken to promote rural development in India?

(a) Enhancing agricultural productivity and diversification

(b) Improving access to education and healthcare services

(c) Developing rural infrastructure and connectivity

(d) All of the above

Q11. Which of the following factors/policies were affecting the price of rice in India in the recent past? (UPSC-2020)

1. Minimum Support Price

2. Government's trading

3. Government's stockpiling

4. Consumer subsidies

Select the correct answer using the code given below:

(a) 1, 2 and 4 only (b) 1, 3 and 4 only

(c) 2 and 3 only (d) 1, 2, 3 and 4

Q12. The economic cost of food grains to the Food Corporation of India is Minimum Support Price and bonus (if any) paid to the farmers plus (UPSC-2019)

(a) Transportation cost only

(b) Interest cost only

(c) Procurement incidentals and distribution cost

(d) Procurement incidentals and charges for warehouses.

Q13. With reference to the provisions made under the National Food Security Act, 2013, consider the following statements: (UPSC-2018)

1. The families coming under the category of 'below poverty line (BPL)' only are eligible to receive subsidised food grains.
2. The eldest woman in a household, of age 18 years or above, shall be the head of the household for the purpose of issuance of a ration card.
3. Pregnant women and lactating mothers are entitled to a 'take-home ration' of 1600 calories per day during pregnancy and for six months thereafter.

Which of the statements given above is / are correct?

(a) 1 and 2 only (b) 2 only

(c) 1 and 3 only (d) 3 only

Answer Key

Q1.	b	Q2.	d	Q3.	a	Q4.	b
Q5.	a	Q6.	a	Q7.	a	Q8.	b
Q9.	c	Q10.	d	Q11.	d	Q12.	c
Q13.	b						

Model Questions for Main Examination

Q1. Discuss the importance of rural banking in India and what are the difficulties faced it?

Q2. What are the advantages of organic farming? What are the challenges faced by farmers in the beginning years of organic farming?

UNIT 7

Employment: Growth, Information and Other Issues

In This Unit

Comprehensive and profound coverage of the following NCERT's chapter:

✓ NCERT Class- 11th (Indian Economic Development), Chapter- 7

Introduction

People work to earn a living. An individual, while living in society works to earn his/her livelihood. Being employed gives self-worth and satisfaction to a person. People indulging in various activities produce various goods and services, which in turn would help the economy of a country to grow. Studying about trends in employment would lead us to study the type of economic activities happening in a country. It also helps the policy makers tackle some of the problems of the society like **child labour, lack of women's participation in workforce and unemployment.**

Workers and Employment

- **Economic activities** are those that have an impact on the gross national product.
- Everyone involved in economic activity, regardless of their position, is a **worker**.
- They are workers too, even if some of them take a temporary leave of absence owing to illness, accidents, physical disabilities, inclement weather, holidays, social or religious events, etc.
- All others who assist the primary workers in these tasks are also considered workers.
- **Workers** include self-employed individuals as well as people who receive compensation from their employers for their labour.

Participation of People in Employment

- An indicator used to analyse the employment situation in the nation is the **worker-population ratio.**
- The percentage of a population that actively contributes to a country's production of goods and services may be found using this ratio.
- A higher ratio indicates a higher level of engagement among the populace; a medium or low ratio indicates a high percentage of the population not directly engaged in economic activity inside a country.
- **The worker-population ratio** can be calculated by dividing the worker's population with total population and multiplying it by 100.

Sex	Worker-Population Ratio		
	Total	Rural	Urban
Men	76.0	75.2	69.3
Women	35.9	33.2	21.8
Total	56.0	54.2	46.0

Worker Population Ratio in India (2022-2023)

- If we see the above-mentioned table, we can analyse that there 56 (round off) workers per 100 people in India.
- This ratio is 36 in urban area and 40 in rural area.
- A higher ratio indicates a higher level of engagement among the populace; a medium or low ratio indicates a high percentage of the population not directly engaged in economic activity inside a country.
- If we see the **female worker-population ratio**, the ratio is greater in rural region than urban region.

- One possible explanation for this could be that men do the majority of high-paying professions in metropolitan areas, and women do not migrate to these areas at a higher rate than men do.
- Most significantly, household chores are performed by women in the workforce, which are not included in the GDP calculation as economic activities in general.

Self-employed and Hired Workers

- One facet of the quality of employment in a country can potentially be ascertained by understanding the position of an employee inside an organisation.
- Workers who own and operate an enterprise to earn their livelihood are known as **self-employed workers.** About 52 per cent workforce in India belongs to this category.
- Another category of workers is **casual wage labourers.** Such labourers are casually engaged in others' farms and, in return, get a remuneration for the work done. They make about thirty percent of India's labour force.
- **Regular salaried employees** are those that are employed by an individual or business and receive their wages on a regular basis. They account for 18 per cent of India's workforce.

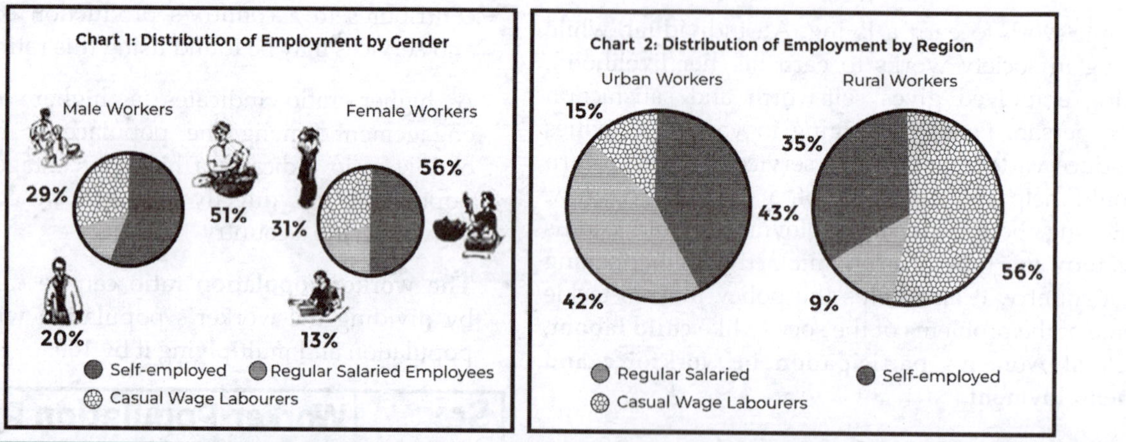

Distribution of Employment by Gender and Region

- The distribution of workers across gender shows approximately same trend.
- Most of them are engaged in self-employed work, followed by casual wage labourer and finally regular salaried employees.
- If we analyse the **distribution of employment across regions,** the trend differs in urban and rural region.
- In **urban region** regular salaried employees are in larger number than that in rural region.
- Similar thing can be analysed for **casual wage labourers**. They form major chunk of employment in rural region compared to that in urban region.

Work in Factories, Offices, and Enterprises

- A nation's workforce pool shifts from agriculture and other related industries to industry and services as it develops economically.
- Workers move from rural to urban areas as a result of this process.
- Ultimately, and at a much later time, the industrial sector starts to lose its percentage of overall employment as the service sector starts to grow quickly.
- An understanding of this movement can be gained by examining the labour distribution by industry.
- In general, there are eight distinct industrial divisions into which we separate all economic activities.
- They include

(i) Agriculture

(ii) Mining

(iii) Manufacturing

(iv) Electricity, Gas and Water Supply

(v) Construction

(vi) Trade

(vii) Transport and Storage

(viii) Services

- To keep things simple all the working persons working in this classification can be combined into three major sectors viz., (a) **primary sector** which includes (i), (b) **secondary sector** which includes (ii), (iii), (iv) and (v) and (c) **Tertiary sector** which includes divisions (vi), (vii) and (viii).
- The distribution of working people across various industries in 2011–12 is displayed in Table on 'Distribution of Employment based on Region'.

Industrial Category	Place of Residence		Sex		Total
	Rural	Urban	Men	Women	
Primary Sector	64.1	6.7	43.6	62.8	48.9
Secondary Sector	20.4	35.0	25.9	20.0	24.3
Tertiary/Service Sector	15.5	58.3	30.5	17.2	26.8
Total	100.0	100.0	100.0	100.0	100.0

Distribution of Workforce by Industry

- **Primary sector forms** the major chunk of work in rural region and the female workforce is largely employed in primary sector.
- It employs 48.9% of total workforce of India.
- The **secondary sector** employs more people in urban region than in rural region.
- Men are employed more than women in this sector.
- It employs a quarter of India's total workforce.
- The **tertiary sector** employs major chunk of urban workforce, here also male workforce is more than female workforce.
- The tertiary sector employs less workforce than primary sector, which is the reason of high unemployment in India.

Growth and Changing Structure of Employment

- There is a **positive relation between economic growth and employment** generation.

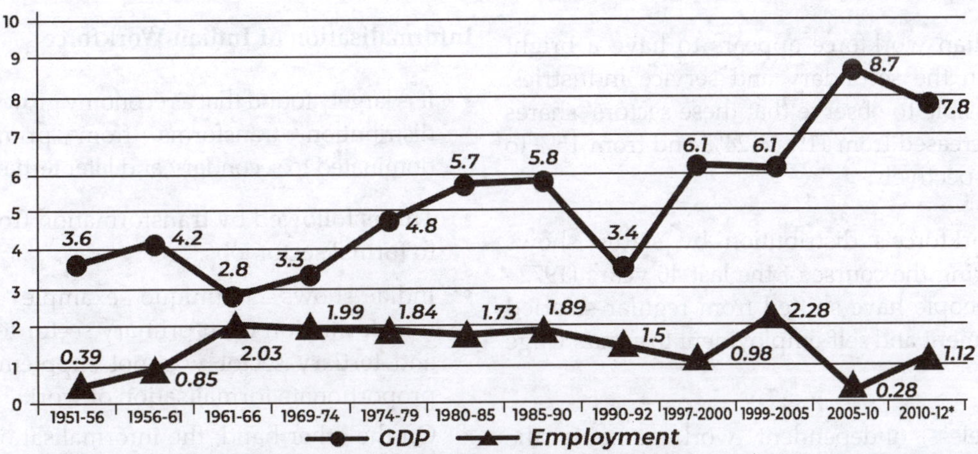

Growth of Employment and Gross Domestic Product (1951-2012)

- When an economy grows, it generates jobs.
- In Indian context, this has always not been the case.
- The following chart shows that **the employment generation growth in India has been always less than GDP growth rate.**
- This problem became more severe after 1991 reforms, where GDP growth rate jumps manifolds, while employment growth rate declined.
- This gap between GDP growth rate and employment rate gave rise to a peculiar problem of **'jobless growth in India'.**
- There is a noticeable shift away from agricultural labour and towards non-farm jobs in the workforce distribution by industrial sectors.

ITEM	1972-73	1983	1993-94	1999-2000	2011-2012
SECTOR					
Primary	74.3	68.6	64	60.4	48.9
Secondary	10.9	11.5	16	15.8	24.3
Services	14.8	16.9	20	23.8	26.8
Total	100.0	100.0	100.0	100.0	100.0
STATUS					
Self-employed	61.4	57.3	54.6	52.6	52.0
Regular Salaried Employees	15.4	13.8	13.6	14.6	18.0
Casual Wage Labourers	23.2	28.9	31.8	32.8	30.0
Total	100.0	100.0	100.0	100.0	100.0

Trends in Employment Pattern (in %)

- The primary sector employed around 74% of the workforce in 1972–73; by 2011–12, that percentage had dropped to roughly 50%.
- The Indian workforce appears to have a bright future in the secondary and service industries. It is possible to observe that these sectors' shares have increased from 11% to 24% and from 15% to 27%, respectively.
- The workforce's distribution by status shows that during the course of the last 40 years (1972–2012), people have shifted from regular salaried employment and self-employment to casual wage labour.
- Nonetheless, independent work remains the primary source of employment.
- The transition from self-employment and regular salaried job to casual wage work is referred to by scholars as the "**casualisation of workforce.**"

Informalisation of Indian Workforce

- It is largely found that as economy grows, workforce distribution transforms from primary sector dominated to secondary and later tertiary sector.
- This is followed by transformation from informal to formal sector jobs.
- India shows a unique example where the transformation from primary sector to secondary and tertiary sector was not supplemented with proportionate formalisation of work.
- On the other hand, the informalisation of Indian workforce started.

- The informal workforce would be devoid of any social security, workers have to work in less regularises environment, on less payments etc.

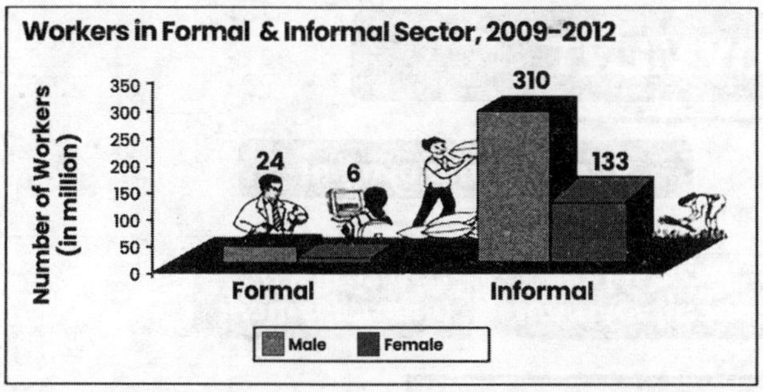

Workers in Formal/Informal Sector (2009-12)

- There are about 473 million workers in the country. There are about 30 million workers in the formal sector which amounts to about 6%. The rest 94% work in the unorganised sector.
- Of the 30 million workers in the formal sector, only 6 million, or roughly 21% (30/6×100), are women. In the informal sector, male workers account for 69 per cent of the workforce.
- Given that employment in the official sector is stagnating, several developing nations, including India, have begun to focus on businesses and workers in the informal sector since the late 1970s.
- Workers and enterprises functioning in the unofficial sector do not get a consistent salary and are not bound by any laws or safeguards from the government.
- Employees are let go without receiving any pay. In addition to using antiquated technology, informal sector businesses don't keep any records.
- Employees in this industry are squatters and live in slums.
- In recent times, the **Indian government has taken steps to modernise informal sector** firms and **provide social security provisions** to workers in this sector, thanks to the efforts of the International Labour Organisation (ILO).

Unemployment

- The term unemployment refers to a situation where a person actively searches for employment but is unable to find work.
- **Unemployment is considered to be a key measure of the health of the economy.**
- The most frequently used measure of unemployment is the unemployment rate.
- It's calculated by dividing the number of unemployed people by the number of people in the labour force.
- In recent times, the Indian government has taken steps to modernise informal sector firms and provide social security provisions to workers in this sector, thanks to the efforts of the International Labour Organisation (ILO).
- The following types of unemployment are usually found in any economy-
- **Frictional Unemployment:** It occurs when people voluntarily change jobs. After a person leaves a company, it naturally takes time to find another job. Similarly, graduates just starting to look for jobs to enter the workforce add to frictional unemployment.
- **Cyclical Unemployment:** Cyclical unemployment is the variation in the number of unemployed workers over the course of economic upturns and downturns, such as those related to changes in oil prices. Unemployment rises during recessionary periods and declines during periods of economic growth.
- **Structural Unemployment:** Structural unemployment comes about through a technological change in the structure of the economy in which labour markets operate. Technological changes can lead to unemployment among workers displaced from jobs that are no longer needed. Examples of such changes include the replacement of horse-drawn transport by automobiles and the automation of manufacturing.
- **Seasonal Unemployment:** Seasonal jobs are limited to a certain time period, sometimes leaving people who work in those jobs without employment after the season ends. Seasonal unemployment is the result of the decreased demand in labour that occurs at each season's end, making the seasonal rate more predictable than other types of unemployment. Seasonal unemployment often occurs in tourist areas, where attractions often are open only during a certain time of the year.

- **Underemployment:** Underemployment differs from unemployment in that it describes people who are working, but aren't employed at their full capability. Measuring underemployment shows how effectively the economy is using the labour force's skills, experience, and work availability.

Types of Unemployment

Government and Employment Generation

- Since independence the **Union and State Governments have played a central role in employment generation in India.**
- The employment generation can be of two types.
- **One** is **indirect employment generation**, where government policies generate economic activities like infrastructure development, capacity expansion etc.
- After these activities a spillover effect is felt and both public and private sectors respond to these activities by expanding their operations and employing more workers.
- **Another type** is **direct employment generation**, where governments launch direct employment generation programs like MGNREGA, *Pradhan Mantri Employment Generation Schemes* etc.

Conclusion

Indulging in any kind of economic activity is fundamental to lead a dignified life by an individual. The job to provide employment is usually undertaken by governments and private sector. In normal circumstances the growing economy provides enough employment opportunity. **India shows many diversions from normal trends.** Here, **decline of share of primary sector** in GDP is not matched with similar decline in dependence of workforce on primary sector. As a result of which a **'jobless growth problem'** is attached to Indian economy. The informalisation and casualisation of workforce has made **Indian workforce prone to social vulnerabilities.** The employment generation programs whether it is direct or indirect have not proved successful in India. A way forward for employment generation could be a growth of secondary sector in India to absorb the surplus labours from primary sector.

TEST YOURSELF

Multiple Choice Questions

Q1. What is the primary goal of employment growth?

(a) Reducing poverty and inequality.

(b) Maximizing corporate profits.

(c) Achieving high economic growth rates.

(d) Promoting urbanisation.

Q2. Which of the following is NOT a source of employment information?

(a) Employment Exchanges

(b) Newspaper advertisements

(c) Social media platforms

(d) Census data

Q3. What is the role of the National Sample Survey Organisation (NSSO) in employment data collection?

(a) Conducting regular surveys and collecting employment-related data.

(b) Providing unemployment benefits to individuals.

(c) Ensuring compliance with labour laws and regulations.

(d) Promoting skill development programs.

Q4. Which sector of the economy is the largest employer in most developing countries?

(a) Agriculture (b) Manufacturing

(c) Services (d) Construction

Q5. What is disguised unemployment?

(a) When individuals are unemployed but actively seeking work.

(b) When individuals are employed but not productive.

(c) When individuals work less than the full-time hours they desire.

(d) When individuals work in low-paying jobs despite having higher qualifications.

Q6. What is the significance of the organised sector in employment?

(a) It provides secure and formal employment with social security benefits.

(b) It contributes to higher economic growth rates.

(c) It offers more entrepreneurial opportunities.

(d) It promotes rural development.

Q7. What are the major challenges in the measurement of employment in developing countries?

(a) Insufficient data collection methods.

(b) Inaccurate reporting by individuals and firms.

(c) Informal sector activities and underemployment.

(d) All of the above.

Q8. What is the role of the Mahatma Gandhi National Rural Employment Guarantee Act (MGNREGA) in employment generation?

(a) Providing unemployment benefits to urban workers.

(b) Facilitating skill development programs in rural areas.

(c) Guaranteeing 100 days of wage employment in rural areas.

(d) Encouraging self-employment through microfinance schemes.

Q9. What is the impact of technological advancements on employment?

(a) It leads to job losses and unemployment.

(b) It enhances productivity and creates new job opportunities.

(c) It promotes a shift from rural to urban areas.

(d) It reduces income inequality.

Q10. What is the role of entrepreneurship in employment generation?

(a) It leads to job losses and unemployment.

(b) It encourages self-employment and job creation.

(c) It increases dependency on government jobs.

(d) It promotes capital-intensive industries.

Q11. The situation of underemployment, where people are apparently working but all of them are made to work less than their potential is known as

(a) Disguised unemployment

(b) Cyclical unemployment

(c) Structural unemployment

(d) Frictional unemployment

Q12. Which of the following benefits are enjoyed by the workers in the organised sector?

1. They enjoy security of employment.
2. They are expected to work only a fixed number of hours and if they work more, they have to be paid overtime by the employer.
3. They also get other benefits from the employers such as get paid leave, payment during holidays, provident fund, gratuity etc.
4. They are supposed to get medical benefits and facilities like drinking water and a safe working environment.

Select the correct answer using the code given below:

(a) 1 only (b) 1 and 2 only

(c) 1, 2 and 3 only (d) 1, 2, 3 and 4

Q13. With reference to casual workers employed in India, consider the following statements: (UPSC 2019)

1. All casual workers are entitled for Employees Provident Fund coverage.
2. All casual workers are entitled for regular working hours and overtime payment.
3. The government can by a notification specify that an establishment or industry shall pay wages only through its bank account.

Which of the above statements are correct?

(a) 1 and 2 only (b) 2 and 3 only

(c) 1 and 3 only (d) 1, 2 and 3

Q14. Disguised unemployment generally means (UPSC 2013)

(a) Large number of people remain unemployed.

(b) Alternative employment is not available.

(c) Marginal productivity of labour is zero.

(d) Productivity of workers is low.

Answer Key

Q1.	a	Q2.	d	Q3.	a	Q4.	a
Q5.	b	Q6.	a	Q7.	d	Q8.	c
Q9.	b	Q10.	b	Q11.	a	Q12.	d
Q13.	b	Q14.	c				

Model Questions for Main Examination

Q1. Define unemployment and discuss all the causes of unemployment in India?

Q2. Discuss the differences between rural and urban unemployment?

UNIT 8

Infrastructure

In This Unit

Comprehensive and profound coverage of the following NCERT's chapter:

✓ NCERT Class- 11th (Indian Economic Development), Chapter- 8

Introduction

The regional development of India is not equal. The **western and southern regions are more developed than eastern and North-eastern region**. One of the reasons for uneven distribution of development could be the presence of developed infrastructure in the western and southern regions. **Infrastructure is essential for any kind of economic activity to become possible**. An investment in infrastructure development provides a spillover effect to other sectors of the economy.

What is Infrastructure?

- **Infrastructure** is defined as the basic physical systems of a business, region, or nation and often involves the production of public goods or production processes. Examples of infrastructure include transportation systems, communication networks, sewage, water, and school systems.
- **Support services are provided by infrastructure** in the primary domains of industrial and agricultural production, as well as local and international trade and commerce.
- Roads, railroads, ports, airports, dams, power plants, oil and gas pipelines, telecommunication facilities, the nation's educational system, which consists of colleges and universities, its health system, which consists of hospitals, its sanitary system, which consists of facilities for clean drinking water, and its monetary system, which consists of banks, insurance, and other financial institutions, are some examples of these services.
- While some of these facilities **directly influence the production** of goods and services, others **benefit the economy indirectly** by fostering the growth of the social sector.
- Some distinguish between two types of infrastructure: **social and economic.** Infrastructure connected to energy, transportation, and communication falls under the latter group, while infrastructure relating to housing, health, and education is under the former.

Relevance of Infrastructure

- A modern industrial economy's **ability to function efficiently** is reliant on its infrastructure.
- Moreover, modern agriculture heavily relies on it for the large-scale, quick transportation of seeds, fertilisers, pesticides, and products via contemporary roads, railroads, and shipping facilities.
- Because agribusiness must operate on a very big scale, it now depends on banking and insurance institutions.
- Infrastructure enhances a nation's economic growth by raising the productivity of its production factors and raising the standard of living for its citizens.
- Poor infrastructure can **negatively impact health** in a number of ways.
- Encouraging changes to the water supply and sanitation system have a significant effect by lowering the morbidity of major waterborne diseases and the severity of the disease when it does occur.

- Apart from the apparent connection between water, sanitation, and health, the state of transportation and communication infrastructure can also impact health care accessibility.
- Transportation-related air pollution and safety risks have an impact on morbidity as well, especially in places with high population density.

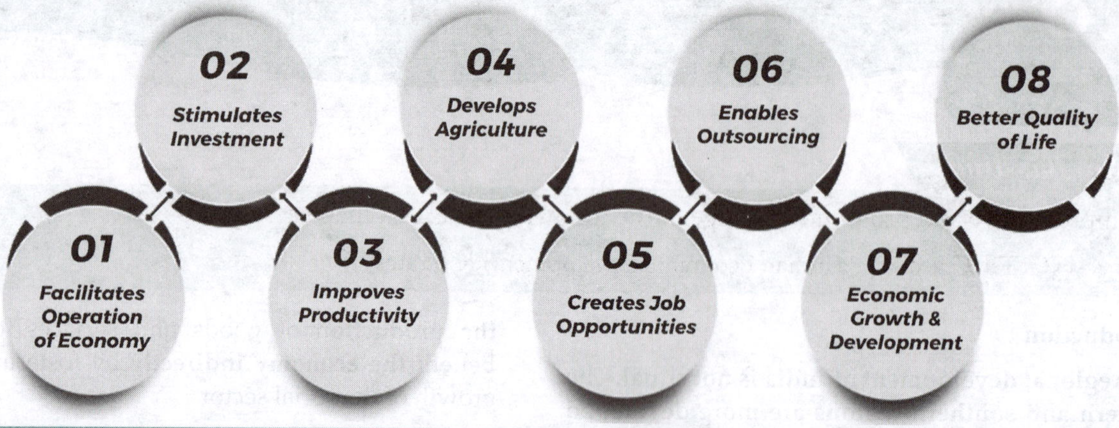

Importance of Infrastructure

India's Current Level of Infrastructure

- **The creation and maintenance of infrastructure** have been the sole responsibility of governments.
- But lately Public-private-partnership (PPP) mode of **infrastructure creation and maintenance has become popular.**
- As far as India is concerned, there has been a dearth of infrastructure in approximately in all sector.
- After 75 years of independence, the rural households still use bio-fuels, fuelwood, cow-dung cakes etc. for cooking purposes.
- The pucca house is still a dream for many households in India.
- **Census 2001 shows scarcity of infrastructure in rural** area:
  - ➢ 56% households do not have electricity connections,
  - ➢ 43% still uses kerosene for cooking and heating,
  - ➢ About 90% households use bio-fuels for cooking,
  - ➢ Tap water availability is limited to 24% of rural households,
  - ➢ 76% households bring drinking water from distant or open sources, outside their house,
  - ➢ Access to improved sanitation is limited to only 20% of households.

Some Infrastructure in India and other Countries

Country	Investment* in Infrastructure as a % GDP (2014)	Access to Improved Water Source (%) (2015)	Access to Improved Sanitation (%) (2015)	Mobile Subscribers/ 100 People (2015)	Power Generation (billion kwh) (2016)
China	46	96	77	93	6015
Hong Kong	24	92	100	229	39
India	34	94	40	79	1423
South Korea	29	98	100	119	549
Pakistan	15	91	64	70	105**
Singapore	29	10	100	146	49*
Indonesia	35	0	61	132	249

Infrastructural Comparisons between Countries from Asia

- The accompanying table compares India's infrastructure situation to that of a few other nations.
- Despite the general consensus that infrastructure is the cornerstone of development, India has not yet heeded this advice.
- 3.4 percent of India's GDP is invested in infrastructure, a much lower percentage than that of China and Indonesia.
- Some economists have projected that India will become the third biggest economy in the world a few decades from now.
- For that to happen, **India will have to boost its infrastructure investment.**
- In any country, as the income rises, the composition of infrastructure requirements changes significantly.
- For low-income countries, basic infrastructure services, like irrigation, transport and power, are more important.
- **As economies mature and most of their basic consumption demands are met,** the share of agriculture in the economy shrinks and more **service-related infrastructure** is required.
- This is why, the share of power and telecommunication infrastructure is greater in high-income countries.
- Thus, development of infrastructure and economic development go hand in hand.
- **Agriculture depends,** to a considerable extent, on the adequate expansion and development of irrigation facilities.
- **Industrial progress depends** on the development of power and electricity generation, transport and communications.
- Obviously, if proper attention is not paid to the development of infrastructure, it is likely to act as a severe constraint on economic development.

Energy

- Energy has been the basic need for any development process.
- From agriculture to manufacturing to service sector, all of them need constant and 24*7 energy source.
- As the country steps up the ladders of development, its demand for energy swells up.

Sources of Energy

- Energy comes from both commercial and non-commercial sources.
- Coal, oil, and electricity are **commercial sources** since they are traded.
- Dried dung, firewood, and agricultural waste are **non-commercial energy sources**. Since they are found in forests and other natural settings, these are not for sale.
- Non-commercial energy sources are typically **renewable**, whereas commercial energy sources are typically **exhaustible** (except from hydropower).
- Over 60% of Indian homes rely on conventional energy sources to fulfil their regular heating and cooking requirements.

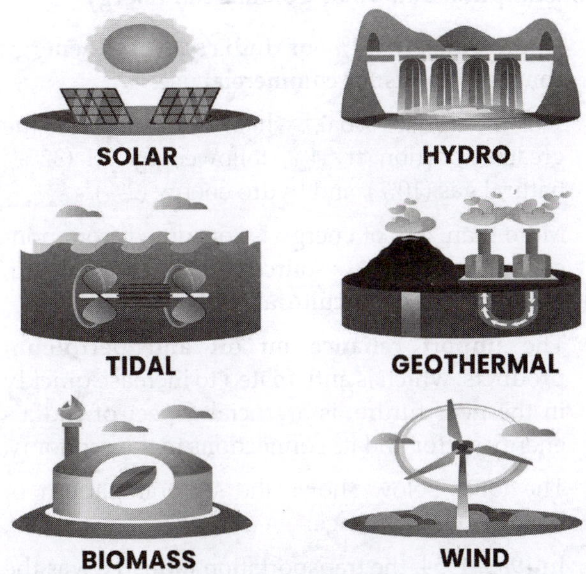

Sources of Energy

Non-conventional Sources of Energy

- Both commercial and non-commercial sources of energy are known as **conventional sources of energy.**
- There are three other sources of energy which are commonly termed as non-conventional sources — **solar energy, wind energy and tidal power.**

- Being a tropical country, India has almost unlimited potential for producing all three types of energy if some appropriate cost-effective technologies that are already available are used. Even cheaper technologies can be developed.

Different Sources of Electricity Generation in India, 2023

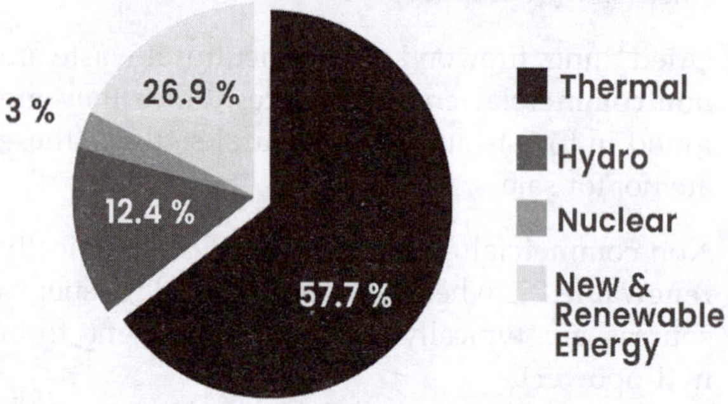

Sources of Electricity Generated (2023)

Consumption Pattern of Commercial Energy

- Approximately **74% of India's overall energy consumption is for commercial** use.
- This comprises **coal**, which accounts for the greatest portion at 54%, followed by oil (32%), natural gas (10%), and hydro energy (2%).
- More than 26% of energy is consumed from non-commercial energy sources, such as firewood, cow dung, and agricultural waste.
- The **import reliance on oil and petroleum** products, which is anticipated to increase quickly in the near future, is a crucial aspect of India's energy sector and its connections to the economy.
- The table below shows the sectoral pattern of business energy usage.
- In 1953–1954, the transportation industry was the biggest user of commercial energy. Nonetheless, the transportation sector's share has been steadily declining while the household, agricultural, and industrial sectors' shares have been rising.
- Of all the energy used for commercial purposes, the largest percentage is derived from oil and gas.
- The use of energy has increased in tandem with the economy's explosive growth.

Sector	1953-54	1970-71	1990-91	2014-15	2021-22
Household	10	12	12	23	20
Agriculture	01	03	08	18	25
Industries	40	50	45	44	40
Transport	44	28	22	2	20
Others	5	07	13	13	5
Total	100	100	100	100	100

Trends in Sectoral Share in Energy Usage (in %)

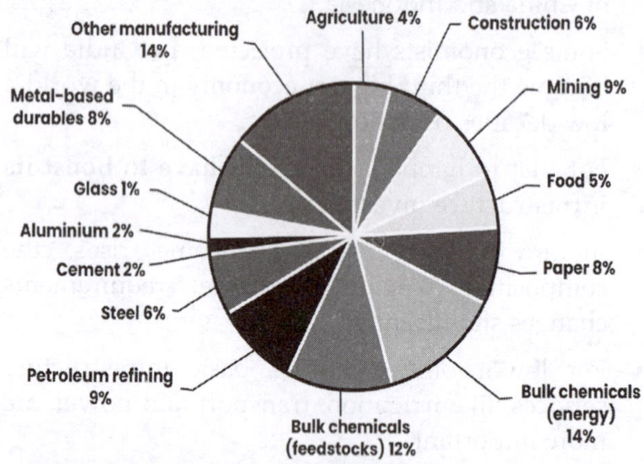

Composition of Commercial Energy Usage

Power/Electricity

- The most obvious kind of energy, power—also known as electricity—is frequently associated with advancement in contemporary society.
- Infrastructure plays a crucial role in determining a nation's economic success.
- Generally speaking, the demand for power is growing faster than the GDP.
- Research indicates that a yearly rise of 8% in GDP requires an annual growth of approximately 12% in the power supply.
- In India, **67% of power generation capacity was derived from thermal sources** in 2016.
- Nuclear power made up only two percent, and hydropower made up fourteen percent.
- India's energy policy supports wind and hydropower because they don't use fossil fuels and so emit less carbon dioxide.
- However, this has not led to a quicker increase in the amount of electricity generated from these two sources.

- **Atomic energy** is a valuable source of electricity and offers financial benefits. At the moment, nuclear energy accounts for only 2% of worldwide energy consumption, whereas the average is 13%. This is much too low.
- Therefore, some academics argue that more power should be produced by atomic (nuclear) sources, while others disagree, citing concerns for the environment and sustainable growth.

Some Challenges in the Power Sector

- Among the difficulties the Indian power industry is currently facing are:

(i) India's **installed energy generation capacity is insufficient** to support 7-8% yearly economic growth. India's commercial energy supply has to develop at a rate of approximately 7% in order to fulfil the country's increasing demand for electricity. India can currently only build 20,000 MW annually. Plants that are not operated correctly result in an underutilisation of even the installed capacity.

(ii) The **State Electricity Boards** (SEBs), responsible for the distribution of electricity, sustain **losses** over 500 billion rupees. This is brought on by **inefficiencies** in electricity pricing, transmission and distribution losses etc. According to some academics, the primary cause of the losses is the distribution of energy to farmers; however, **theft of electricity** occurs in many locations, exacerbating the situation for SEBs.

(iii) Foreign investors and private sector power generators have not yet fully fulfilled their roles.

(iv) There is widespread discontent among the population as a result of **high electricity costs and protracted blackouts** in many regions of the nation, and

(v) There is a shortage of coal and raw materials for thermal power plants, which are the backbone of India's electricity industry. Therefore, population increase and ongoing economic development are boosting the need for energy faster than India can now produce it.

- Additional supply of electricity can be ensured through increased public investment, improved research and development efforts, exploration, technical innovation, and utilisation of renewable energy sources.
- The government has opted for privatisation of the power sector, namely in the area of distribution, rather than investing in it by increasing installed capacity. This has resulted in significantly higher electricity prices, which have negatively affected certain sectors.

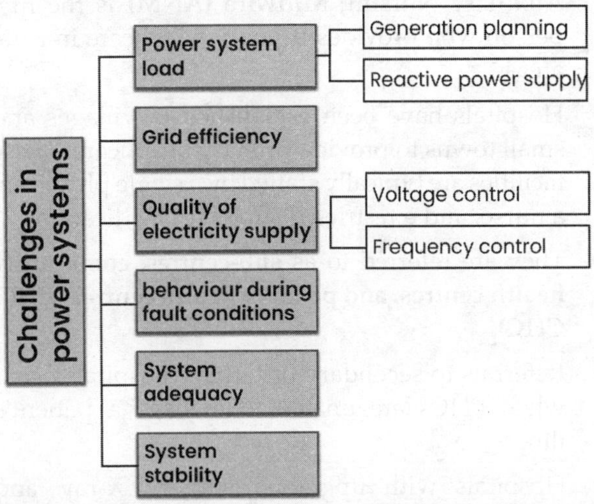

Challenges in Power System

Health

- Health encompasses not only the lack of illness but also the **capacity to reach one's full potential**.
- It serves as a **gauge of someone's wellbeing**.
- For a country to prosper, its populace must be in good health. A sick workforce would act as a drag to nation's development.
- The **health infrastructure** is concerned with health and wellness centres, health professionals, medicines etc.
- The presence of health infrastructure and its affordability make sure that the population stay healthy.
- Various health indicators like infant mortality rates, maternal mortality rates, nutrition, life expectancy etc. are used to compare the status of health infrastructure and it's functioning in any country.

Health System in India

- India's primary, secondary, and tertiary health care systems comprise **a three-tiered health infrastructure.**

- **Primary healthcare** comprises immunisation against major infectious diseases and injuries, promotion of mental health, provision of necessary medications, education about prevalent health issues and how to identify, prevent, and control them. It also includes promotion of food supply, proper nutrition, adequate water supply, and basic sanitation.
- **Auxiliary Nursing Midwife (ANM)** is the first person who provides primary healthcare in rural areas.
- Hospitals have been established in villages and small towns to provide primary healthcare. These facilities are typically staffed by a single physician, a nurse, and a restricted supply of medications.
- They are referred to as **sub-centres, community health centres, and primary health centres (PHC, CHC).**
- Referrals to secondary or tertiary hospitals occur when PHCs are unable to manage a patient's illness.
- Hospitals with upgraded surgery, X-ray, and electrocardiogram (ECG) facilities are considered **secondary health care institutions**. In addition to offering superior healthcare facilities, they serve as primary healthcare providers. The majority of them are found in large towns and district headquarters.
- The **tertiary sector includes all hospitals with cutting-edge technology** and medications that handle complex medical issues that primary and secondary hospitals are unable to handle.
- In addition, the **tertiary sector** is home to numerous prestigious institutions that offer specialised medical care in addition to doing research and offering top-notch medical education.
- A few of these are the Jawaharlal Institute of Postgraduate Medical Education and Research in Pondicherry; All India Institute of Medical Science in New Delhi; Post Graduate Institute in Chandigarh; National Institute of Mental Health and Neuro Sciences in Bangalore; and All India Institute of Hygiene and Public Health in Kolkata.

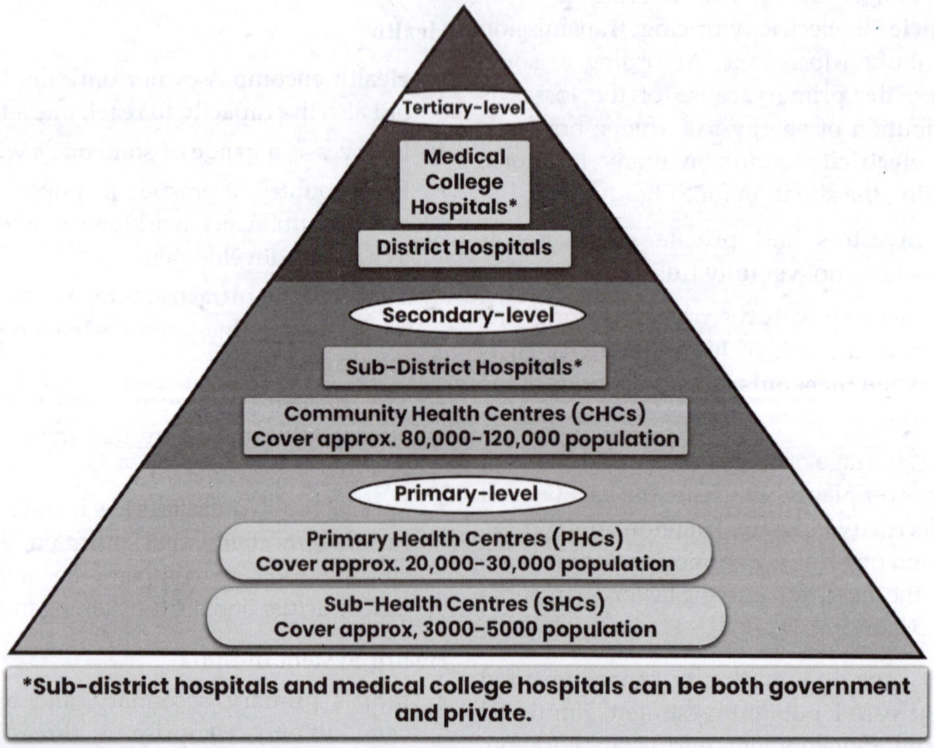

Health System in India

State of Health Infrastructure

- All matters pertaining to health, including medical education, food adulteration, drug and poisoning, the medical profession, vital statistics, mental illness, and insanity, are subject to **constitutional mandates that the government oversee** and control.
- The **Central Council of Health and Family Welfare** is the vehicle through which the Union Government develops broad policies and initiatives.
- In order to carry out major health projects across the country, it collects data and offers financial and technical support to State governments, Union Territories, and other organisations.
- **India has developed a sizable health workforce** at various levels over the years.
- The government has **established a range of hospitals** at the village level, which are officially referred to as **Primary Health Centres (PHCs).**
- India is home to a sizable number of **hospitals that are managed by the private sector** and nonprofit organisations.

Item	1951	1981	2000	2014-15	2018
Hospitals (Govt.)	2694	6,085	15,888	19,653	25,778
Beds (Govt.)	1,17,000	5,04,538	7,19,861	7,54,724	7,13,986
Dispensaries	6,600	16,745	23,065	26,325	2,57,43
PHCs	725	9,115	22,842	25,308	1,58,417
Sub-centres	-	84,736	1,37,311	53,655	5624
CHCs	-	761	3,043	5,396	27,951

Public Health Infrastructure in India

- Professionals and paramedical staff with training from medical, pharmacy, and nursing schools work in these hospitals.
- The **physical delivery of health care has significantly expanded** since Independence.
- From 1951 to 2013, the **number of nurses rose** from 0.18 to 23.44 lakh, while the number of allopathic doctors went from 0.62 to 9.2 lakh.
- The eradication of smallpox, guinea worms, and almost complete eradication of polio and leprosy have been brought about by the development of health infrastructure.

Private Sector Health Infrastructure

- In recent times, private sector has invested big in health infrastructure in India.
- More than 70 per cent of the hospitals in India are run by the private sector.
- They **control nearly two-fifth of the beds** available in the hospitals.
- Nearly **60 per cent of dispensaries are run by the private** sector.
- They provide healthcare for 80 per cent of out-patients and 46 per cent of in-patients.
- In recent times, **private sector has been playing a dominant role** in medical education and training, medical technology and diagnostics, manufacture and sale of pharmaceuticals, hospital construction and the provision of medical services.
- In 2001-02, there were more than 13 lakh medical enterprises employing 22 lakh people; more than 80 per cent of them are single person owned, and operated by one person occasionally employing a hired worker.
- Scholars point out that the private sector in India has grown independently without any major regulation; some private practitioners are not even registered doctors and are known as **quacks**.
- Modern super-specialty hospitals have been established by industrial and pharmaceutical businesses, as well as numerous non-resident Indians, in the 1990s as a result of liberalisation efforts aimed at drawing in medical tourists and India's wealthy.

Indian Systems of Medicine (ISM)

- Ayurveda, Yoga, Unani, Siddha, Naturopathy, and Homoeopathy (**AYUSH**) are the six systems that are included in it.
- Currently, India has up to 7 lakh registered practitioners, 26,000 dispensaries, and 3,167 ISM hospitals.
- However, not much has been done to establish a **framework for research or to standardise instruction.**

- ISMs are safe, affordable, and effective, which means they have a lot of potential to solve many of our healthcare issues.

Indicators of Health and Health Infrastructure—A Critical Appraisal

Indicators	India	China	USA	Srilanka
Infant Mortality Rate/1,000 live births	38	9	6	8
Under-5 mortality/1,000 live-births	48	11	7	10
Birth by skilled attendants (% of total)	74	100	99	99
Infants immunised (DTP) (%)	87	99	95	99
Health expenditure as % of GDP	4.7	5.6	17	3.5
Government health spending to total government spending (%)	5	10.4	21.3	11.2
Out of pocket expenditure as a % of private expenditure on health	89	72	21.4	95

Indicators of Health in India in Comparison with other Countries (2014-15)

- There is **greater scope for the role of government** in the health sector.
- For instance, the table shows expenditure on health sector as 4.7 per cent of the total GDP.
- This is abysmally low as compared to other countries, both developed and developing.
- One study points out that India has about 17 per cent of the world's population but it bears a frightening 20 per cent of the **global burden of diseases (GBD)**.
- **GBD is an indicator used by experts to gauge the number of people dying prematurely due to a particular disease,** as well as, the number of years spent by them in a state of 'disability' owing to the disease.
- In India, **more than half of GBD is accounted for by communicable diseases** such as diarrhoea, malaria and tuberculosis.
- Every year around five lakh children die of water-borne diseases. The danger of AIDS is also looming large. Malnutrition and inadequate supply of vaccines lead to the death of 2.2 million children every year.
- At present, less than 20 per cent of the population utilises public health facilities.
- One study has pointed out that only 38 per cent of the PHCs have the required number of doctors and only 30 per cent of the PHCs have sufficient stock of medicines.

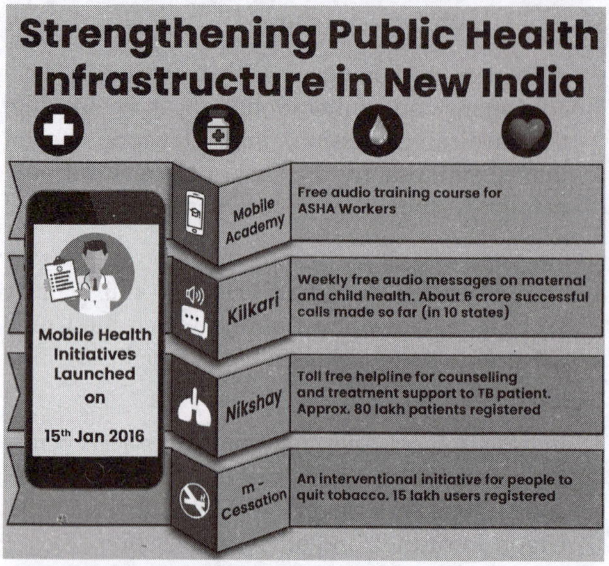

Public Health Infrastructure in India

Urban-Rural and Poor-Rich Divide

- Only **25% of India's hospitals, including private ones, are found in rural areas,** despite the country's 70% rural population.
- There are only roughly half as many dispensaries in rural India.
- Roughly thirty percent of the 6.3 lakh beds that government hospitals have are located in rural areas.
- **Rural residents lack access** to adequate medical facilities as a result. People's health statuses have varied as a result.
- In terms of hospitals, rural areas have just 0.36 hospitals per lakh inhabitants, but urban areas have 3.6 hospitals per lakh inhabitants.
- Even basic healthcare services like blood testing and X-rays, which are provided by city dwellers, are not provided by PHCs situated in rural areas.
- In terms of healthcare facilities, states like Uttar Pradesh, Bihar, Madhya Pradesh, and Rajasthan are somewhat behind.
- Over the past few years, the proportion of people living in rural areas without access to adequate healthcare facilities has increased.
- **Villagers lack access to specialised medical care,** including obstetrics, gynaecology, paediatrics, and anaesthesia.

- Rural areas continue to have a **physician shortage**, despite the fact that there are 380 accredited medical colleges that annually graduate roughly 44,000 medical professionals.
- Approximately **25% of these medical graduates depart the nation** in pursuit of more lucrative possibilities, although the majority opt to work at private hospitals, most of which are located in urban areas.
- Whether they reside in a city or a rural area, the richest 20% of Indians barely spend 2% of their income on healthcare. **The 20% poorest people spend 12%.**
- Many **poor people are forced to sell their land or even pledge their children** in order to pay for medical care.
- The impoverished are forced to go to private hospitals, where they **incur permanent debt**, or they choose to die since government-run hospitals are unable to provide adequate services.

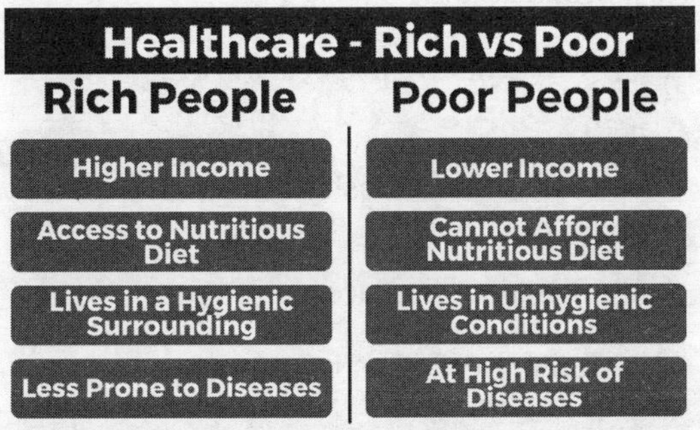

Healthcare for Rich v/s Poor

Women's Health

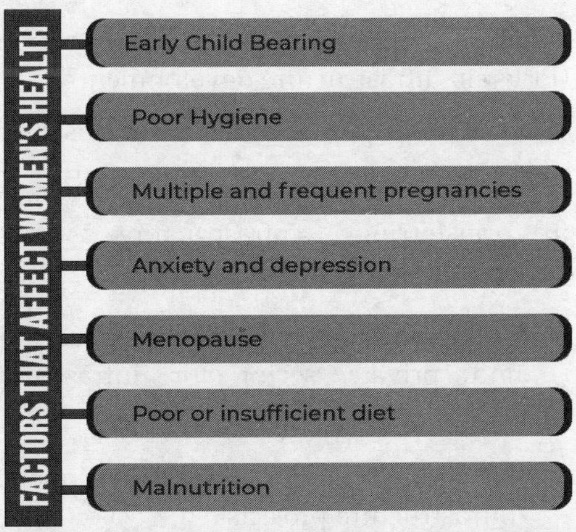

Factors that Affect Women's Health

- In India, women make up roughly 50% of the population.
- When compared to men, they have numerous disadvantages in the fields of healthcare, education, and economic engagement.
- The **decline in the nation's child sex ratio**, which went from 927 in 2001 to 919 in 2011, suggests that the number of female foeticides is increasing.
- Approximately 3,000,00 girls who are younger than 15 have been married and have given birth to a kid at least once.
- **Anaemia and nutritional anaemia** caused by **iron deficiency** affect more than 50% of married women between the age s of 15 and 49. This condition has been connected to **19% of maternal deaths.**
- Abortions are a major cause of maternal illness and mortality in India.
- A vital public good and a basic human right is health.
- If public health services are decentralised, then all citizens will have access to improved healthcare facilities.
- The long-term fight against illnesses requires effective health infrastructure and education.
- Thus, it is essential to raise awareness about health and hygiene issues and to offer effective mechanisms.
- The telecom and IT sectors play a crucial role in this process that cannot be overlooked.
- Moreover, primary healthcare is essential to the efficacy of healthcare programmes.
- The ultimate objective ought to be to assist individuals in achieving a higher standard of living.
- In India, the healthcare systems in urban and rural areas differ significantly. We run the risk of upending our nation's socioeconomic structure if we overlook this growing split.
- Accessibility and affordability must be incorporated into our fundamental health infrastructure in order to offer basic healthcare to everyone.

Conclusion

Any **nation's development depends on its social and economic infrastructure**. It guarantees the expansion of every economic sector. The infrastructure ensures availability of electricity, transportation, sound health etc. to the citizens of a country. Even after 75 years of independence, India is struggling to provide enough infrastructure to its citizens. The rural area is facing lack of roads, communication, health infrastructures. Even if the infrastructure is available, its quality is not satisfactory. Various researches have shown that as a nation moves towards modernity, the requirements of its citizens also evolve. Hence based on those requirements India not only **needs to create more infrastructure but also needs to make it accessible and available to all.**

TEST YOURSELF

Multiple Choice Questions

Q1. What is infrastructure?

(a) The physical and organisational structures needed for the operation of a society

(b) The financial resources of a country

(c) The legal framework governing public utilities

(d) The social services provided by the government

Q2. Which of the following is an example of economic infrastructure?

(a) Schools and hospitals

(b) Transportation networks

(c) Police stations and courts

(d) Parks and recreational facilities

Q3. What is the significance of infrastructure development in economic growth?

(a) It promotes social welfare programs.

(b) It increases government revenue through taxation.

(c) It enhances productivity and facilitates economic activities.

(d) It reduces income inequality.

Q4. What are green infrastructure projects?

(a) Infrastructure projects focused on renewable energy sources

(b) Infrastructure projects with environmentally friendly designs

(c) Infrastructure projects promoting urbanisation

(d) Infrastructure projects in rural areas

Q5. Which government agency is primarily responsible for infrastructure development in India?

(a) Ministry of Finance

(b) Ministry of Infrastructure

(c) Ministry of Road Transport Highways

(d) Ministry of Rural Development

Q6. What is the role of public-private partnerships (PPPs) in infrastructure development?

(a) Providing public funds for infrastructure projects

(b) Transferring infrastructure projects entirely to the private sector

(c) Collaborating between the government and private sector for infrastructure projects

(d) Facilitating foreign direct investment in infrastructure projects

Q7. Which of the following is an example of social infrastructure?

(a) Highways and railways

(b) Power plants and energy grids

(c) Schools and hospitals

(d) Airports and seaports

Q8. What is the role of information and communication technology (ICT) in infrastructure?

(a) Enhancing digital connectivity and communication

(b) Providing physical transportation networks

(c) Improving healthcare facilities

(d) Promoting industrialisation in rural areas

Q9. What is the concept of smart cities in infrastructure development?

(a) Developing cities with advanced technological systems and infrastructure

(b) Constructing sustainable infrastructure in rural areas

(c) Promoting urbanisation without considering environmental concerns

(d) Focusing on traditional infrastructure development in urban areas

Q10. What are the challenges to infrastructure development in India?

(a) Insufficient funding and financial resources

(b) Inadequate planning and coordination

(c) Limited access to skilled labour

(d) All of the above

Q11. Which of the following statements is/are correct about Infrastructure in an economy?

1. Infrastructure provides supporting services in the main areas of industrial and agricultural production, domestic and foreign trade and commerce.
2. Infrastructure contributes to economic development of a country only by increasing the productivity of the factors of production but not by improving the quality of life of its people.
3. Modern agriculture is also largely depends on the Infrastructure.

Select the correct answer using the code given below:

(a) 1 and 2 only (b) 1 and 3 only

(c) 2 and 3 only (d) 1, 2 and 3

Q12. Directions: Given below are two statements labelled as Assertion (A) and Reason (R). In the context of the two statements, which of the following is correct?

Assertion (A): The share of power and telecommunication infrastructure is greater in high-income countries.

Reason (R): As economies mature and most of their basic consumption demands are met, the share of agriculture in the economy shrinks and more service-related infrastructure is required.

Select the Correct answer using the codes given below:

(a) Both A and R are true and R is the correct explanation of A.

(b) Both A and Rare true but R is not the correct explanation of A.

(c) A is true but R is false.

(d) A is false but R is true.

Q13. Which of the following statements is/are correct about energy consumption in India?

1. Non-commercial energy sources consisting of firewood, cow dung and agricultural wastes account for more than half of the total energy consumed in India.
2. The critical feature of India's energy sector is the import dependence on crude and petroleum products.
3. In India, the thermal sources accounts for the largest share of power generation capacity.

Select the correct answer using the code given below:

(a) 1 and 2 only (b) 1 and 3 only

(c) 2 and 3 only (d) 1, 2 and 3

Answer Key

Q1.	a	Q2.	b	Q3.	c
Q4.	b	Q5.	c	Q6.	c
Q7.	c	Q8.	a	Q9.	a
Q10.	d	Q11.	b	Q12.	a
Q13.	c				

Model Questions for Main Examination

Q1. Critically examine the major drawbacks of our healthcare system?

Q2. Discuss the concept of social and economic infrastructure?

UNIT 9 Development

In This Unit

Comprehensive and profound coverage of the following NCERT's chapter:

✓ NCERT Class- 11th (Indian Economic Development), Chapter- 9

What is Development?

- It is a **process in which someone or something grows or changes and becomes more advanced.**
- The meaning of development is different for different individuals. The developmental goals also differ from person to person. Development for one may not be development for others.
- In such a challenging situation a **nation forms developmental policies which take everyone along.** Development can be in many sectors like social, economic, political, art and culture etc.
- Similarly, the measurement of development can be of different types.

Income and other Development Goals

- For most of the people, income from any source can be a goal of development.

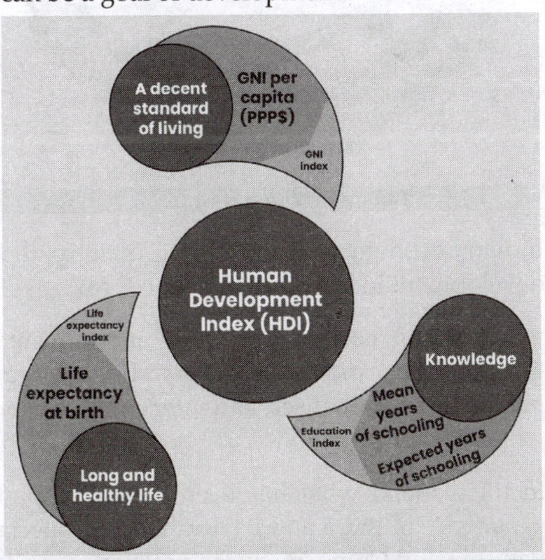

Human Development Index (HDI)

- The money gained from various economic activities can buy the goods and services required to lead a fulfilling life. These materialistic needs can be fulfilled by money.
- But all developmental goals of human cannot be fulfilled by money only.

National Development

- Just like different individuals have different goals for development, their notion for national development can also differ from one and another.
- For some people **economic development** should be sole measure for development.
- For others, the **political and social developments** like more modernisation, liberalisation etc. could be a measure for development.
- While, for some environment and bio-diversity protection, happiness of people can be a measure for national development.

How to Compare Different Countries or States?

Income as a Criteria

- Usually, income is taken as criteria for comparison of different countries and states.
- National and state income become criteria for comparison.
- To rectify the effect of large population average income or per capita income criteria is more preferred.
- In **World Development Report 2006**, brought out by the World Bank, this criterion is used in classifying countries.

- Countries with per capita income of Rs 4,53,000 per annum and above in 2004, are called **rich countries** and those with per capita income of Rs 37,000 or less are called **low-income countries.**
- **India comes in the category of low-income countries because its per capita income in 2004 was just Rs 28,000 per annum.**
- The rich countries, excluding countries of Middle East and certain other small countries, are generally called **developed countries.**
- Income criteria **does not measure the distribution of income** throughout the country or the state.
- It can happen that small number of people occupy larger wealth and this cannot be compared accurately by per capita income criteria.
- Also, the greater per capita income does not indicate developed status every time.
- For example, consider the example of state of **Haryana and Kerala in India**, the per capita income of people in Haryana is greater than that of Kerala.
- Still the human development indicators of people from Kerala like health, education, sanitation etc. are greater for Kerala than Haryana.

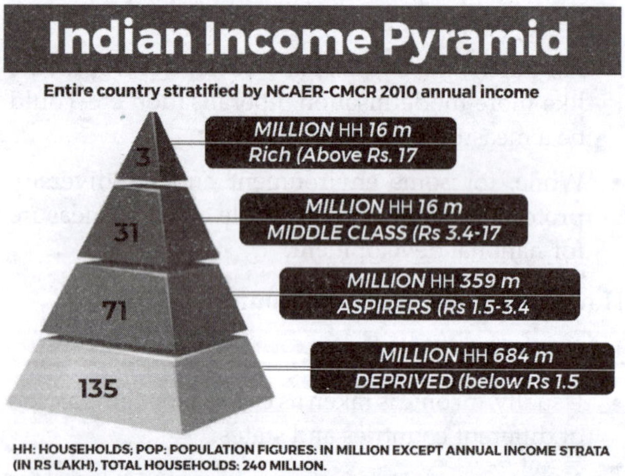

Indian Income Pyramid

Public Facilities as Criteria

- Even though a region has greater per capita income, a lack of public facilities in that region would reduce the impact of greater per capita income.
- For example, if a region lacks public health facilities, then the high per capita income would not give a person the good medical service.
- Similarly, high per capita income cannot ensure medical research, public sanitation and cleanliness, environment protection, security, higher education etc.
- These can be ensured by investment in public facilities by governments and private sectors.
- Hence **presence of good public facilities** can also be a criterion for comparison for development between two regions.
- The **investment in public facilities** would lead to better human development. This becomes a criterion for **UNDP in its Human Development Report** to compare countries based on their human development index.

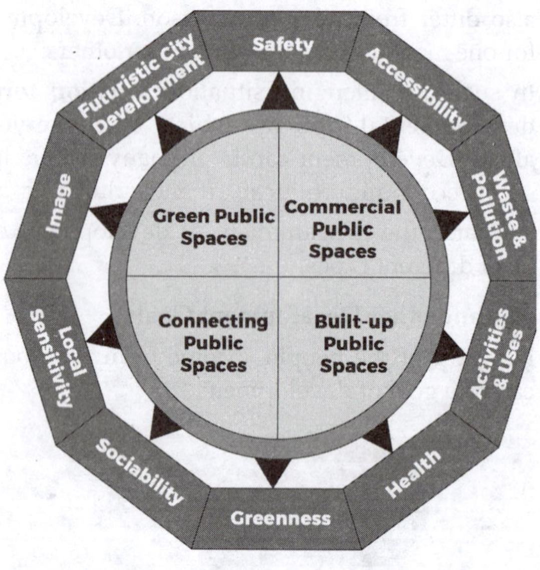

Public Facilities as Criteria

- Indian economy charted its own path of development in post-independence era.
- After 1991's economic reform and advent of globalisation, Indian economy became more liberal, open, globalised and inter connected with world's economy.
- In this context what has been the development experience of India and its neighbours, especially Pakistan and China are worth noticing.

- While one of them remained laggard to economic and human development, other leapfrogged in economic and human development criteria.
- Being a vibrant democratic country different from other two, India faces some extra challenges, while charting its part of development, which are not found in the military-politico power in Pakistan and one-party system in China.

Development Path-A Snapshot View

Strategies Adopted in 5 Year plans		
India **Mixed Economy** (Govt run large industries while private sector owned run small industries)	**Pakistan** **Mixed Economy** (Govt run large industries while private sector owned run small industries)	**China** **Socialist Economy** (All major sectors under government control)
Who Owned Land?		
India **Private Sector** Small Farms Owned by Individual Farmers	**Pakistan** **Private Sector** Small Farms Owned by Individual Farmers	**China** **Government** Govt Owned land. Communes were set up in villages where all the people collectively cultivated land

Strategies Adopted in 5 Year Plans

- All the three nations **India (1947), Pakistan (1947) and China (1949)** gained independence on approximately same time.
- Pakistan had begun planned growth, just like India. In 1956, it began its first five-year plan, which is known as the Medium Term Development Plan.
- In the same way, in 1953, China also began its first five-year plan.
- India, too, operated under a planned economy till 2017.
- Up to the 1980s, the GDP growth rates and per capita income of all three countries were comparable.
- Following that, **China began implementing its reform** plans; India followed suit in the late 1980s, and **Pakistan began denationalising** its assets in the 1980s.

China

- Following the formation of the People's Republic of China, which was governed by a single party system, all significant economic sectors, private businesses, and privately owned land were placed under government supervision.
- The goal of the **1958-launched Great Leap Forward (GLF) effort was to industrialise** the nation extensively. It encouraged people to establish businesses in their backyards.
- Communes were established in rural regions. The Commune system **allowed people to farm land jointly.** In 1958, nearly all farm workers were divided into 26,000 communes. The GLF campaign encountered numerous issues.
- About **30 million people died in China** as a result of a terrible drought.
- Russia withdrew its personnel who had been sent to China to aid in the modernisation process when it had disputes with China.
- **Mao** ushered in the **Great Proletarian Cultural Revolution** (1966–76) in 1965, sending **professionals and students to work in and learn from rural areas.**
- The **1978 reforms** laid the groundwork for China's current rapid industrial growth.
- **China introduced reforms in phases.** Reforms in the investment, international commerce, and agriculture sectors were started in the first phase.
- For example, in agriculture, commune lands were divided into **tiny plots** that were assigned to **individual households for use only, not for ownership**. All land income was theirs to keep after specified taxes were paid. Reforms in the industrial sector were started in the later phase.
- Enterprises in the private sector were permitted to produce items, as were township and village businesses, or businesses owned and run by local collectives.
- Government-owned businesses, also referred to as State Owned Enterprises (SOEs) or public sector businesses in India, were forced to compete at this point.
- In the process of reform, dual pricing was also included.
- This entails setting prices in two ways: farmers and industrial units had to buy and sell set quantities of inputs and products at government-fixed prices, and the remaining goods had to be bought and sold at market rates.

- Over time, as output rose, so did the percentage of items or inputs traded on the market.
- **Special economic zones were established** to draw in foreign investors.

India v/s China Growth Rates

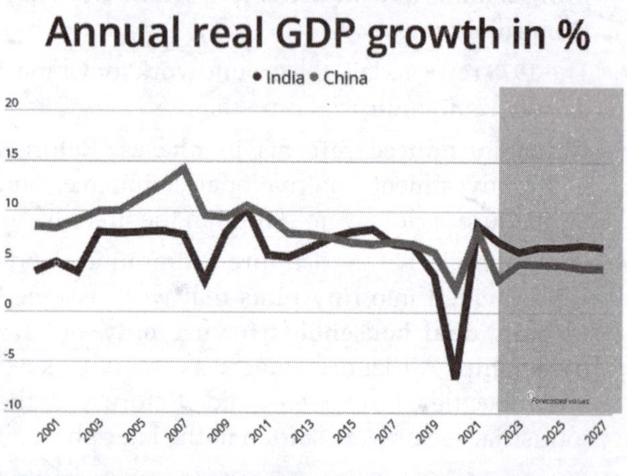

Annual Real GDP Growth Rate (%) India v/s China

Pakistan

- While observing various economic policies followed by Pakistan, we can find various similarities with India.
- **Pakistan also followed mixed economy model like India.**
- In 1950s and 1960s Pakistan introduced various regulation that started import substitutions and tariff-based protection of domestic industries etc.
- **In 1960s Green Revolution came to Pakistan, which started mechanisation of agriculture.**
- **In 1970s Pakistan started nationalisation of capital goods industries like India.**
- Subsequently, in the 1970s and 1980s, **denationalisation** and the advancement of private industry received significant attention.
- **In Pakistan, economic changes commenced subsequent to 1988.**
- It received financial and developmental aid from western nations and institutions and also the remittances started flowing to Pakistan from Middle East during those periods.

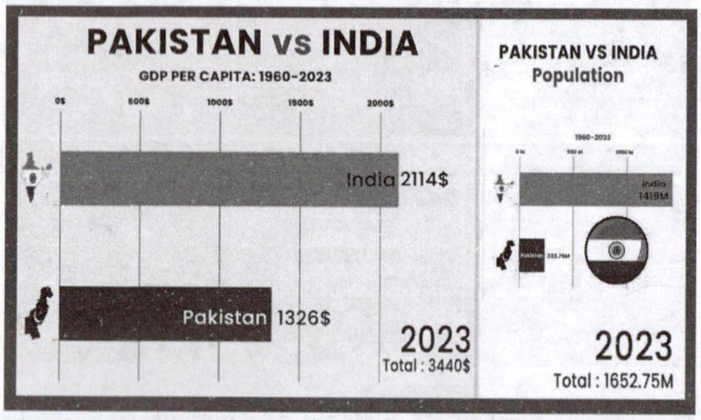

India v/s Pakistan Per Capita GDP

Demographic Indicators

- If we compare demographics of all three countries, India and China have more or less the same population, while Pakistan has one tenth of Chinese population.

Country	Estimated Population (in million) (2015)	Annual Growth of Population (2015)	Density (per sq. km)	Sex Ratio (2015)	Fertility Rate (2015)	Urbanisation (2015)
India	1311	1.2	441	929	2.3	33
China	1371	0.5	146	941	1.6	56
Pakistan	188	2.1	245	947	3.7	39

Comparative Analysis of Select Demographic Indicators

- After observing the above table, we can note that while China has arrested its population growth and fertility rate due to its **'one child policy'**, Pakistan has yet to arrest its population growth.
- India is on path of stabilizing its population growth.
- **The sex ratio is biased against women in all the three nations.** China's one child policy acted against female child; all the three nations have adverse sex ratio due to son preferences in these countries.

- In case of **urbanisation China leads**, followed by Pakistan and then India.

Gross Domestic Product

- China is the world's second largest country, with a GDP (PPP) of $19.8 trillion. In contrast, the GDP (PPP) of Pakistan is $0.94 trillion, or around 12% of India's GDP, but the GDP of India is $8.07 trillion.
- About 40% of China's GDP is made up of India's GDP.
- As the table below shows, China was able to sustain nearly double-digit growth for a decade at a time when many wealthy nations were struggling to maintain growth rates of even 5%.
- Moreover, take note of the fact that in the 1980s, China had double-digit growth while India was at the bottom, with Pakistan leading the way.
- In 2011–15, there has been a decline in China's growth rate, whereas, Pakistan met with drastic decline at 4 per cent. Some academics attribute this trend to the **political instability** that persisted for a considerable amount of time and the reforms that Pakistan implemented in 1988.

ANNUAL GROWTH OF GROSS DOMESTIC PRODUCT (%), 1980-2015

Country	1980-90	2011-20
India	5.7	6.7
China	10.3	7.9
Pakistan	6.3	4.0

Source: Key Indicators for Asia and Pacific 2016, Asian Development Bank, Philippines: World Development Indicators 2016

Annual Growth of Gross Domestic Product (%)

- Various industries in these nations contributed to this trend.
- India has a lower percentage of its population living in cities than China and Pakistan.
- China's climatic and geographical circumstances mean that only roughly 10% of the country's total land area is suitable for farming.
- Forty percent of the cultivable area in India is found in China overall.
- More than 80% of Chinese citizens rely only on farming for their livelihood up until the 1980s.

Sectoral Share of Employment and GDP (%) in 2014-2015

Sector	Contribution to GDP			Distribution of Workforce		
	India	China	Pakistan	India	China	Pakistan
Agriculture	17	9	25	50	28	43
Industry	30	43	21	21	29	23
Services	53	48	54	29	43	34
Total	100	100	100	100	100	100

Sectoral Share of Employment and GDP (%) in 2014-15

- Since then, the government encouraged people to leave their fields and pursue other activities such as handicrafts, commerce and transport.
- In 2014–15, with 28 per cent of its workforce engaged in agriculture, its contribution to the GDP in China is 9 per cent (see table below).
- Agriculture made up 17 and 25% of the GDP in both Pakistan and India, respectively, but a larger share of the labour force in India is employed in this industry.
- In India, 54.6% of the population works in agriculture, compared to roughly 43% in Pakistan.
- The industry and service sectors contribute more to output but have a smaller worker share in all three economies, as indicated by the sectoral shares of employment and output.
- The manufacturing and service sectors account for 43 and 48 percent of GDP in China, respectively, while the service sector accounts for more than 50 percent of GDP in India and Pakistan.
- Normally, as a nation develops, it moves its output and jobs from agriculture to manufacturing and eventually to services. This is the situation in China, as the table below illustrates.

- In India and Pakistan, the percentages of workers involved in manufacturing were quite low, at 21 and 23 percent, respectively.
- In India and Pakistan, industries account for 27.6% and 21% of GDP, respectively.
- There is a direct movement towards the service sector in these countries.
- Thus, in both India and Pakistan, the service sector is emerging as a major player of development.
- It contributes more to GDP and, at the same time, emerges as a prospective employer.
- When comparing the percentage of workers in the 1980s, Pakistan outpaced China and India in the number of workers who moved into the service sector.
- In India, China, and Pakistan, the service sector employed 17, 12, and 27% of the labour force, respectively, in the 1980s. While in 2021, these numbers are 30.7%, 43%, and 34%, respectively.
- During the past thirty years, there has been a decrease in the growth of the agriculture sector, which accounts for the highest share of employment across all three countries.
- China has continued to grow its industrial sector at a nearly double-digit rate, while Pakistan and India have seen their growth rates fall.
- Regarding the service sector, China managed to increase its growth rate between 1980 and 2015, whilst India and Pakistan saw stagnant growth.
- Consequently, the rise of both China and India is primarily driven by their respective industrial and service sectors. Over this period, Pakistan has shown signs of a slowdown in all three industries.

Country	1980-90			2011-15		
	Agriculture	Industry	Service	Agriculture	Industry	Service
India	3.1	7.4	6.9	2.3	5	8.4
China	5.9	10.8	13.5	4.1	8.1	8.4
Pakistan	4	7.7	6.8	2.7	3.4	4.4

Trends in Output Growth in Different Sectors, 1980-2015

Indicators of Human Development

Some Selected Indicators of Human Development, 2016

Item	India	China	Pakistan
Human Development Index (Value)	0.624	0.738	0.550
Rank (based on HDI)	131	91	148
Life Expectancy at Birth (years)	68.3	76	66.4
Mean years of Schooling (% aged 15 and above)	6.3	7.6	5.1
GDP per capita (PPP US$)	6092	14,400	4866
People Below Poverty Line (at $3.10 a day ppp) (%) (2011)	37	32	44
Infant Mortality Rate (per 1000 live births)	38	9	66
Maternal Mortality Rate (per 1 lakh births)	174	27	178
Population using Improved Sanitation (%)	40	77	64
Population with Sustainable Access to Improved Water Source (%)	94	96	91
Percentage of Undernourished Children	39	9	45

Source: Human Development Report 2016 and World Development Indicators (www.worldbank.org)

Indicators of Human Development, 2016

- The table above indicates that **China is overtaking** Pakistan and India in indicators of human development.
- This is true for a wide range of measures, including those measuring **income** (such as GDP per capita), the percentage of the population living in **poverty**, or **health** (such as mortality rates, life expectancy, literacy, and sanitation availability) and **malnourishment** rates.
- However, neither of these two nations has been successful in preventing maternal death in women.
- Only 23 women per lakh births die in China, compared to roughly 103 and 154 deaths per lakh births in India and Pakistan, respectively.
- Remarkably, the majority of the populations in all three countries report having access to **better sources of drinking water.**
- It can be observed that, out of the three countries, **India has the highest percentage of the poor**, with an average daily income below the international poverty threshold of $3.65.
- However, we should be aware of an issue when using the aforementioned human development indices to such questions and passing judgement on them. This happens because, while all of these indications are very significant, they are insufficient. We also require what could be referred to as "**liberty-indicators**" in addition to these.
- As a gauge of "the **extent of democratic participation** in social and political decision-making," one such indicator has actually been added, but it has not been given much weight.
- Several apparent "liberty indicators," such as the degree of constitutional protection provided to citizens' rights or the degree of protection afforded to the judiciary and the rule of law, have not been considered.
- It might be argued that the creation of a **human development index is inadequate** and that its applicability is restricted if these (and maybe a few others) are left out and are not given top priority on the list.

HUMAN DEVELOPMENT INDEX (H.D.I.)

Definition	Human Development - Indicators
Human development index is used to measure how development has improved human life	1. Human development index rank 2. Life Expectancy 3. Infant Mortality Rate 4. Maternal Mortality Rate 5. Adult Literacy Rate 6. Percentage of population below poverty line 7. Per capita G.D.P etc.

Human Development Index

Development Tactics: A Review

- It is imperative for any country to learn from its competitors.
- India has much to learn from the success and failures of its neighbours.
- All the three countries, which were following more or less similar growth paths started reforming their economies.
- **China started it in 1978, Pakistan started it in 1988, India in 1991.**
- The compulsion for China to start economic reform was not imposed from external institutions. Chinese communist government was not happy with slow growth of its economy.
- They believed that the **Maoist concept of economic growth**, which emphasised decentralisation, self-sufficiency, and rejecting foreign commodities, capital, and technology, **had failed.**
- The **Great Leap Forward**, widespread land reforms, collectivisation, and other programmes **did not increase the per capita grain output** from the mid-1950s to 1978.
- The development of health and education facilities, land reforms, a protracted period of decentralised planning, and the presence of small businesses were all found to have contributed favourably to the improvement of social and economic indices throughout the post-reform era.
- Prior to the implementation of the reforms, basic health services had already been widely expanded into rural areas.

- The **distribution of food grains was more egalitarian** under the communal system.
- Additionally, experts point out that every reform proposal was originally introduced on a lesser scale before being expanded widely.
- Decentralised government experimentation made it possible to evaluate the political, social, and economic consequences of success or failure.
- As previously mentioned, the implementation of agricultural reforms, such as granting individual land plots for cultivation, resulted in the wealth of a large number of impoverished individuals.
- It established a solid foundation of support for more changes and set the stage for the later extraordinary expansion of rural industry.
- Scholars cite numerous instances were reform initiatives resulted in China's swift economic expansion.
- Scholars contend that Pakistan's reform approach caused all economic metrics to deteriorate. As we saw in a previous part, the GDP growth rate and its sectoral components have decreased in the 1990s as compared to the 1980s.
- Despite Pakistan's relatively healthy international poverty line data, researchers utilising Pakistan's government data point to rising poverty in the country.
- More over 40% of people lived in poverty in the 1960s; this percentage fell to 25% in the 1980s before beginning to rise once more in the 1990s.
- According to academics, the causes for Pakistan's economy's slowing growth and reappearance of poverty include that the country's agricultural growth and food supply situation were dependent more on a successful harvest than on an institutionalised process of technological improvement.
- The economy was in good shape during a good harvest; when it wasn't, the economic indicators revealed stagnation or negative tendencies.
- Recall that in order to resolve its balance of payments crisis, India had to borrow money from the IMF and World Bank; foreign cash is a necessary resource for any nation, and it's critical to understand how to obtain it.
- A nation should not worry if it can increase its foreign exchange profits through the sustainable export of manufactured goods.
- The majority of Pakistan's foreign cash profits came from the export of highly volatile agricultural products and remittances from Pakistani workers in the Middle East. On the one hand, there was a rising reliance on foreign loans, and on the other, there was growing difficulties in repaying the loans.
- Nonetheless, Pakistan's economy has stabilised and grown during the past few years.
- According to the Annual Plan 2016–17, the GDP grew by 4.7% in 2015–16, which was the highest growth rate during the preceding eight years.
- Although the growth rate in agriculture was considerably below desired levels, the industrial and service sectors experienced growth rates of 6.8% and 5.7%, respectively.
- Additionally, a lot of macroeconomic indices started to exhibit steady and encouraging trends.

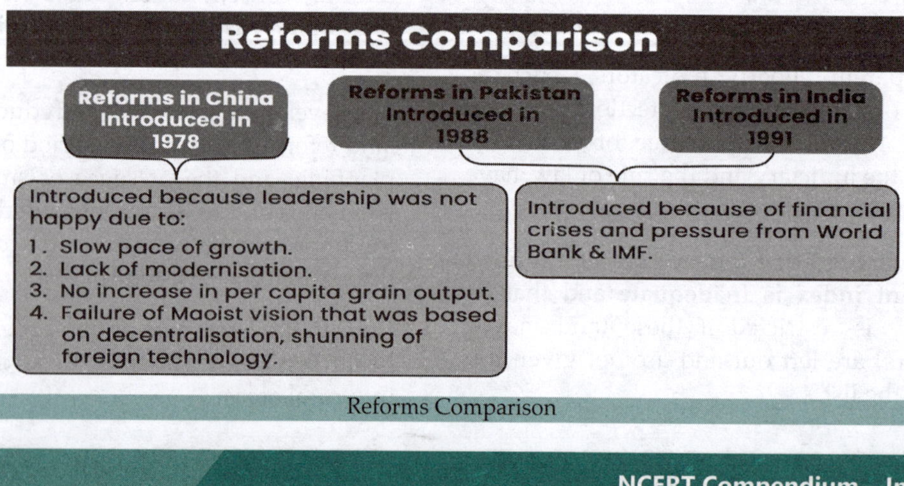

Reforms Comparison

Environment and Sustainable Development

In the earlier sections, we have seen how the development model has led to the economic growth of India and the world. The current development method does not consider the **highly exploitative way for development**. The current model has led to many problems like **depletion of non-renewable energy** sources, **degradation of environment**, global warming, loss of biodiversity etc. Hence a need is felt to chart a sustainable development path which would help the world to develop without compromising the potential for future generations to develop.

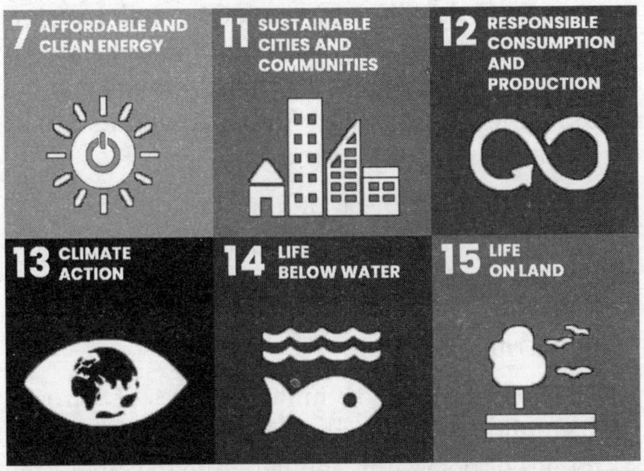

Sustainable Development

The definition and Uses of the Environment

The **entirety of all resources and the planetary inheritance are together referred to as the environment**. It encompasses all the **interdependent biotic and abiotic elements**. Therefore, an examination of the environment necessitates an examination of the interactions between these biotic and abiotic environmental elements.

Functions of the Environment

- The environment carries out four essential tasks:
  1. It **provides resources**, which comprise both non-renewable and renewable resources,
  2. it **assimilates waste**,
  3. it **sustains life** by providing genetic and bio diversity and
  4. it also **provides aesthetic** services like scenery etc.
- The environment is able to perform these functions without any interruption as long as the demand on these functions is within its **carrying capacity**. This implies that the **resource extraction is not above the rate of regeneration** of the resource and the wastes generated are within the assimilating capacity of the environment.
- When this is not so, the environment fails to perform its third and vital function of life sustenance and this results in an environmental crisis.
- This is the situation today all over the world.
- Many resources have become extinct and the wastes generated are beyond the absorptive capacity of the environment.
- **Absorptive capacity** means the **ability of the environment to absorb degradation.**
- The result — we are today at the **threshold of environmental crisis.**
- The past development has polluted and dried up rivers and other aquifers making **water an economic good.**
- Besides, the intensive and extensive extraction of both renewable and non-renewable resources has exhausted some of these vital resources and we are compelled to spend huge amounts on technology and research to explore new resources.
- Added to these are the **health costs of degraded environmental** quality — decline in air and water quality (seventy per cent of water in India is polluted) have resulted in increased incidence of respiratory and water-borne diseases.
- Hence the expenditure on health is also rising.
- To make matters worse, **global environmental issues such as global warming and ozone depletion** also contribute to increased financial commitments for the government.
- Thus, it is clear that the opportunity costs of negative environmental impacts are high.

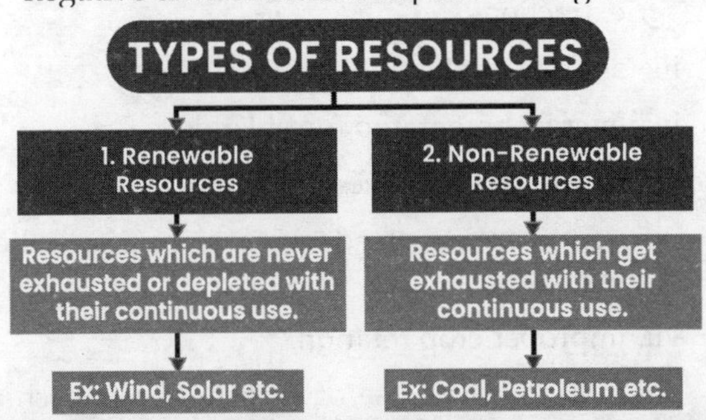

Types of Resources

The Environmental Situation in India

- Large deposits of iron-ore, coal and natural gas are found in the country.
- India alone accounts for nearly 20 per cent of the **world's total iron-ore reserves.**
- **Bauxite, copper, chromate, diamonds, gold, lead, lignite, manganese, zinc, uranium, etc.** are also available in different parts of the country.
- However, the developmental activities in India have resulted in pressure on its finite natural resources, besides creating impacts on human health and well-being.
- **The threat to India's environment poses a dichotomy**—threat of poverty-induced environmental degradation and, at the same time, threat of pollution from affluence and a rapidly growing industrial sector.
- The priority issues identified are:
  - i. land degradation,
  - ii. biodiversity loss,
  - iii. air pollution with special reference to vehicular pollution in urban cities,
  - iv. management of fresh water and
  - v. solid waste management.
- Land in India suffers from varying degrees and types of degradation stemming mainly from unstable use and inappropriate management practices.
- Some of the factors responsible for land degradation are:
  - i. loss of vegetation occurring due to **deforestation**,
  - ii. unsustainable **fuel wood** and fodder extraction,
  - iii. shifting cultivation,
  - iv. **encroachment** into forest lands,
  - v. **forest fires** and over grazing ,
  - vi. non-adoption of adequate soil conservation measures,
  - vii. improper crop rotation,
  - viii. indiscriminate use of **agrochemicals** such as fertilizers and pesticides,
  - ix. **improper planning** and management of irrigation systems,
  - x. **extraction of ground water** in excess of the recharge capacity,
  - xi. open access resource and
  - xii. **poverty** of the agriculture-dependent people.
- India supports approximately 17 per cent of the world's human and 20 per cent of livestock population on a mere 2.5 per cent of the world's geographical area.
- The **high density of population and livestock** and the **competing uses of land** for forestry, agriculture, pastures, human settlements and industries exert an enormous pressure on the country's finite land resources.
- The per capita forest land in the country is only 0.08 hectare against the requirement of 0.47 hectare to meet basic needs, resulting in an excess felling of about 15 million cubic meter forests over the permissible limit.
- The country loses 0.8 million tonnes of nitrogen, 1.8 million tonnes of phosphorus, and 26.3 million tonnes of potassium annually due to soil erosion, which is estimated to be occurring at a pace of 5.3 billion tonnes year nationwide.
- The Indian government estimates that between 5.8 and 8.4 million tonnes of nutrients are lost annually as a result of erosion.
- India is among the world's 10 most industrialised countries. However, this position has resulted in unwelcome and unforeseen repercussions like pollution, unplanned urbanisation, and an increased risk of accidents.
- Seventeen large- and medium-sized industry sectors have been classified by the Central Pollution Control Board (CPCB) as highly polluting.

Sustainable Development

- Historically, there has been a notion that development and environmental degradation have an antagonistic relationship.
- Since industrial revolution the development strategy has degraded the environment.

- Any conservation effort is usually tagged as an anti-development strategy.
- For developing world like India, development is must for poor people.
- At the same time conservation of environment and the interests of future generation can also not be compromised.
- This scenario asks for a new development strategy, which is sustainable development strategy.
- The concept of sustainable development was emphasised by the **United Nations Conference on Environment and Development (UNCED)**, which defined it as: **'Development that meets the need of the present generation without compromising the ability of the future generation to meet their own needs'.**
- The seminal report—**Our Common Future**—that gave the above definition explained sustainable development as **'meeting the basic needs of all and extending to all the opportunity to satisfy their aspirations for a better life'.**
- Meeting the needs of all requires redistributing resources and is hence a moral issue.
- ***Edward Barbier*** defined sustainable development as one which is directly concerned with increasing the material standard of living of the poor at the grass root level — this can be quantitatively measured in terms of increased income, real income, educational services, health care, sanitation, water supply etc.
- In more specific terms, **sustainable development aims at decreasing the absolute poverty of the poor** by providing lasting and secure livelihoods that minimise resource depletion, environmental degradation, cultural disruption and social instability.
- Sustainable development is, in this sense, a development that meets the basic needs of all, particularly the poor majority, for employment, food, energy, water, housing, and ensures growth of agriculture, manufacturing, power and services to meet these needs.
- The **Brundtland Commission** emphasises on **protecting the future generation.**
- This is in line with the argument of the environmentalists who emphasise that we have a moral obligation to hand over the planet earth in good order to the future generation; that is, the **present generation should bequeath a better environment to the future generation.**
- At least we should leave to the next generation a stock of **'quality of life'** assets no less than what we have inherited.
- The present generation can promote development that enhances the natural and built environment in ways that are compatible with:
  i. conservation of natural assets,
  ii. preservation of the regenerative capacity of the world's natural ecological system,
  iii. avoiding the imposition of added costs or risks on future generations.
- According to ***Herman Daly,*** a leading environmental economist, to achieve sustainable development, the following needs to be done:

17 Goals to Transform our World

i. Limiting the human population to a level within the carrying capacity of the environment. The carrying capacity of the environment is like a ***'plimsoll line'*** of the ship which is its load limit mark. In the absence of the ***plimsoll line*** for the economy, human scale grows beyond the carrying capacity of the earth and deviates from sustainable development.

ii. Instead of requiring a lot of input, technological advancement should be input-efficient.

iii. It is important to harvest renewable resources in a sustainable manner, meaning that the rate of extraction must not outpace the rate of regeneration.

iv. The rate at which non-renewable resource depletion surpasses the rate at which renewable equivalents are created.

v. Pollution-related inefficiencies ought to be fixed.

Techniques for Long-Term and Sustainable Growth

Utilising Non-Traditional Energy Sources

- India's energy requirements have been met by thermal and hydroelectric power facilities.
- They cause native communities to be displaced in addition to environmental degradation.
- To arrest the environment loss and to conserve the non-renewable energy sources, we must start using the non-conventional energy sources like **wind, solar, biomass etc.**

LPG, Gobar (Bio) Gas in Rural Areas

- Rural area use biomass, woods and cow dung cakes etc. for their energy needs. **They cause pollution and hardship to rural people.** Governments are encouraging LPG and gobar (Bio) gas for cooking and other energy requirements.

CNG in Urban Area

- Vehicular emission is one of the biggest sources of urban air pollution. To reduce this pollution CNG gas use must be promoted in urban areas. For example, use of CNG in Delhi has reduced air pollution in Delhi.

Wind Power

- In areas where speed of wind is usually high, wind mills can provide electricity without any adverse impact on the environment.
- Wind turbines move with the wind and electricity is generated.
- No doubt, the initial cost is high. **But the benefits are such that the high cost gets easily absorbed.**

Solar Power through Photovoltaic Cells:

- India is naturally endowed with a **large quantity of solar energy in the form of sunlight.**
- Now, with the help of **photovoltaic cells,** solar energy can be converted into electricity.
- To catch solar energy and transform it into electricity, these cells employ specialised materials.
- This technology is highly helpful in isolated areas and places where electricity supply via grid or power lines is either impractical or prohibitively expensive.
- This technique is also totally free from pollution.

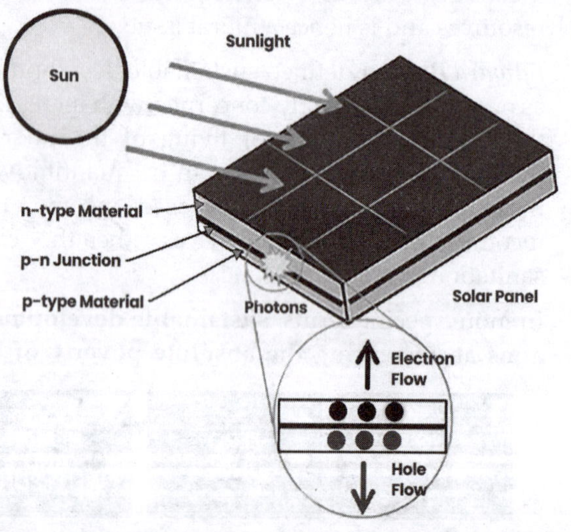

Solar Power and Photovoltaic Cells

Mini-Hydel Plants

- Streams are almost **ubiquitous** in mountainous areas. A significant portion of these streams are **evergreen.**
- These streams' energy is used by mini-hydel plants to power tiny turbines.

- Local users can utilise the electricity produced by the turbines.
- Because these power plants produce enough electricity to meet local demands and do not alter the land use pattern in the areas where they are located, they are relatively environmentally beneficial.
- This implies that they can **prevent transmission loss** and do away with the requirement for massive transmission towers and cables.

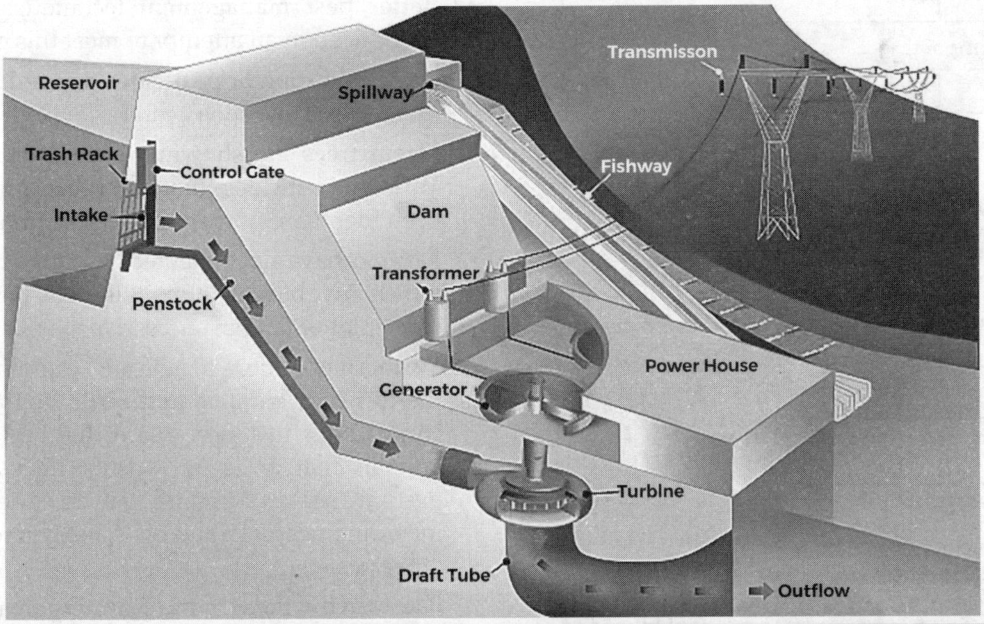

Mini Hydel Plants

Traditional Knowledge and Practices

- Traditionally, Indian people have been close to their environment. They have been more a component of the environment and not its controller.
- If we look back at our **agriculture system, healthcare system, housing, transport etc**., we find that all practices have been environment friendly.
- Only recently have we drifted away from the traditional systems and caused large scale damage to the environment and also our rural heritage.
- One apt example is in healthcare. India is very much privileged to have about 15,000 species of plants which have medicinal properties. About 8,000 of these are in regular use in various systems of treatment including the folk tradition. While these were previously overlooked, they are being resorted to not due to their organic and safe nature.
- All cosmetic products of days, including face cream, body lotion, hair oil, and toothpaste, are made with herbal ingredients.
- These items are not only safe for the environment, but they also don't require extensive industrial or chemical processing and have few to no negative side effects.

Bio-Composting

- The advent of modern, intensive agriculture has led to use of chemical fertilizers.
- This has led to many problems like **bioaccumulation, biomagnification, pollution** of water bodies etc. **Farmers are now becoming aware of the ill effects of chemical fertilisers.**
- They are now using the organically made fertilizers.
- In certain parts of the country, cattle are maintained only because they produce **dung** which is an important fertilizer and soil conditioner.
- **Earthworms** can convert organic matter into compost faster than the normal composting process.
- This process is now being widely used.

- Indirectly, the civic authorities are benefited too as they have to dispose off reduced quantity of waste.

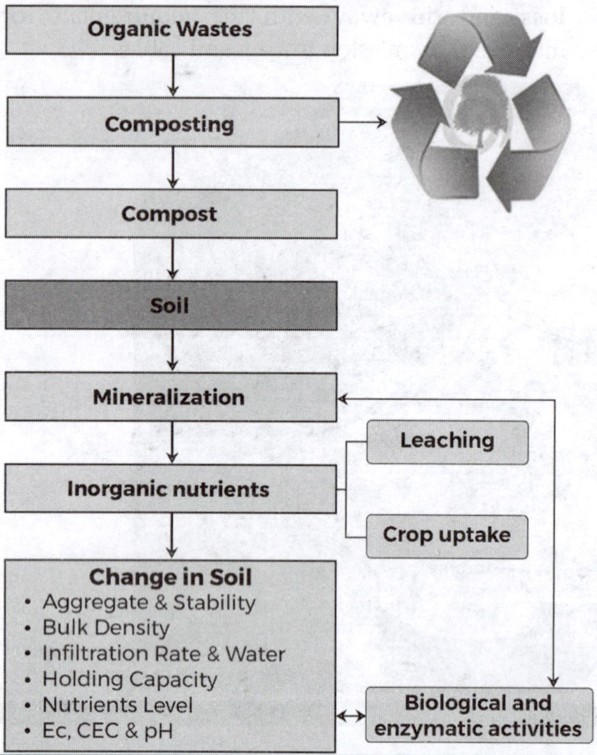

Bio Composting

Bio-Pest Control

- The entire nation went into a frenzy to apply more and more chemical pesticides in an attempt to increase production with the arrival of the Green Revolution.
- The negative effects soon became apparent; food products were tainted, and pesticides contaminated the soil, waterways, and even the groundwater. It was discovered that even fish, pork, and milk were affected.
- **Better pest management** techniques are being introduced in an attempt to meet this challenge.
- The application of **pesticides derived from plant materials** is one such action.
- **Neem trees** are showing to be quite beneficial. Various pesticides that suppress growth have been identified in neem and are currently in use.
- Farmers have also benefited from **mixed cropping,** which involves planting different crops on the same plot of land in successive years.
- Furthermore, more people are becoming aware of the different **animals and birds that aid in pest control**. For instance, one of the best groups of animals that feeds on rodents, mice, and other pests are snakes. Similarly, a wide variety of birds, including peacocks and owls, feed on rodents and other pests.
- If let to live in the vicinity of farming areas, these can eradicate a wide range of pests, including insects. Lizards are significant in this context as well.
- These days, sustainable development is a buzzword. **It is 'indeed' a paradigm shift in development thinking.**
- Though it has been interpreted in a number of ways, adherence to this path ensures lasting development and non-declining welfare for all.

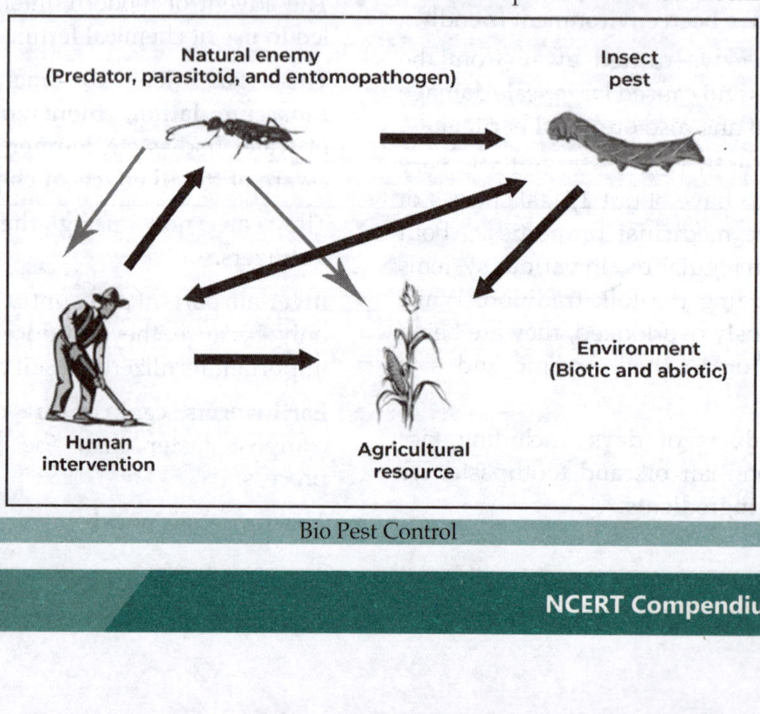

Bio Pest Control

Conclusion

Development is a multidimensional concept. What is development for one is restriction for others. Nations are compared on various criteria to check the extents of development they have achieved. India, which adopted a planned economy in its initial days and later privatisation and globalisation after 1991 reforms has performed well in some aspects while faltered in human development indicators and employment generation when compared to its peers. The comparison with Pakistan and China has shown that India has yet to achieve the demographic, economic and human development indicators like China.

The current mode of development is very resource intensive. The ill impact that the development is producing has put the present as well as future generation at severe risk. To deal with the limitations of current development methods, a new method that is **sustainable development is significant.**

TEST YOURSELF

Multiple Choice Questions

Q1. Which of the following can lead to development in the country?

(a) The process of increasing the GDP of a country.

(b) The improvement in the standard of living and well-being of a population.

(c) The expansion of industrial sectors within an economy.

(d) All of the above.

Q2. What is the Human Development Index (HDI)?

(a) An index that measures a country's economic growth rate.

(b) An index that measures a country's education and healthcare indicators.

(c) An index that measures a country's infrastructure development.

(d) An index that measures a country's income inequality.

Q3. What is sustainable development?

(a) Development that focuses on economic growth at any cost.

(b) Development that meets the needs of the present without compromising the needs of future generations.

(c) Development that emphasises social welfare programs.

(d) Development that promotes urbanisation and industrialisation.

Q4. What is the role of education in development?

(a) It increases income inequality.

(b) It enhances agricultural productivity.

(c) It promotes entrepreneurship and innovation.

(d) It reduces the dependency on foreign trade.

Q5. What is the concept of inclusive development?

(a) Development that benefits only the urban population

(b) Development that prioritises industrial growth over social welfare

(c) Development that ensures equal access to resources and opportunities for all segments of society

(d) Development that focuses on reducing the population growth rate

Q6. Which of the following is an example of a poverty alleviation program in India?

(a) Make in India

(b) Swachh Bharat Abhiyan

(c) Mahatma Gandhi National Rural Employment Guarantee Act (MGNREGA)

(d) Goods and Services Tax (GST)

Q7. What is the role of technology in development?

(a) It increases income inequality.

(b) It enhances agricultural productivity.

(c) It promotes import dependency.

(d) It reduces the role of domestic industries.

Q8. What is the significance of infrastructure development in economic development?

(a) It promotes social welfare programs.

(b) It increases government revenue through taxation.

(c) It enhances productivity and facilitates economic activities.

(d) It reduces income inequality.

Q9. What are the challenges to development in developing countries?

(a) Poverty and income inequality

(b) Insufficient infrastructure and human capital

(c) Lack of access to credit and financial services

(d) All of the above

Q10. What is the role of globalisation in development?

(a) It promotes import substitution and protectionist policies.

(b) It increases income inequality.

(c) It facilitates international trade and economic integration.

(d) It discourages foreign direct investment.

Q11. Which of the following statements is/are correct about the Demographic Indicators of India, Pakistan and China?

1. The population of Pakistan is very small and accounts for roughly about one-tenth of China.
2. Among the three nations, the population density of India is the lowest.
3. The annual growth rate of population is high in India than China and Pakistan.

Select the correct answer using the code given below:

(a) 1 only (b) 1 and 2 only

(c) 1, 2 and 3 (d) None of the above

Q12. Consider the following statements:

1. China introduced structural reforms on its own initiative while they were forced upon India by international agencies.
2. Though China has followed the classical development pattern of gradual shift from agriculture to manufacturing and then to services, India's shift has been directly from agriculture to service sector.

Which of the statements given above is/are correct?

(a) 1 only (b) 2 only

(c) Both 1 and 2 (d) Neither 1 nor 2

Q13. Which of the following statements is/are correct about the Sustainable Development?

1. It is the development that will allow all future generations to have a potential average quality of life that is at least as high as that which is being enjoyed by the current generation.
2. The concept of sustainable development was emphasised by the United Nations Conference on Environment and Development (UNCED).

Select the correct answer using the code given below:

(a) 1 only (b) 2 only

(c) Both 1 and 2 (d) Neither 1 nor 2

Q14. Which of the following are among the major strategies for the Sustainable Development in India?

1. Use of Non- conventional Sources of Energy
2. Bio composting
3. Biopest Control
4. Using Gobar Gas in Rural Areas

Select the correct answer using the code given below:

(a) 2 and 3 only (b) 2, 3 and 4 only

(c) 1, 2 and 4 only (d) 1, 2, 3 and 4

Answer Key					
Q1.	d	Q2.	b	Q3.	b
Q4.	c	Q5.	c	Q6.	c
Q7.	b	Q8.	c	Q9.	d
Q10.	c	Q11.	a	Q12.	c
Q13.	c	Q14.	d		

Model Questions for Main Examination

Q1. Explain intra-generational and inter-generational issues of equity from the perspective of inclusive growth and sustainable development. (UPSC 2020)

Q2. Define the concept of carrying capacity of an ecosystem as relevant to an environment. Explain how understanding this concept is vital while planning for sustainable development of a region. (UPSC 2019)

UNIT 10 Introduction to Macroeconomics

In This Unit

Comprehensive and profound coverage of the following NCERT's chapter:

- ✓ NCERT Class- 12th (Introductory Macroeconomics), Chapter- 1

What is Macroeconomics?

It is a branch of economics that **studies how an overall economy behaves**. It tries to address situations facing the economy as a whole. It includes the study of the effects of taxation and other budgetary policies on markets, change in money supply, rate of interest, wages, employment and output.

Variable of Macro Economics

Some Basic Concepts in Macroeconomics

Economic Agents: By economic units or economic agents, we mean those individuals or institutions which take economic decisions. They can be **consumers** who decide what and how much to consume. They may be **producers of goods and services** who decide what and how much to produce. They may be entities like the government, corporations, banks which also take different economic decisions like **how much to spend, what interest rate to charge on the credits, how much to tax, etc.**

Capitalist Economy: A type of economic model, where production activities are mainly carried out by capitalist enterprises. A capitalist economy can be defined as an economy in which most of the economic activities have the following characteristics:

(a) there is **private ownership** of means of production,

(b) production takes place for **selling the output** in the market,

(c) there is sale and purchase of labour services at a price which is called the **wage rate** and the labour which is sold and purchased against wages is referred to as **wage labour**.

Entrepreneurs: People who exercise **control over major decisions** and bear a large part of the risk associated with the **firm/enterprise**.

Capital: Capital is a broad term that can describe **anything that confers value or benefit to its owners,** such as a factory and its machinery, intellectual property like patents, or the financial assets of a business or an individual.

Labour: The **work done by a group of workers** or by a particular worker is referred to as their labour.

Factors of Production: Factors of production are the **inputs needed for creating** a good or service, and the factors of production **include land, labour, entrepreneurship, and capital**.

Revenue: After producing output with the help of these three factors of production, namely capital, land and labour, the entrepreneur sells the product in the market. The **money that is earned is called revenue.**

Profit: the part of revenue left after paying the rents of land, interest of capital and wage to labour is called as profit incurred by the firm.

Investment Expenditure: Profits are often used by the producers in the next period to buy new machinery or to build new factories, so that production can be expanded. **These expenses which raise productive capacity** are examples of investment expenditure.

Firm: A firm is **production unit in capitalist economy**. Here entrepreneur hires wage labour from market, employs the services of capital and land. After hiring these inputs, the firm undertakes the task of production with a clear **motive to earn profit**.

State: It is also a player in production process. The role of the state **framing laws, enforcing them and delivering justice**. The state, in many instances, **undertakes production** – apart from imposing taxes and spending money on building public infrastructure, running schools, colleges, providing health services etc.

Household Sector: A household is a **single individual** who takes **decisions relating to her own consumption,** or a group of individuals for whom decisions relating to consumption are jointly determined. Households also **save and pay taxes.**

External Sector: It is also a significant sector in the study of macroeconomics. Trade with the external sector can be of two kinds:

1. The domestic country may sell goods to the rest of the world. These are called ***exports***.
2. The economy may also buy goods from the rest of the world. These are called ***imports***. Besides exports and imports, the rest of the world affects the domestic economy in other ways as well.
3. Capital from foreign countries may flow into the domestic country, or the domestic country may be exporting capital to foreign countries.

Final Goods: An item that is meant for final use and will not pass through any more stages of production or transformations is called a final good. Once it has been sold it passes out of the active economic flow. It will not undergo any further transformation at the hands of any producer. It may, however, undergo transformation by the action of the ultimate purchaser. In fact, many such final goods are transformed during their consumption. Thus, it is not in the nature of the good but in the economic nature of its use that a good becomes a final good.

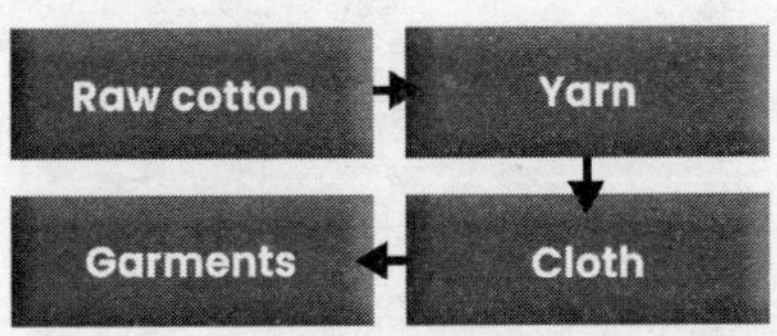

How Garments Become Final Goods

Types of Final Goods: based on **timescale of consumption** of final goods, there are two types of goods. They are **Consumption goods and capital goods.**

Consumption goods: Goods like food and clothing, and services like recreation that are consumed when purchased by their ultimate consumers are called consumption goods or consumer goods.

Capital goods: There are goods that are of durable character which are used in the production process. These are tools, implements and machines. While they make production of other commodities feasible, they themselves don't get transformed in the production process. They are also final goods yet they are not final goods to be ultimately consumed.

Consumer Durables: **Consumer durables, also known as "durable goods,"** are a category of consumer goods that do not wear out quickly and therefore do not have to be purchased frequently. E.g., **television sets, automobiles etc.**

Intermediate Goods: Of the total production taking place in the economy a large number of products don't end up in final consumption and are not capital goods either. Such goods may be used by other producers as material inputs. These are **intermediate goods**, mostly used as raw material or inputs for production of other commodities. Examples are steel sheets used for making automobiles and copper used for making utensils. **These are not final goods.**

Stock variables/goods: Stocks are defined at a particular point of time. It represents the amount of inventory and intermediate goods available to the firm at a particular time. The building, machine etc. can be termed as stocks in production process.

Flow variables/goods: **They are defined over a period of time.** We need to delineate a time period to get a quantitative measure of them. Since a lot of accounting is done annually in an economy, many of these are expressed annually like annual profits or production.

Gross investment: Part of our **final output that comprises of capital goods** constitutes gross investment of an economy. These may be machines, tools and implements; buildings, office spaces, storehouses or infrastructure like roads, bridges, airports or jetties.

Depreciation: A significant part of final output does not become the part of gross investment in an economy. It is needed to be maintained to deal with wear and tear, replacement and maintenance of already existing capital goods. Hence a significant amount of final goods must be subtracted from the gross investment to reach a new value, that is **net investment**. This deletion, which is made from the value of gross investment in order to accommodate regular wear and tear of capital, is called depreciation.

Net investment: Any new addition to capital stock in an economy is measured by net investment or new capital formation, which is expressed as

Net Investment = Gross investment – Depreciation

TEST YOURSELF

Multiple Choice Questions

Q1. Which of the following statements is/are correct about 'Capital Goods'?

1. These are mostly used as raw materials or inputs for the production of other commodities.
2. It is generally observed that more sophisticated and heavy capital goods raise the ability of a labourer to produce goods.

Select the correct answer using the code given below:

(a) 1 only (b) 2 only
(c) Both 1 and 2 (d) Neither 1 nor 2

Q2. Which of the following is NOT true about a firm in an economy:

(a) Firms are the engines of production, transforming resources into goods and services.

(b) Firms hire labor, acquire capital (equipment, machinery), and utilize land, all through market mechanisms.

(c) The primary driver for firms is to generate profit by selling their outputs at a price exceeding the cost of inputs

(d) It frames laws and enforces them to ensure market functions smoothly.

Answer Key	
Q1.	b
Q2.	d

Model Questions for Main Examination

1. What is the external sector of economy?

2. What are the different types of goods in an economy? Describe briefly, consumption goods, capital goods and consumer durable goods.

UNIT 11 National Income Accounting

In This Unit

Comprehensive and profound coverage of the following NCERT's chapter:

✓ NCERT Class- 12th (Introductory Macroeconomics), Chapter- 2

Introduction

National income accounting is a set of principles and methods used to measure the income and production of a country. There are basically **two ways of measuring national economic activity**. Either, as the **money value of the total production** of goods and services during a given period (usually a year), or, as the **total of incomes derived** from economic activity after allowance has been made for capital consumption. It involves the study of the **ways to calculate national income;** study of various sub-categories of national income; **defining various price indices** like GDP deflator, consumer price indices, wholesale price indices; and problems associated with taking GDP of a country as an indicator of the aggregate welfare of the people of the country.

Circular Flow of Income and Methods of Calculating National Income

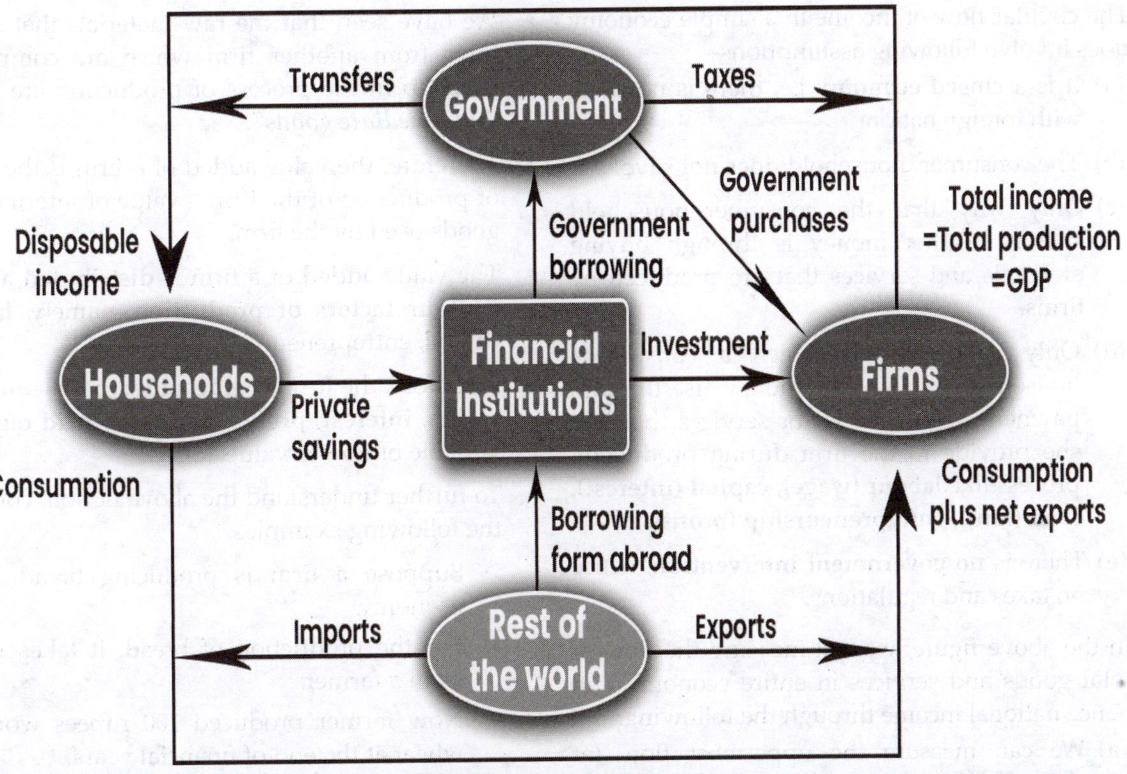

The Circular Flow of Income

- Before understanding various methods to calculate national income, one must first understand the **circular flow of income in an economy.**
- For simplicity, we assume only a simple model of economy.
- As studied earlier there are only four factors of production. These are land, labour, capital and entrepreneurship.
- Also, there may be fundamentally four kind of contribution that can be made during the production of goods and services.
- They are-
  (a) contribution made by human labour, remuneration for which is called **wage**
  (b) contribution made by capital, remuneration for which is called **interest**
  (c) contribution made by entrepreneurship, remuneration of which is **profit**
  (d) contribution made by fixed natural resources (called 'land'), remuneration for which is called **rent.**
- The circular flow of income in a simple economy does involve following assumptions-
  (a) It is a **closed economy** i.e. there is no trade with foreign nation.
  (b) The consumer/household **does not save**.
  (c) Only way that the consumer/household spends his/her money is through buying of goods and services that are produced by firms.
  (d) Only way through which a consumer/household earns the money is through payment of various factor services that he/she provide to the firm during production process like **labour (wage), capital (interest), land (rent), entrepreneurship (profit).**
  (e) There is **no government intervention**, hence no taxes and regulations.
- In the above figure, we can measure the flow of total goods and services in entire economy and hence national income through the following:
  (a) We can measure the uppermost flow (at point A) by measuring the aggregate value of spending that the firms receive for the final goods and services which they produce. This method will be called the ***expenditure method***.
  (b) If we measure the flow at B by measuring the aggregate value of final goods and services produced by all the firms, it will be called ***product method***.
  (c) At C, measuring the sum total of all factor payments will be called ***income method***.
- In simple economic model we can say that spending done by the **households must be equal to the factor payments that they receive from the firm.**
- Hence it is usually found that national income accounting through expenditure method and income method consider similar approaches.

The Product or Value-Added Method

- The term that is used to denote the net contribution made by a firm is called **its value added.** This includes the inventories, stocks etc., which cannot be used in the calculation of GDP under this method.
- We have seen that the raw materials that a firm buys from another firm which are completely used up in the process of production are called ***"intermediate goods"***.
- Therefore, the value added of a firm is the value of production of the firm – value of intermediate goods used by the firm.
- The value added of a firm is **distributed among its four factors of production,** namely, labour, capital, entrepreneurship and land.
- Therefore, the firm's **value added must equal the wages, interest, profits, and rents paid out.** The variable of flow is value added.
- To further understand the above notion, consider the following examples:
  - ➢ Suppose a firm is producing bread in an economy.
  - ➢ For the production of bread, it takes wheat from a farmer.
  - ➢ Now farmer produced 100 rupees worth of wheat at the end of financial years.
  - ➢ Here, total value addition by the farmer would be 100 rupees.

- Now, he sells 50 rupees worth of wheat to bread making firm.
- Firm uses this wheat as input and produces bread worth of 200 rupees.
- Here, value added by the firm is equal to 200-50, i.e. 150 rupees.
- Because 50 rupees worth of wheat has already been calculated, while we are calculating value added by the farmer, to avoid 'double counting', the 50 rupees value added by farmer is subtracted from 200 rupees.
- Hence value added by both farmer and firm is equal to 100+150=250 rupees.

- **Gross value added by firm**: i (GVA_i) ≡ Gross value of the output produced by the firm i (Q_i) – Value of intermediate goods used by the firm (Z_i)
  - **GVA_i** ≡ Value of sales by the firm (V_i) + Value of change in inventories (A_i) – Value of intermediate goods used by the firm (Z_i).
- If we sum up the gross value added of all the firms of the economy in a year, we get a measure of the value of aggregate amount of goods and services produced by the economy in a year (just as we had done in the wheat-bread example). Such an estimate is called *Gross Domestic Product (GDP).*
- Hence, if we take N numbers of firms, then-

GDP ≡ Sum total of the gross value added of all the firms in the economy

$$\equiv GVA_1 + GVA_2 + \ldots\ldots + GVA_N$$

- Therefore,

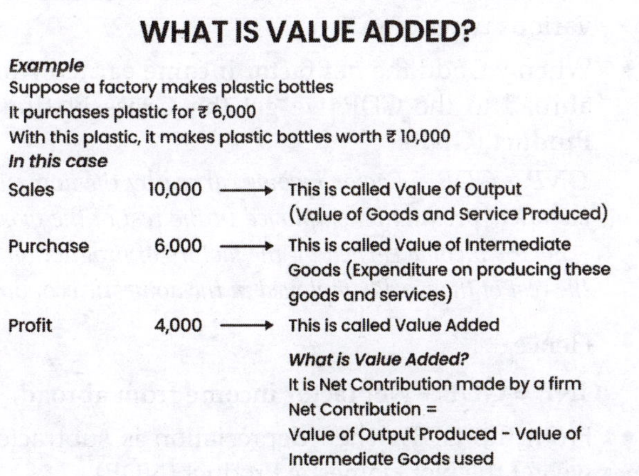

Calculating Value Added

Expenditure Method

In our **circular flow of income** in simple economy, we saw that the national income can also be calculated by summing up all the spending done by consumers/households or all the goods and services that are bought by consumer/household.

The total consumption expenditure constitutes:

Final Consumption Expenditure (C): This includes consumption expenditure by private households for the consumption of goods and services. This may also include the consumption expenditure made by firms to treat their guests and employees.

Final Investment Expenditure (I): Investment is an addition to capital stock of an economy in a given time period. This includes investments by firms as well as government sector. This also includes investment on intermediate goods.

Government Expenditure (G): The expenditure that the government makes on the final goods and services produced by firms. It is to be noted that the final expenditure incurred by the government includes both the consumption and investment expenditure.

Net Export (X-M): This part includes export earning that is earned by firms in an economy. The net export includes total earning from export minus total spending on import.

Hence GDP would be total sum of all the expenditure incurred by all the firms involved in production process in an economy **i.e.** ***GDP=C+I+G+X-M***

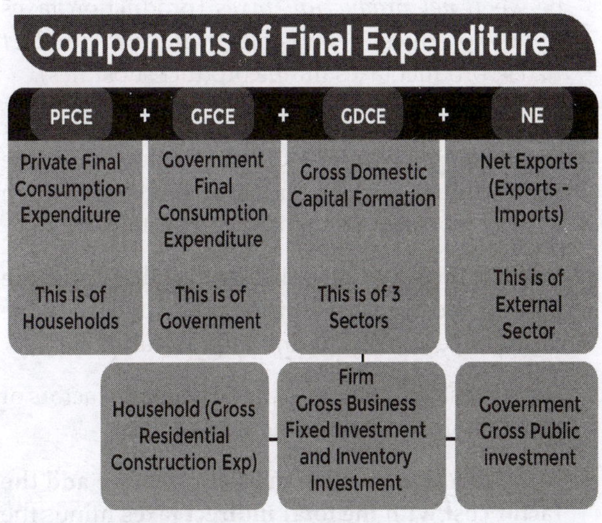

Components of Final Expenditure

Income Method

- In our circular flow of income in simple economy model we have seen that the consumer / household provide factor services to the firm in production process.
- In this transaction, the firm provides factor payments to the households for their factor services.
- This payment is given in the terms of **wages (for labour), profit (for entrepreneurship), interest (for capital) and rent (for land).**
- The income method of calculating GDP takes into consideration the sum total of factor payments earned by every household in an economy. Hence,

GDP = Sum total of all factor payments of all the household in an economy.

GDP = W (wages) + P (profits) + In (interests) + R (rents)

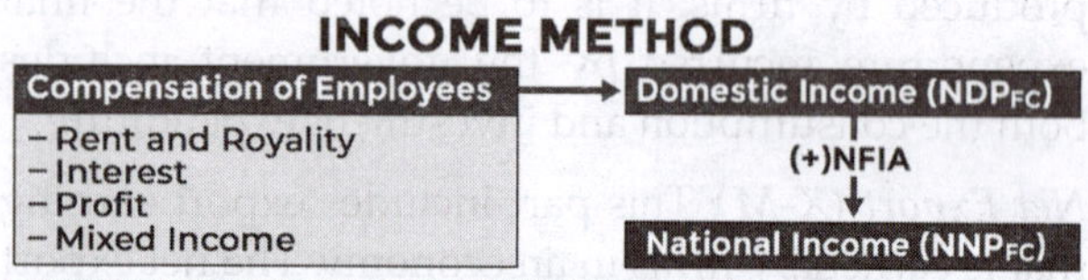

Income Method

Factor Cost, Basic Prices And Market Prices

- The **distinction** between factor cost, basic prices and market prices is based on the distinction between ***net production taxes*** (production taxes minus production subsidies) and ***net product taxes*** (product taxes minus product subsidies).
- **Production** taxes and subsidies are **paid or received in relation to production** and are **independent of the volume of production** such as land revenues, stamp and registration fee etc.
- **Product taxes** and subsidies on the other hand, **are paid or received per unit or product,** e.g., excise tax, service tax, export and import duties etc.
- **Factor cost** includes only the payment to factors of production, it **does not include any tax.**
- In order to arrive at the **market price, we add the factor cost with the total indirect taxes** minus the total subsidies.
- **Basic prices** lie in between. It is obtained when **factor cost is added with the net production taxes.**
- In basic prices when net product subsidies are added, we get the **market price.**
- Hence,

GVA at factor costs + Net production taxes = GVA at basic prices

GVA at basic prices + Net product taxes = GVA at market prices

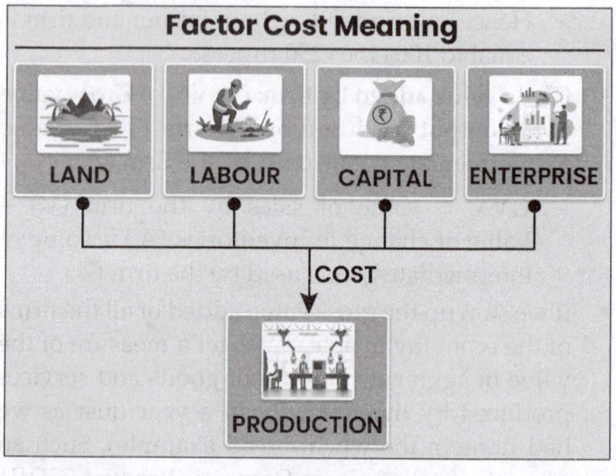

Factor Cost

- In its revision in January 2015 the **Central Statistics Office (CSO) replaced GDP at factor cost with the GVA at basic prices** and the **GDP at market prices**, which is now called **only GDP.**

Some Macroeconomic Identities

- We have already seen the GDP and GVA and also various types of prices.
- When we add the **net factor income earned from abroad** to the GDP, we get the **Gross National Product (GNP).**

  GNP ≡ GDP + Factor income earned by the domestic factors of production employed in the rest of the world – Factor income earned by the factors of production of the rest of the world employed in the domestic economy

- Hence,

GNP ≡ GDP + Net factor income from abroad.

- From the GDP, when depreciation is subtracted we get the Net Domestic Product (NDP).

NDP = GDP - Depreciation

- When, from, depreciation is subtracted, we get the Net National Product (NNP).

NNP = GNP – Depreciation

- The above expression gives us NNP at market price. When from NNP at market price we deduct the net indirect taxes (total indirect taxes – total subsidies), we get the **NNP at factor cost.**
  - ➢ The National Income is this NNP at factor cost.

NNP at factor cost ≡ National Income (NI) ≡ *NNP at market prices – (Indirect taxes – Subsidies) ≡ NNP at market prices – Net indirect taxes (Net indirect taxes ≡ Indirect taxes – Subsidies)*

- The transfer of this national revenue to families is not complete.
- Some of them are deducted as undistributed profits, some of them are deducted as net interest payment by the household for previous loans, some are deducted as corporate tax, and some are added as transfer payment to households by governments and private firms.
- Thus,

Personal income (PI) *≡ National Income – Undistributed profits – Net interest payments made by households – Corporate tax + Transfer payments to the households from the government and firms.*

- From this personal income if we deduct personal and non-personal taxes, then we would get the **personal disposable income.**

Personal Disposable Income (PDI) ≡ PI – Personal tax payments – non tax payments.

- Personal Disposable Income is the part of the aggregate income which belongs to the households. They may decide to consume a part of it, and save the rest.

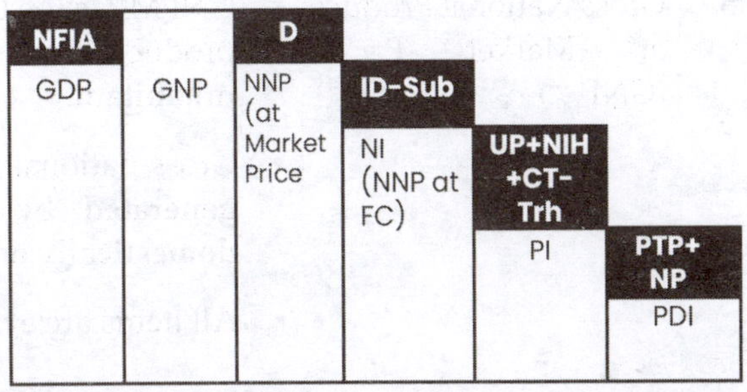

Diagrammatic representation of the subcategories of aggregate income. NFIA: Net Factor Income from Abroad, D: Depreciation, ID: Indirect Taxes, Sub: Subsidies, UP: Undistributed Profits, NIH: Net Interest payments by Households, CT: Corporate Taxes, TrH: Transfers recived by Households, PTP: Personal Tax Payments, NP: Non-Tax Payments.

Subcategories of Aggregate Income

Basic National Income Aggregates

1.	Gross Domestic Product at Market Prices (GDP_{MP})	• GDP is the market worth, measured in a year, of all final goods and services produced inside a **nation's domestic territory.** • All work produced by **citizens or non-residents** of a nation is included, regardless of whether the work is owned by a domestic business or a foreign organisation. • Everything is priced according to **market value.** $GDP_{MP} = C + I + G + X - M$
2.	GDP at Factor Cost (GDP_{FC})	• Gross domestic product at market prices **less net product taxes** is known as GDP at factor cost. • Market pricing are what consumers are willing to pay. Subsidies and product taxes are included in market prices. The prices of the goods as received by the producers are referred to as factor cost. Therefore, market prices less net indirect taxes equals factor cost. GDP at factor cost calculates the monetary value of the production generated by domestic businesses in a nation during a given year. $GDP_{FC} = GDP_{MP} - NIT$

3.	Net Domestic Product at Market Prices (NDP_{MP})	• Policymakers can use this indicator to calculate the amount of **money the nation must spend in order to retain its existing GDP**. GDP will decline if the nation is unable to replenish the capital stock that depreciation has destroyed. $NDP_{MP} = GDP_{MP}$ - Depreciation
4.	NDP at Factor Cost (NDP_{FC})	• NDP at factor cost is the income earned by the factors in the form of wages, profits, rent, interest, etc., **within the domestic territory of a country.** $NDP_{FC} = NDP_{MP}$ - Net Product Taxes - Net production Taxes
5.	Gross National Product at Market Prices (GNP_{MP})	• GNPMP is the **total value**, evaluated at market prices, of all the finished products and services generated in a year **by the average Indian inhabitant**. • Gross national product (GNP) is the total amount of economic **output generated by a country's average citizen, whether they dwell domestically or outside.** • All items are evaluated according to their market worth. $GNP_{MP} = GDP_{MP}$ + NFIA
6.	GNP at Factor Cost (GNP_{FC})	• The GDP at factor cost calculates the annual value of the output that a nation's factors of production get. $GNP_{FC} = GNP_{MP}$ - Net Product Taxes - Net Production Taxes
7.	**Net National Product at Market Prices (NNP*MP*)**	• This is the maximum amount that a nation can consume in a specific amount of time. Regardless of the location of production (whether local or foreign), **NNP measures output.** $NNP_{MP} = GNP_{MP}$ - Depreciation $NNP_{MP} = NDP_{MP}$ + NFIA
8.	NNP at Factor Cost (NNP_{FC}) Or National Income (NI)	• NNP at factor cost is the **sum of income earned by all factors in the production** in the form of wages, profits, rent and interest, etc., **belonging to a country** during a year. • It is the National Product and is not bound by production in the national boundaries. It is the net domestic factor income added with the net factor income from abroad. NI = NNP_{MP} - Net Product Taxes - Net production Taxes $= NDP_{FC}$ + NFIA $= NNP_{FC}$
9.	GVA at Market Prices	GDP at market prices
10.	GVA at basic prices	GVA_{MP} - Net Product Taxes
11.	GVA at factor cost	GVA at basic prices - Net Production Taxes

National Disposable Income and Private Income

- Apart from these categories of aggregate macroeconomic variables, in India, a few other aggregate income categories are also used in National Income accounting
- National Disposable Income = Net National Product at market prices + Other current transfers from the rest of the world
- The idea behind National Disposable Income is that it gives an idea of what is the maximum amount of goods and services the domestic economy has at its disposal.
- **Current transfers from the rest of the world** include items such as gifts, aids, etc.

Private Income *= Factor income from net domestic product accruing to the private sector + National debt interest + Net factor income from abroad + Current transfers from government + Other net transfers from the rest of the world*

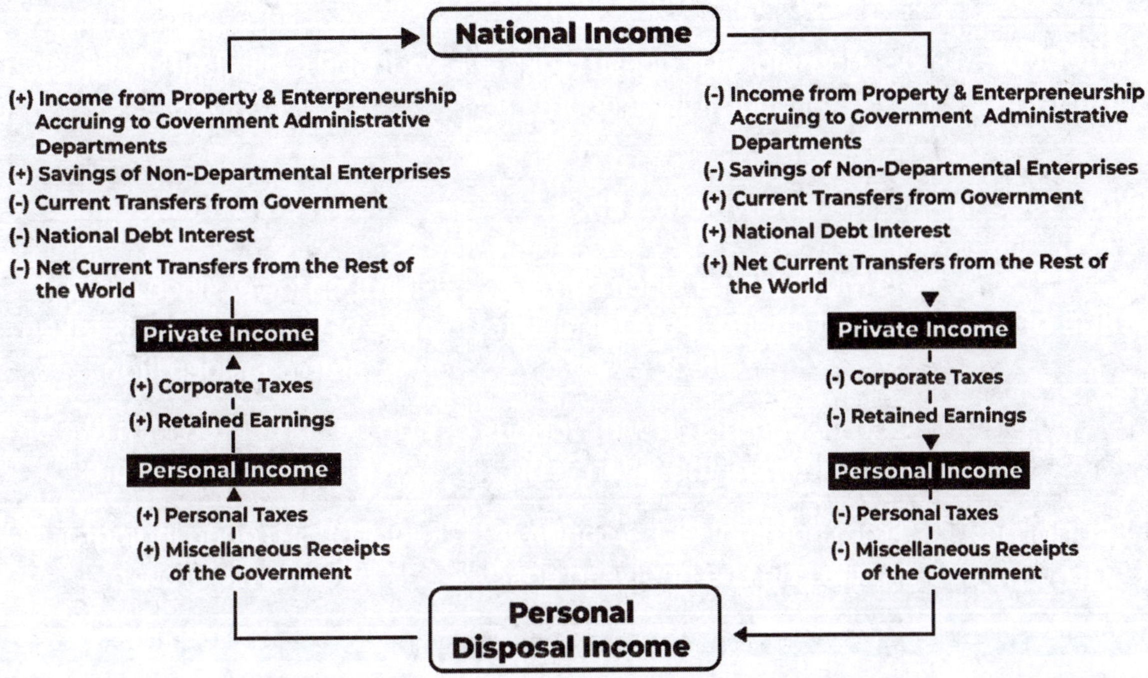

National Income v/s Personal Income

Nominal and Real GDP

- **Real GDP** is calculated in a way such that the goods and services are evaluated at some constant set of prices (or **constant prices**).
- Since these **prices remain fixed**, if the Real GDP changes, we can be sure that it is the volume of production which is undergoing changes.
- **Nominal GDP**, on the other hand, is simply the value of GDP at the current prevailing prices.
- The ratio of nominal GDP to real GDP provides insight into how prices have changed between the base year, whose values are used to determine the real GDP, and the current year.
- The production volume is fixed while determining the real and nominal GDP for the current year.
- Consequently, the only reason these measurements differ is if the **price level changed** between the base year and the current year.
- The nominal to real GDP ratio is a well-recognised measure of prices. We refer to this as the GDP Deflator.
- Consequently, if GDPn represents nominal GDP and GDP represents real GDP, then,
- Sometimes the deflator is also denoted in percentage terms. In such a case:

Comparing Nominal GDP & Real GDP

Basis For Comparison	Nominal GDP	Real GDP
Meaning	Nominal GDP is sum-total of economic output produced in a year valued at current market price	Real GDP is sum-total of economic output produced in a year valued at a pre-determined base market price
Effect of Inflation	Nominal GDP doesn't take inflation into account	Real GDP is a inflation-adjusted GDP
Expressed in	Current Market Price	Base year's market price
Value of GDP	Is much higher since current market changes are taken into effect	Is much lower since market price of the base year is taken into consideration
Uses	Can be compared with various quarters of the given year	Can be compared with two or more financial years
Economic Growth	From nominal GDP, economic growth can't be analysed easily	Real GDP is a good Indicator of economic growth

Comparing Nominal GDP and Real GDP

Consumer Price Index (CPI): This is the index of prices of a given basket of commodities which are bought by the representative consumer. CPI is generally expressed in percentage terms.

Wholesale Price Index (WPI): Many commodities have two sets of prices. One is the **retail price** which the consumer actually pays. The other is the **wholesale price,** the price at which goods are traded in bulk. These two may differ in value because of the margin kept by traders. Goods which are traded in bulk (such as raw materials or semi-finished goods) are not purchased by ordinary consumers. Like **CPI, the index for wholesale prices is called Wholesale Price Index (WPI).**

Difference between CPI/WPI and GDP Deflator

CPI (and analogously WPI) may differ from GDP deflator because:

1. The goods purchased by consumers do not represent all the goods which are produced in a country. **GDP deflator takes into account all such goods and services.**

2. CPI includes prices of goods consumed by the representative consumer; hence it includes prices of imported goods. **GDP deflator does not include prices of imported goods.**

3. The **weights are constant in CPI** – but they differ according to production level of each good in GDP deflator.

GDP and Welfare

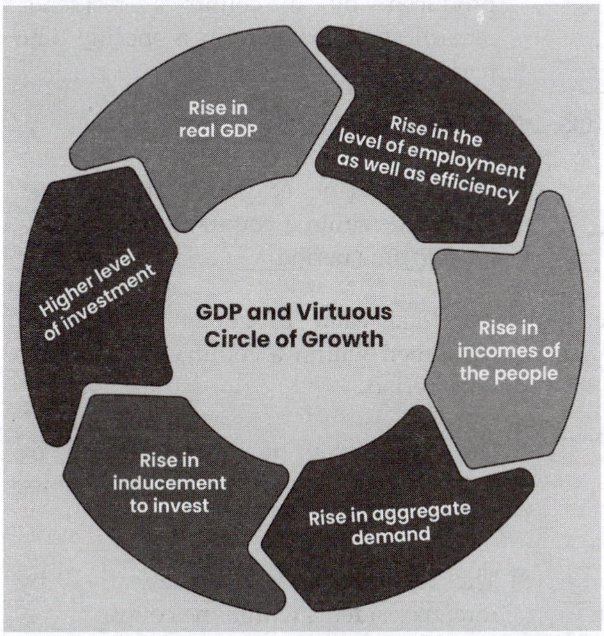

GDP and Virtuous Circle of Growth

Across world GDP has become the indicator of economic progress. **GDP number is taken as benchmark to judge the progress made by people of a country.** But there are some limitations to see the GDP as indicator for wellbeing of common people. They are as follows:

- Distribution of GDP is not Uniform
- GDP does not show the distribution of income and wealth across nation.
- GDP numbers also hide the actual performance by each and every sectors.
- For example, in India's context, the bourgeoning GDP number does not show the true contribution made by MSME sectors.
- The service sector's contribution hides the plight of the agriculture sector.
- In similar ways, the unequal distribution of wealth and unequal distribution of development are also not shown properly by GDP numbers.
- Non-monetary Exchanges
- GDP number does not include some non-monetary activities like domestic help.
- It also does not take the contribution of barter type transaction, which does not involve monetary transaction.
- In this ways GDP does not involve each and every production and service-related activities in an economy.

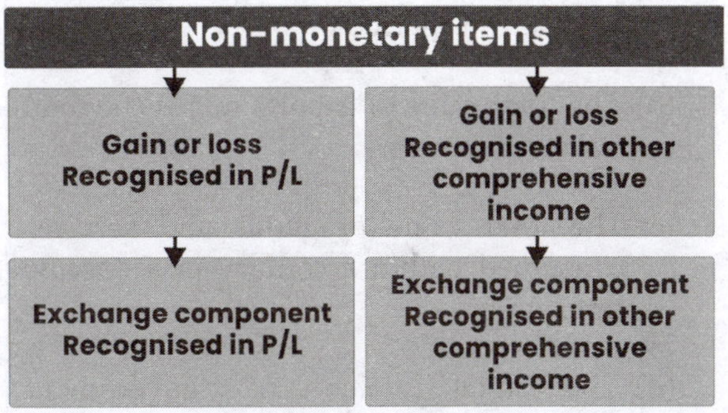

Non-Monetary Items

- Externalities
- GDP number does not take into consideration externalities and cost of lost opportunities.
- For example, GDP takes into consideration coal mining and electricity generation from thermal powerplants using coal, but it does **not consider the negative impact** of air pollution on environment and public health.
- These negative externalities are not assigned any measurable number.
- Similarly, the **cost of lost opportunity** like if a farmer chose to cultivate sugarcane in the place of wheat, then what would be the cost of lost opportunity incurred on economy. It is also not included in GDP calculation.

TEST YOURSELF

Multiple Choice Questions

Q1. What is national income accounting?

(a) The process of calculating the income of individuals within a nation.

(b) The process of calculating the total output and income of a nation.

(c) The process of calculating the income of government agencies within a nation.

(d) The process of calculating the income of foreign entities within a nation.

Q2. What is Gross Domestic Product (GDP)?

(a) The total value of goods and services produced within a country's borders in a specific time period.

(b) The total value of exports minus the total value of imports.

(c) The total value of goods and services consumed within a country in a specific time period.

(d) The total value of government expenditures within a country in a specific time period.

Q3. Which of the following is included in GDP?

(a) Income earned by foreign residents within the country.

(b) Income earned by domestic residents abroad.

(c) Government transfer payments.

(d) Capital gains from the sale of stocks and bonds.

Q4. What is Net Domestic Product (NDP)?

(a) GDP minus depreciation

(b) GDP plus depreciation

(c) GDP minus indirect taxes

(d) GDP plus indirect taxes

Q5. What is Gross National Product (GNP)?

(a) The total value of goods and services produced within a country's borders in a specific time period.

(b) The total value of exports minus the total value of imports.

(c) The total value of goods and services consumed within a country in a specific time period.

(d) The total value of goods and services produced by a country's residents, regardless of location, in a specific time period.

Q6. What is National Income (NI)?

(a) The total value of goods and services produced within a country's borders in a specific time period.

(b) The total value of goods and services consumed within a country in a specific time period.

(c) The total value of income earned by domestic residents, including wages, rents, and profits.

(d) The total value of income earned by foreign residents within the country.

Q7. What is Disposable Income?

(a) The income left after paying taxes and other deductions.

(b) The income left after saving a portion of the total income.

(c) The income left after paying for necessities like food and shelter.

(d) The income left after paying off all debts and loans.

Q8. What is the difference between nominal GDP and real GDP?

(a) Nominal GDP is measured at current market prices, while real GDP is adjusted for inflation.

(b) Nominal GDP is adjusted for inflation, while real GDP is measured at current market prices.

(c) Nominal GDP includes indirect taxes, while real GDP does not.

(d) Nominal GDP includes government transfer payments, while real GDP does not.

Q9. Which of the following statements is/are correct about the Value Added Method of calculating National Income?

(a) It is a way to calculate the GDP or national income by looking at the demand side of the products.

(b) In this method we calculate the aggregate annual value of goods and services produced.

(c) It is a way to calculate of GDP Equation by total income generated by goods and services.

(d) None of the above.

Q10. Consider the following statements about GDP at Factor Cost:

1. In India currently, the most highlighted measure of national income is GDP at factor cost.

2. National Sample Survey Office (NSSO) calculates the GDP at factor cost and at market prices in India.

3. Factor cost includes only the payment to factors of production and it does not include any tax.

Which of the above statements is/are correct?

(a) 3 only (b) 2 and 3 only

(c) 1 and 2 only (d) 1, 2 and 3

Q11. Which of the following is a National Income of a country?

1. Net National Product at factor cost

2. NNP at market prices – (Indirect taxes – Subsidies)

3. GDP at Market Price + Net factor income from abroad

4. GNP – Depreciation

Select the correct answer using the codes given below:

(a) 1 only (b) 1 and 2 only

(c) 1, 2 and 3 only (d) 1, 2, 3 and 4

Q12. Out of Total National Income, the income that goes to the firms and households is known as:

(a) Private Income

(b) Public Income

(c) Personal Income

(d) Personal Disposable Income

Q13. Increase in absolute and per capita real GNP do not connote a higher level of economic development, if (2018)

(a) Industrial output fails to keep pace with agricultural output.

(b) Agricultural output fails to keep pace with industrial output.

(c) Poverty and unemployment increase.

(d) Imports grow faster than exports.

Answer Key					
Q1.	b	Q2.	a	Q3.	a
Q4.	a	Q5.	d	Q6.	c
Q7.	a	Q8.	a	Q9.	b
Q10.	a	Q11.	b	Q12.	c
Q13.	c				

Model Questions for Main Examination

Q1. What is the value-added method in calculation of national income?

Q2. Write a note on GDP and welfare.

UNIT 12

Money and Banking

In This Unit

Comprehensive and profound coverage of the following NCERT's chapters:

✓ NCERT Class- 11th (Introductory Macroeconomics), Chapter- 3

Introduction

Money is considered as the most common mode of exchange in an economy. It acts as an intermediate whenever two people transact in an economy. Money was brought to deal with the difficulties and limitations found while doing the transaction in barter system. Money can be saved, stored and it is handy compared to any other system. Money is most trusted mode for **storing value**. It has longest **shelf-life**.

Function of Money

- Money is the most efficient, hassle free and handy mode of exchange.
- It is a convenient unit of account. The values to all goods and services can be assigned by using money. For example, monetary values can be assigned to 1 kg of rice, similarly value can be assigned as per hour of labour work.
- Money is **transferrable, storable, inheritable mode of exchange.**

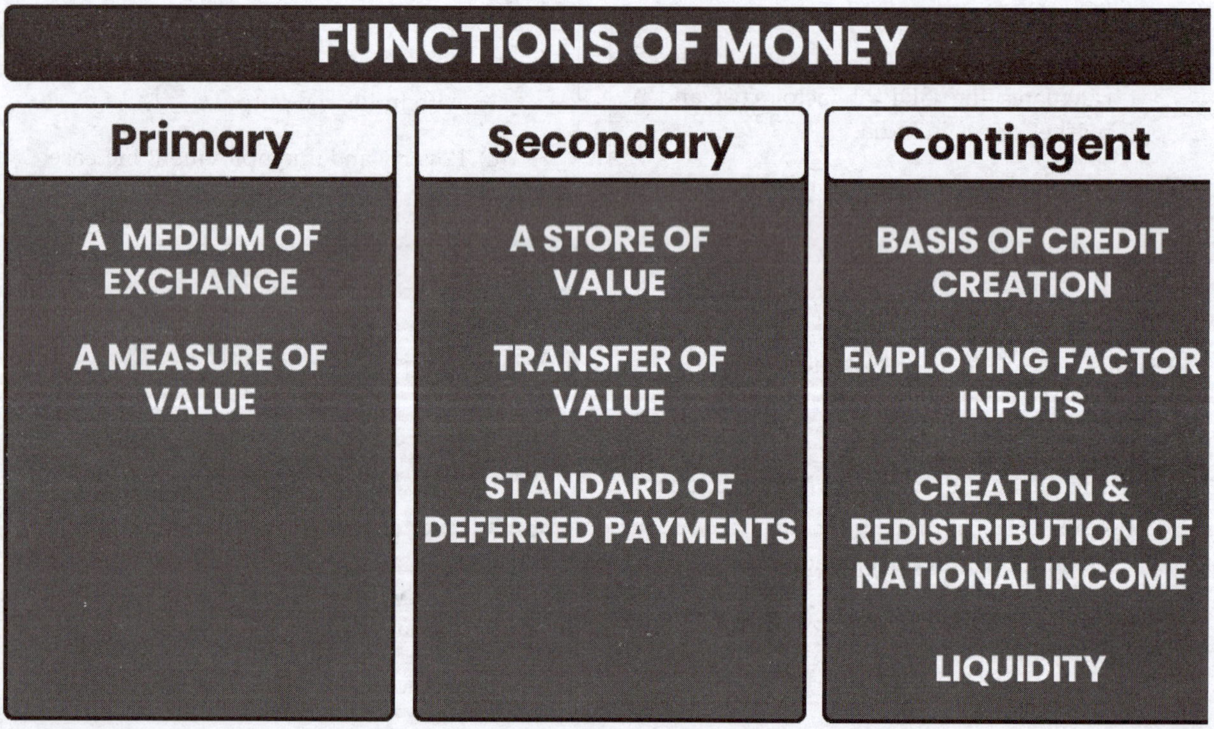

Functions of Money

Cashless Economy

- Some countries have made an attempt to move towards an economy which uses less of cash and more of digital transactions.
- A **cashless society** describes an economic state whereby financial transactions are not connected with money in the form of physical bank notes or coins but rather through the transfer of digital information (usually an electronic representation of money) between the transacting parties.
- In India, government has been consistently investing in various reforms for greater **financial inclusion**. During the last few years' initiatives such as **Jan Dhan accounts, Aadhar enabled payment systems, e –Wallets, National financial Switch (NFS)** and others have strengthened the government resolve to go cashless.
- Today, financial inclusion is seen as a realistic dream **because of mobile and smart phone penetration across the country.**

Demand for Money and Supply of Money

Demand for Money

- The demand of money depends on transaction being made by people.
- It also depends on income of people, i.e., when income of people rises, demand for money rises.
- People save money in bank to earn interest. Hence, when **interest rate increases in economy, demand for money goes down.**

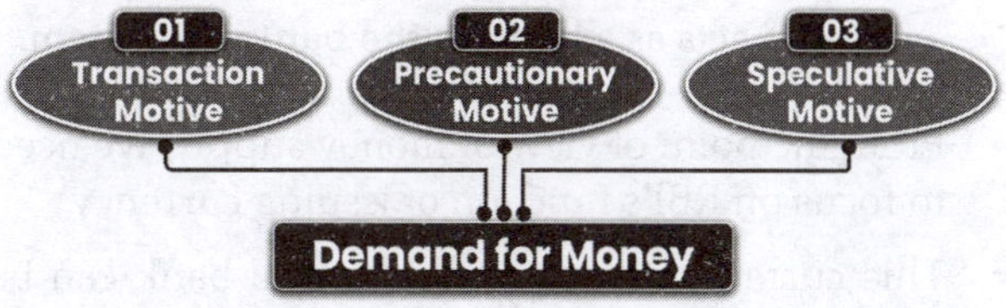

Demand for Money

Supply of Money

Money in a contemporary economy consists of bank deposits and cash. There are several measures of money depending on the kinds of bank deposits that are being considered. These are produced by a system that consists of the commercial banking sector and the central bank of the economy.

Central Bank

- Central Bank is a very important institution in a modern economy.
- **Almost every country has one central bank.** India got its central bank in 1935. Its name is the **'Reserve Bank of India' (RBI).**
- Central bank has several important functions:
  - It **issues the currency** of the country.
  - It **controls money supply** of the country through various methods, like bank rate, open market operations and variations in reserve ratios.

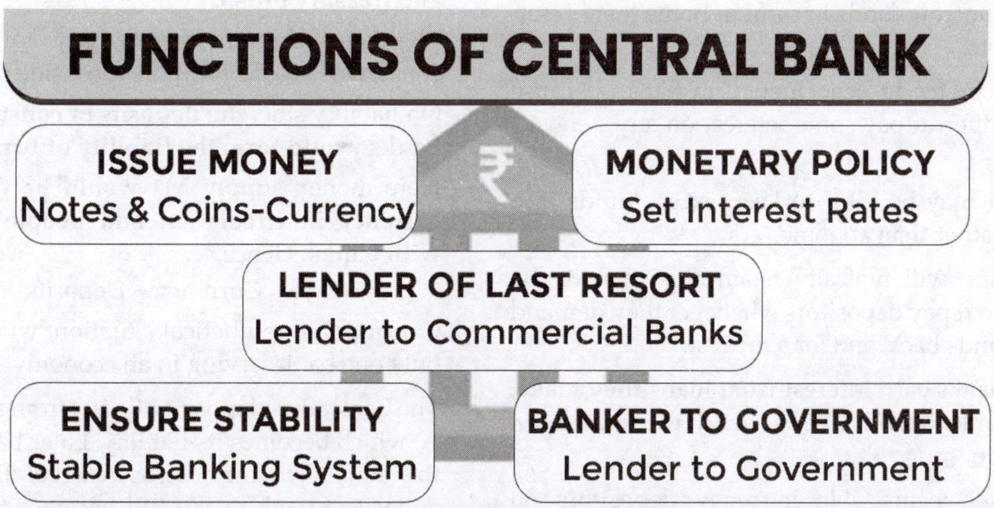

Functions of Central Bank

- ➢ It acts as a **banker to the government**.
- ➢ It is the **custodian of the foreign exchange** reserves of the economy.
- ➢ It also acts as a **bank to the banking system**.

- From the point of view of money supply, we need to focus on RBI's function of issuing currency.
- This currency issued by the central bank can be held by the public or by the commercial banks, and is called the ***'high-powered money' or 'reserve money' or 'monetary base'*** as it acts as a basis for credit creation.

Commercial Banks

- **Commercial banks** are the other type of institutions which are a part of the money-creating system of the economy.
- They accept deposits from the public and lend out part of these funds to those who want to borrow.
- The interest rate paid by the banks to depositors is lower than the rate charged from the borrowers.
- This difference between these two types of interest rates, called the **'spread', is the profit appropriated by the bank.**
- Commercial banks mediate between individuals or firms with excess funds and lend to those who need funds.
- People with excess funds can keep their funds in the form of **deposits** in banks and those who need funds, **borrow** funds in form of home loans, crop loans, etc.
- People prefer to keep money in banks because banks offer to pay some interest on any deposits made.
- Also, it may be safer to keep excess funds in a bank, rather than at home.
- The bank will typically retain a portion of the funds to repay depositors whenever they demand their funds back, and loan the rest.
- Since banks earn **interest from loans they make, any bank would like to lend the maximum possible.**
- However, being able to repay depositors on demand is crucial to the bank's survival.
- Depositors would keep their funds in a bank only if they are fully confident of getting them back on demand.
- A bank must, therefore, **balance its lending activities so as to ensure that sufficient funds are available to repay any depositor on demand.**

Commercial Banks in India

Money Creation by Banking System

- Banking system creates money by providing loans and by giving interest to the depositor's deposits.
- The basic accounting system dictates that the balance sheet of any firm would have **assets** on one side and a matching **liability** on the other side.
- For commercial banks, the **assets** side would consist of reserves and loans. The reserves for banks would consist of **Capital assets of banks like building, land, furniture etc. and deposits with RBI (Partly in the form of cash and partly in the form of financial instruments like bonds and treasury bills.).**
- The **loans** that the banks have forwarded to consumers would form the asset side of banks.
- On liability side, **the deposits of consumers with banks would form the liability of banks.**
- Here money supply **M1 would be the sum of currency in circulation and people's deposits with banks.** Hence,

  M1 = Currency + Deposits
- Consider a hypothetical situation, where there is only one bank serving in an economy.
- The bank takes deposit of Rs 100 from a consumer A, which becomes its liability. Later bank deposit this Rs 100 to the RBI as reserve. This Rs 100 deposit of bank to the RBI becomes the asset of the bank.

Assets		Liabilities	
Reserves	Rs 100	Deposits	Rs 100
		Net worth	Rs 0
Total	Rs 100	Total	Rs 100

Table: Balance Sheet of a Bank

- Now, what would be money supply M1 in this case?

  M1 = Currency in circulation + Deposits = 0 + 100 = 100.
- Here we observe that as bank is not allowed to give any loan. Therefore, bank was not able to create new money in the system. Here **money multiplier was 1 only.**
- Now suppose there would be no restriction of keeping reserves with the RBI, and banks are free to forward all the money of deposits as loan.
- In this situation, a challenging situation would arise, when the consumer A would come to withdraw his deposit of Rs 100.
- To save banks from over lending and to maintain the trust of people in banking system, RBI (or central banks around world) prescribe certain part of deposit amount as **reserves** with RBI.
- These reserves can be in the form of cash, which is called **Cash reserve ratio (CRR)** or in the form of liquid instruments, which is known as **Statutory Liquidity Ratio (SLR).**

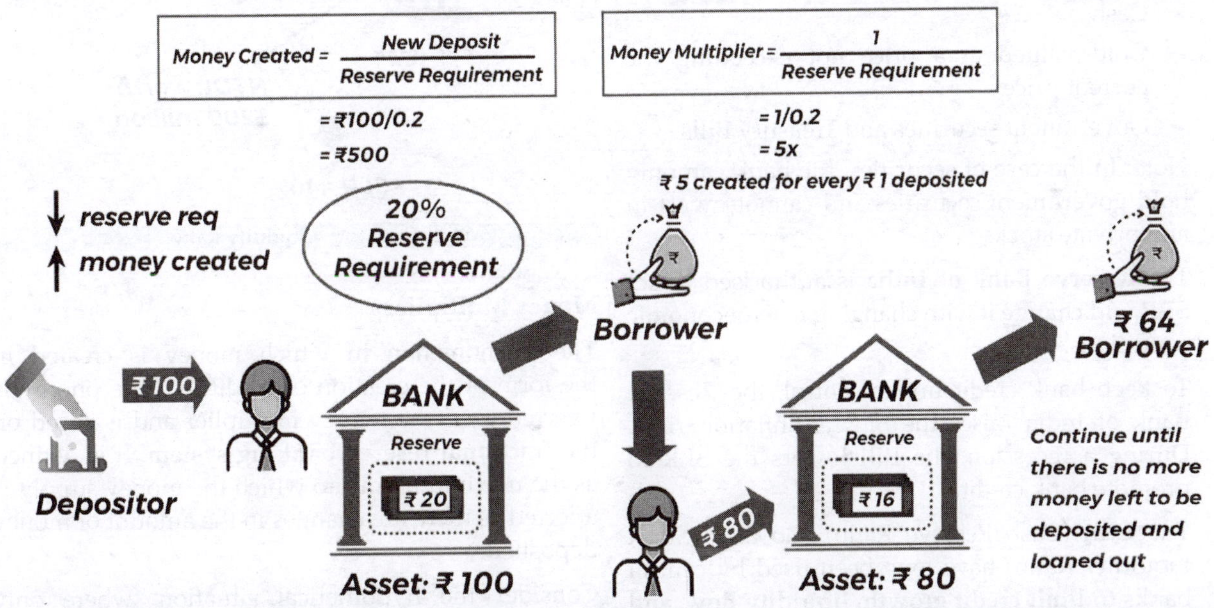

Money Creation By Banking System

Limits to Credit Creation and Money Multiplier

Cash Reserve Ratio (CRR)

- CRR is the percentage of deposits which a bank must keep as cash reserves with the bank.
- Cash Reserve Ratio Rate is **computed as a percentage of the net demand and time liabilities of each bank.** Net Demand and Time Liability is total of the savings account, current account, and fixed deposit balances.
- **CRR is governed by the provisions of Section 42 of the Reserve Bank of India Act, 1934.** It allows RBI to announce a CRR between 3%-15%. This was amended in 2007 by removing the lower ceiling making it 0-15%.
- It is applicable to all **Scheduled commercial banks.**

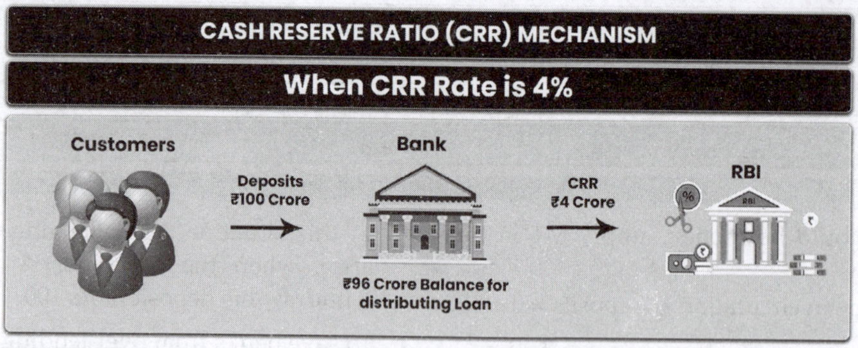

Cash Reserve Ratio (CRR)

Statutory Liquidity Ratio (SLR)

- **Statutory Liquidity Ratio (SLR)** is the minimum percentage of deposits (i.e., Net Demand and Time Liabilities (NDTL)) that a commercial bank must keep with itself.
- This asset can be in the form of the following:
  - Cash
  - Gold valued at a price not exceeding the current price
  - Government securities and Treasury Bills
- Note: In the case of securities, the bank can only hold government securities and cannot invest in any private stocks.
- The **Reserve Bank of India** is authorised to **set SLR and change it** with changing macroeconomic conditions.
- To keep bank credit under control, the Reserve Bank of India raises the SLR as inflation rises. During a recession, the RBI lowers the SLR to promote bank credit.
- The CRR (Cash Reserve Ratio) and SLR (Stock Liquidity Ratio) have long been used by central banks to **limit credit growth, liquidity flow, and inflation in the economy.**
- A bank is liable to pay a penalty to the Reserve Bank of India if it fails to maintain the prescribed SLR. On the deficient amount for that particular day, the defaulter bank must pay a penalty of 3% above the bank rate.
- The 2007 amendment to the Banking Regulation Act of 1949 removed the lower ceiling of SLR which implied it can be set between 0-40% of NDTL of the banks.

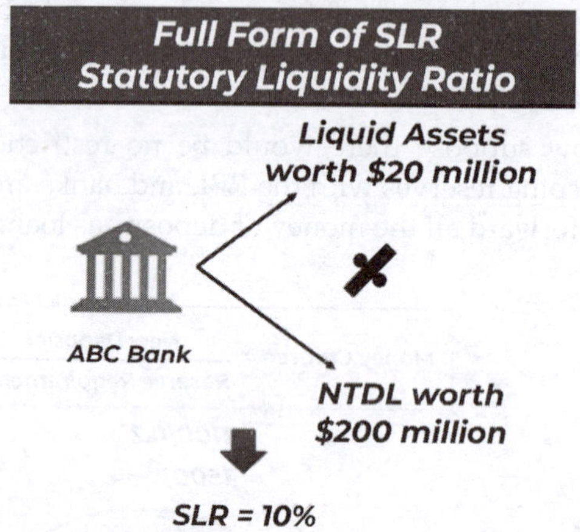

Statutory Liquidity Ratio

Money Multiplier

The phenomenon in which money is created in the form of the creation of credit in the economy is referred to as the money multiplier and is based on the **fractional reserve banking system.** It is defined as the maximum limit to which the money supply is affected as there are changes in the amount of money deposited.

Consider the hypothetical situation, where only one bank is serving all people. There is N numbers of consumers. All deposits their money in the said bank and take loans from the same bank. The RBI has mandated a CRR of 20% for all banks. Here, money multiplier process would take place in the following ways:

- Let us assume that our bank starts with a deposit of Rs 100 made by 'A'.
- The reserve ratio is 20 per cent. Thus, our bank has Rs 80 (100 – 20) to lend and the bank lends out Rs

80 to 'B', which shows up in the bank's deposits in the next round as liabilities, making a total of Rs 180 as deposits.

- Now our bank is required to keep 20 per cent of 180 i.e., Rs 36 as cash reserves.
- Recall that our bank had started with Rs 100 as cash.
- Since it is required to keep only Rs 36 as reserves, it can lend Rs 64 again (100 – 36 = 64).
- The bank lends out Rs 64 to 'C'. This in turn shows up in the bank as deposits.
- The process keeps repeating itself till all the required reserves become Rs 100.
- The required reserves will be Rs 100 only when the total deposits become Rs 500.
- This is because for deposits of Rs 500, cash reserves would have to be Rs 100 (20 per cent of 500 = 100).

Round	Deposit in Bank	Required Reserve	Loan made by bank
1	100.00	20.00	80.00
2	180.00	36.00	64.00
.	.	.	.
.	.	.	.
.	.	.	.
Last Nth consumer	500.00	100.00	400.00

Money Multiplier Process

From the above table, we can see that a deposit of Rs 100 became a deposit of Rs 500 through N round of operations. Here, RBI's CRR is 20%. Therefore, the Rs 100 can be taken out as CRR and Rs 400 can be circulated as loan amount by the bank. Here, bank created Rs 400 as new money. Hence CRR decides what would be the amount of money multiplier in an economy.

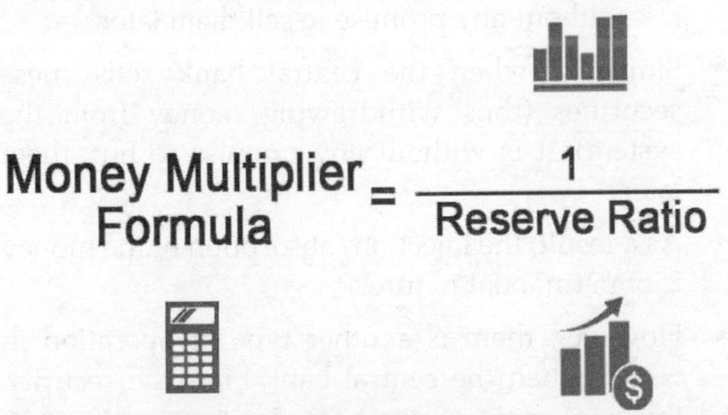

Money Multiplier Formula

The Money multiplier is given by following formula,

In our example,

Thus, reserves of Rs 100 create deposits of Rs (5 X 100) =Rs 500.

Policy Tools To Control Money Supply

- Reserve Bank of India is the only institution which can issue currency.
- With that function, it also acts as '**lender of last resort**', that is when commercial banks need more funds to create more credit, they go to RBI.
- RBI through various qualitative and quantitative tools controls the money circulation and creation of credit in the market.
- **The qualitative tools** of RBI consist of Cash Reserve Ratio (CRR), Statutory Liquidity ratio (SLR), Bank rate and Open Market Operations (OMO).
- **The quantitative tools** include Fixed Margin Requirements, Consumer Credit Regulations, Credit Rationing, Moral Suasion, Persuasion and Direct Action.

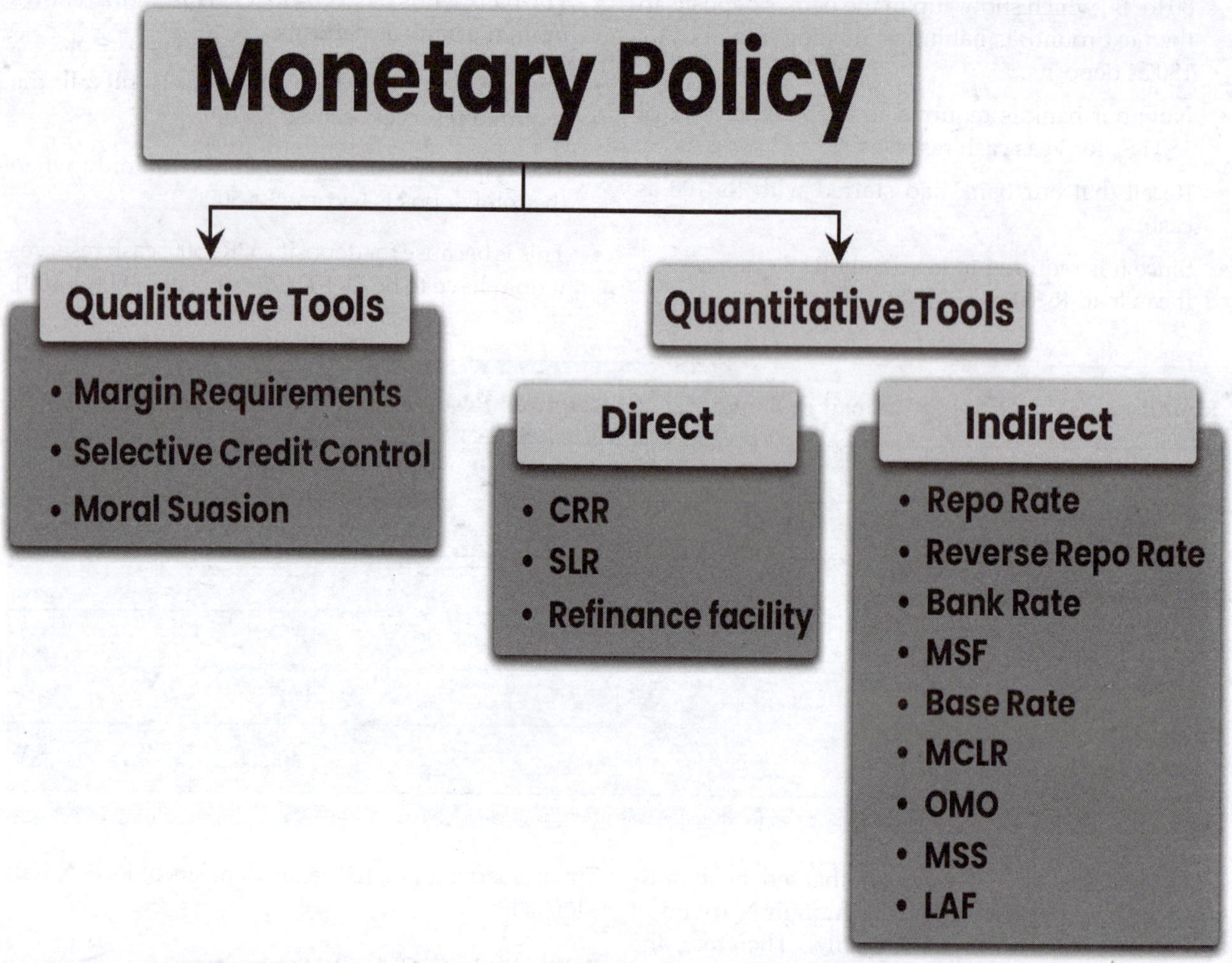

Tools of Monetary Policy

Open Market Operations

- It refers to **buying and selling of bonds issued by the Government** in the open market.
- This purchase and sale are entrusted to the Central bank on behalf of the Government.
- When RBI buys a government bond in the open market, it pays for it by giving a cheque.
- This cheque increases the total amount of reserves in the economy and thus increases the money supply.
- **Selling of a bond by RBI** (to private individuals or institutions) leads to reduction in quantity of reserves and hence the money supply.
- There are two types of open market operations: outright and repo.
- **Outright open market operations are permanent in nature:** when the central bank buys these securities (thus injecting money into the system), it is without any promise to sell them later.
- Similarly, when the central bank sells these securities (thus withdrawing money from the system), it is without any promise to buy them later.
- As a result, the injection/absorption of the money is of permanent nature.
- However, there is another type of operation in which when the central bank buys the security, this agreement of purchase also has specification about date and price of resale of this security. This type of agreement is called a **repurchase agreement or repo**.

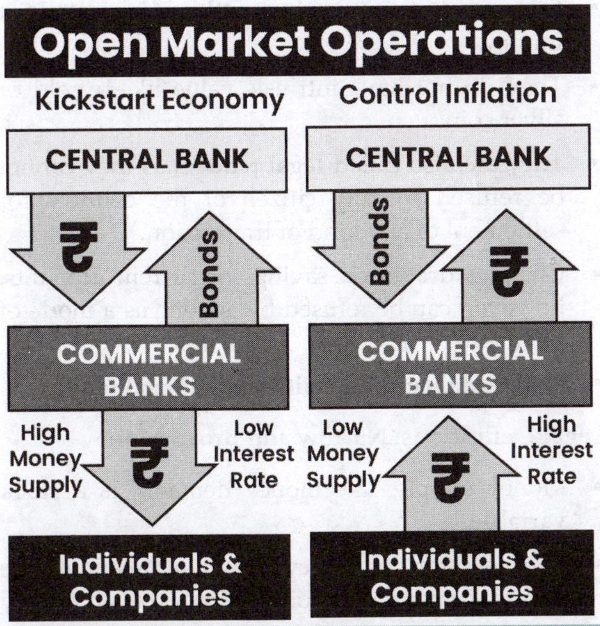

Open Market Operations

Repo Rate

- The term 'Repo' stands for **'Repurchase agreement'**.
- Repo is a form of short-term, **collateral-backed borrowing instrument and the interest rate charged for such borrowings is termed as repo rate.**
- In India, **repo rate is the rate at which Reserve Bank of India lends money to commercial banks in India if they face a scarcity of funds.**
- Commercial banks sell government securities and bonds to Reserve Bank of India with an agreement to repurchase the securities and bonds from Reserve Bank of India on a future date at a pre-determined price including interest charges.

Reverse Repo Rate

- Reverse repo as the name suggests is an opposite contract to the Repo Rate.
- Reverse Repo rate is the rate at which the **Reserve Bank of India borrows funds** from the commercial banks in the country.
- In other words, it is the rate at which commercial **banks in India park their excess money with Reserve Bank** of India usually for a short-term.
- The Reserve Bank of India conducts repo and reverse repo operations **at various maturities: overnight, 7-day, 14- day**, etc.
- This has now become the **main tool of monetary policy of the Reserve Bank of India.**

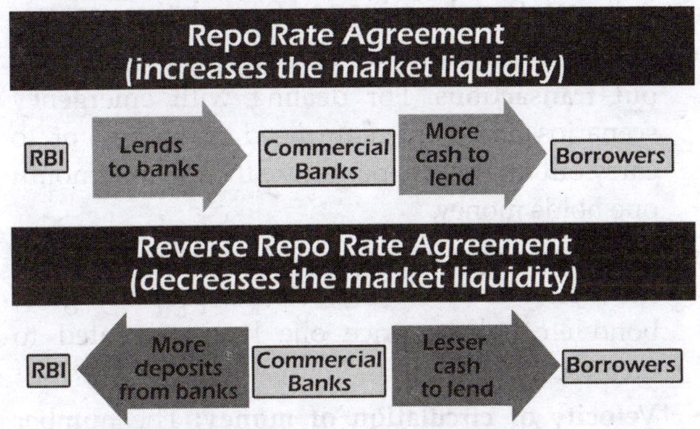

Repo and Reverse Repo Rate

Bank Rate

- A bank rate is the interest rate at which a nation's **central bank lends money** to domestic banks, often in the form of **very long-term loans**, when compared to repo loans.
- Managing the bank rate is a method by which central banks affect economic activity.
- Lower bank rates can help to expand the economy by lowering the cost of funds for borrowers, and higher bank rates help to reign in the economy when inflation is higher than desired.
- A fall in the bank rate can increase the money supply.

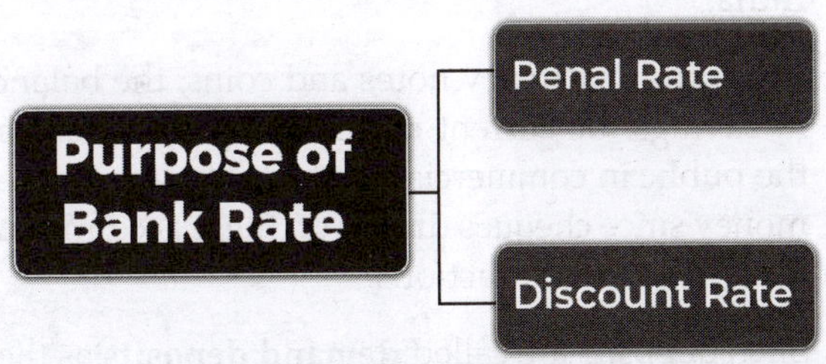

Purpose of Bank Rate

Why Do People Hold Money?

- **Money is the most liquid of all assets. It is universally accepted medium of exchange.** Economists have found out that there is an opportunity cost associated with people holding money or storing it in bank. There is a bargain between availability of liquid money and earning interest rate on money by keeping it in banks under simple or time deposits.

- The two motives that drive people to hold money is **Transactional motive and Speculative motive.**
- The principal motive for holding money is to **carry out transactions**. For dealing with emergency scenarios and immediate need of money, or to carry out monthly expenditure throughout month one holds money.
- The **speculative motive** drives a person to hold the money to invest in assets like property, gold, bond etc. whose price one has speculated to increase in future.
- **Velocity of circulation of money:** The number of times a unit of money changes hands during the unit period is called the velocity of circulation of money. For example, if the Rs 100 note change the hands three times in a month. And this is the online currency in circulation. Then after one month the velocity of circulation of money would be three.

The Supply of Money: Various Measures

- In a modern economy money consists mainly of **currency notes and coins** issued by the monetary authority of the country.
- In India **currency notes are issued by the Reserve Bank of India (RBI)**, which is the monetary authority in India.
- However, **coins are issued by the Government of India.**
- Apart from currency notes and coins, the balance in savings, or current account deposits, held by the public in commercial banks is also considered money since cheques drawn on these accounts are used to settle transactions.
- Such deposits are called **demand deposits** as they are payable by the bank on demand from the account-holder.
- Other deposits, e.g., fixed deposits, have a fixed period to maturity and are referred to as time deposits.
- **Currency notes and coins are therefore called fiat money.**
- They do not have intrinsic value like a gold or silver coin.
- They are also called **legal tenders** as they cannot be refused by any citizen of the country for settlement of any kind of transaction.
- Cheques drawn on savings or current accounts, however, can be refused by anyone as a mode of payment.
- **Hence, demand deposits are not legal tenders.**

Legal Definitions: Narrow and Broad Money

- Money supply, like money demand, is a **stock variable.**
- The total stock of money in circulation among the public at a particular point of time is called **money supply**.
- RBI publishes figures for four alternative measures of money supply, viz. **M1, M2, M3 and M4.**
- They are defined as follows-

1. **M1** = CU + DD
2. **M2** = M1 + Savings deposits with Post Office savings banks
3. **M3** = M1 + Net time deposits of commercial banks
4. **M4** = M3 + Total deposits with Post Office savings organisations (excluding National Savings Certificates)

- Where, CU is currency (notes plus coins) held by the public and DD is net demand deposits held by commercial banks.
- The word **'net'** implies that only deposits of the public held by the banks are to be included in money supply.
- The **interbank deposits**, which a commercial bank holds in other commercial banks, are not to be regarded as part of money supply.
- **M1 and M2** are known as **narrow money**.
- **M3 and M4** are known as **broad money**.
- **These measures are in decreasing order of liquidity.**

- M1 is most liquid and easiest for transactions whereas M4 is least liquid of all.
- M3 is the most commonly used measure of money supply. It is also known as **aggregate monetary resources**.

Broad Money & Narrow Money

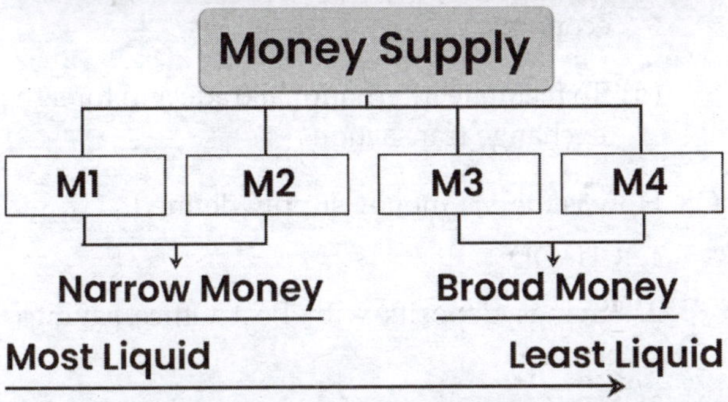

Broad Money and Narrow Money

Demonetisation

- Demonetisation was a new initiative taken by the Government of India in November 2016 to tackle the problem of corruption, black money, terrorism and circulation of fake currency in the economy.
- Old currency notes of Rs 500, and Rs 1000 were no longer legal tender. **New currency notes in the denomination of Rs 500 and Rs 2000 were launched.**
- **Negatives Impacts of Demonetisation** include:
  - There were long queues outside banks and ATM booths.
  - The shortage of currency in circulation had an adverse impact on the economic activities. However, things improved with time and normalcy returned.
- **Positive Impacts of Demonetisation** include:
  - It improved tax compliance as a large number of people were bought in the tax ambit.
  - The savings of an individual were channelised into the formal financial system.
  - As a result, banks have more resources at their disposal which can be used to provide more loans at lower interest rates.
  - It is a demonstration of State's decision to put a curb on black money, showing that tax evasion will no longer be tolerated.
  - Tax evasion will result in financial penalty and social condemnation.
  - Tax compliance will improve and corruption will decrease.
  - Demonetisation could also help tax administration in another way, by shifting transactions out of the cash economy into the formal payment system.
  - Households and firms have begun to shift from cash to electronic payment technologies.

TEST YOURSELF

Multiple Choice Questions

Q1. What is money?

(a) The total amount of wealth in an economy.

(b) The medium of exchange used to facilitate transactions.

(c) The interest rate charged by banks for loans.

(d) The measure of a country's economic growth.

Q2. What are the functions of money?

(a) Store of value, medium of exchange, and unit of account.

(b) Medium of exchange, barter system, and unit of account.

(c) Store of value, barter system, and standard of living.

(d) Unit of account, barter system, and economic growth.

Q3. What is a central bank?

(a) A bank that provides services to individuals and businesses.

(b) A bank that regulates and supervises other banks in an economy.

(c) A bank that facilitates international trade and exchange of currencies.

(d) A bank that offers specialised financial services to corporations.

Q4. What is a commercial bank?

(a) A bank that operates internationally and deals with foreign exchange.

(b) A bank that offers financial services to the general public and businesses.

(c) A bank that focuses on agricultural lending and rural development.

(d) A bank that provides loans and financial support to government projects.

Q5. What is the role of the Reserve Bank of India (RBI)?

(a) To regulate and supervise commercial banks in India.

(b) To provide loans to individuals and businesses.

(c) To facilitate international trade and foreign exchange transactions.

(d) To promote industrial growth and investment in the country.

Q6. What is a demand deposit?

(a) A deposit that earns interest over a specific period.

(b) A deposit held in a foreign currency account.

(c) A deposit that can be withdrawn on demand by the depositor.

(d) A deposit made by a commercial bank with the central bank.

Q7. What is the role of the cash reserve ratio (CRR)?

(a) To determine the interest rates offered by commercial banks

(b) To regulate the amount of money commercial banks must keep as reserves

(c) To control the supply of money in the economy

(d) To facilitate international trade and foreign exchange transactions

Q8. How is the M4 money supply defined?

1. CU+DD
2. Savings deposits with Post Office savings banks.
3. Net time deposits of commercial banks.
4. Total deposits with Post Office savings organisations (excluding National Savings Certificates).

Select the correct answer using the code given below:

(a) 1 only (b) 1, 3 and 4 only

(c) 1 and 2 only (d) 1 , 2, 3 and 4 only

Q9. Which of the following is not a qualitative tool?

(a) Margin requirements (b) Moral suasion

(c) Selective credit control (d) Repo rate

Q10. Which of the following statements is/are correct about Barter System?

(a) Economic exchanges without the mediation of money are referred to as barter exchanges.

(b) The Barter Exchanges requires double coincidence of wants.

(c) Both 'a' and 'b'

(d) Neither 'a' nor 'b'

Q11. Which of the following statements is/are correct about the Reserve Bank of India?

1. It controls money supply of the country through various methods, like bank rate, open market operations and variations in reserve ratios.
2. It acts as a banker to the government.
3. It is the custodian of the foreign exchange reserves of the economy.
4. It measures and publishes important inflation indices such as CPI, WPI and IIP.

Select the correct answer using the code given below:

(a) 1 only (b) 1 and 2 only

(c) 1, 2 and 3 only (d) 1, 2, 3 and 4

Q12. Which of the following statements is/are correct about Commercial Banks?

1. Commercial banks are type of institutions which are a part of the money-creating system of the economy.
2. The difference between interest rate paid by the banks to depositors and the rate charged from the borrowers is called the 'spread'.
3. This currency issued by the commercial bank is called the high-powered money.

Select the correct answer using the code given below:

(a) 1 and 2 only (b) 2 and 3 only

(c) 1 and 3 only (d) 1, 2 and 3

Q13. Which of the following statements is/are correct about 'Cash Reserve Ratio' (CRR)?

1. CRR is a percentage of deposits which a bank must keep as cash reserves.
2. CRR is a legal requirement and is binding on the banks.
3. The provisions of CRR is made to ensure that no bank is 'over lending'.

Select the correct answer using the code given below:

(a) 1 and 2 only (b) 2 and 3 only

(c) 1 and 3 only (d) 1, 2 and 3

Q14. The total stock of money in circulation among the public at a particular point of time is called money supply. With reference to this, identify the M1 concept of Money Supply includes which of the following items?

1. Currency held by the public
2. Net demand deposits held by commercial banks
3. Savings deposits with Post Office savings banks
4. Net time deposits of commercial banks.

Select the correct answer using the code given below:

(a) 1 only (b) 1 and 2 only

(c) 1, 2 and 3 only (d) 1, 2, 3 and 4

Q15. Which of the following is/are considered as the positive impact of Demonetisation initiative taken by the Government of India in November 2016?

1. It improved tax compliance as a large number of people were bought in the tax ambit.
2. The savings of an individual were channelised into the formal financial system.
3. Banks have more resources at their disposal which can be used to provide more loans at lower interest rates.

Select the correct answer using the code given below:

(a) 1 and 2 only (b) 2 and 3 only

(c) 1 and 3 only (d) 1, 2 and 3

Q16. Which of the following statements is/are correct?

(a) Collateral is an asset that the borrower owns (such as land, building, vehicle, livestock, deposits with banks) and uses this as a guarantee to a lender until the loan is repaid.

(b) In India, the, the lender does not have the right to sell the asset or collateral to obtain payment unless ordered by the Courts.

(c) Both 'a' and 'b'

(d) Neither 'a' nor 'b'

Q17. Which of the following statements is/are correct about the Informal loans in India?

1. The RBI and NABARD supervise the credit activities of lenders in the informal sector.
2. In order to reduce the dependence of rural areas on informal sources of credit, banks and cooperatives need to increase their lending particularly in the rural areas.

Select the correct answer using the code given below:

(a) 1 only (b) 2 only

(c) Both 1 and 2 (d) Neither 1 nor 2

Q18. Consider the following statements: (UPSC 2022)

1. In India, credit rating agencies are regulated by Reserve Bank of India.
2. The rating agency popularly known as ICRA is a public limited company.
3. Brickwork Ratings is an Indian credit rating agency.

Which of the statements given above are correct?

(a) 1 and 2 only (b) 2 and 3 only

(c) 1 and 3 only (d) 1, 2 and 3

Q19. With reference to the 'Banks Board Bureau (BBB)', which of the following statements are correct? (UPSC 2022)

1. The Governor of RBI is the Chairman of BBB.
2. BBB recommends the selection of heads for Public Sector Banks.
3. BBB helps the Public Sector Banks in developing strategies and capital raising plans.

Select the correct answer using the code given below:

(a) 1 and 2 only (b) 2 and 3 only

(c) 1 and 3 only (d) 1, 2 and 3

Q20. The money multiplier in an economy increases with which one of the following? (UPSC 2021)

(a) Increase in the Cash Reserve Ratio in the banks.

(b) Increase in the Statutory Liquidity Ratio in the banks.

(c) Increase in the banking habit of the people.

(d) Increase in the population of the country.

Q21. In India, the central bank's function as the 'lender of last resort' usually refers to which of the following? (UPSC 2021)

1. Lending to trade and industry bodies when they fail to borrow from other sources.
2. Providing liquidity to the banks having a temporary crisis.

3. Lending to governments to finance budgetary deficits.

Select the correct answer using the code given below.

(a) 1 and 2 only (b) 2 only

(c) 2 and 3 only (d) 3 only

Q22. Consider the following statements: (UPSC 2021)

1. The Governor of the Reserve Bank of India (RBI) is appointed by the Central Government.
2. Certain provisions in the Constitution of India give the Central Government the right to issue directions to the RBI in public interest.
3. The Governor of the RBI draws his power from the RBI Act.

Which of the above statements are correct?

(a) 1 and 2 only (b) 2 and 3 only

(c) 1 and 3 only (d) 1, 2 and 3

Q23. If you withdraw ₹1,00,000 in cash from your Demand Deposit Account at your bank, the immediate effect on aggregate money supply in the economy will be (UPSC 2020)

(a) To reduce it by ₹1,00,000

(b) To increase it by ₹1,00,000

(c) To increase it by more than ₹1,00,000

(d) To leave it unchanged

Q24. If the RBI decides to adopt an expansionist monetary policy, which of the following would it not do? (UPSC 2020)

1. Cut and optimise the Statutory Liquidity Ratio.
2. Increase the Marginal Standing Facility Rate.
3. Cut the Bank Rate and Repo Rate.

Select the correct answer using the code given below:

(a) 1 and 2 only (b) 2 only

(c) 1 and 3 only (d) 1, 2 and 3

Q25. Which of the following is not included in the assets of a commercial bank in India? (UPSC 2019)

(a) Advances

(b) Deposits

(c) Investments

(d) Money at call and short notice

Q26. With reference to the governance of public sector banking in India, consider the following statements: (UPSC 2018)

1. Capital infusion into public sector banks by the Government of India has steadily increased in the last decade.
2. To put the public sector banks in order, the merger of associate banks with the parent State Bank of India has been affected.

Which of the statements given above is/are correct?

(a) 1 only (b) 2 only

(c) Both 1 and 2 (d) Neither 1 nor 2

Q27. Which one of the following statements correctly describes the meaning of legal tender money? (UPSC 2018)

(a) The money which is tendered in courts of law to defray the fee of legal cases

(b) The money which a creditor is under compulsion to accept in settlement of his claims

(c) The bank money in the form of cheques, drafts, bills of exchange, etc.

(d) The metallic money in circulation in a country

Q28. An increase in the Bank Rate generally indicates that the (UPSC 2013)

(a) Market rate of interest is likely to fall

(b) Central Bank is no longer making loans to commercial banks

(c) Central Bank is following an easy money policy

(d) Central Bank is following a tight money policy

Answer Key

Q1.	b	Q2.	a	Q3.	b
Q4.	b	Q5.	a	Q6.	c
Q7.	b	Q8.	b	Q9.	d
Q10.	C	Q11.	c	Q12.	a
Q13.	d	Q14.	b	Q15.	d
Q16.	a	Q17.	b	Q18.	b
Q19.	b	Q20.	c	Q21.	b
Q22.	c	Q23.	d	Q24.	b
Q25.	b	Q26.	b	Q27.	b
Q28.	d				

Model Questions for Main Examination

Q1. Discuss all the functions of money?

Q2. What are the various tools of monetary policy?

UNIT 13 Government Budget and the Economy

In This Unit

Comprehensive and profound coverage of the following NCERT's chapter:

✓ NCERT Class- 12th (Introductory Macroeconomics), Chapter- 5

Government Budget – Meaning and its Components

- **There is a Constitutional requirement in India (Article 112)** to present before the Parliament a statement of estimated receipts and expenditures of the government in respect of every financial year which runs from 1 April to 31 March.
- This *'Annual Financial Statement'* constitutes the main budget document of the government.
- Although the budget document relates to the ***receipts and expenditure*** of the government for a particular financial year, its impact is felt in subsequent years as well.
- There is a need therefore to have two accounts- those that relate to the current financial year only are included in the ***revenue account*** (also called revenue budget) and those that concern the assets and liabilities of the government into the ***capital account*** (also called capital budget).

Objective of Government Budget

The government plays a very important role in increasing the welfare of the people. In order to do that the government intervenes in the economy in the following ways:

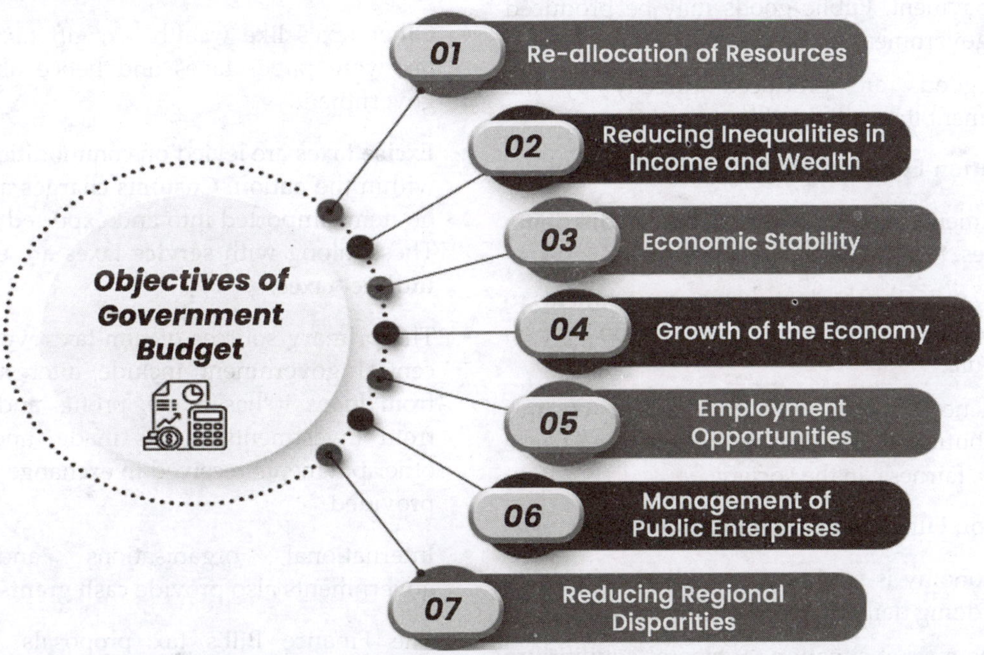

Objective of Government Budget

Allocation Function of Government Budget

- The objective for any government is the welfare of the society. Among various function for welfare of people, **providing public goods is one of the main functions.** The budget must ensure proper allocation to public goods.
- **Public goods** can be defined as a **commodity or service that is provided without profit to all members of a society**, either by the government or by a private individual or organisation.
- There are two major characteristics of public goods, those are-
    - It is ***non-rivalrous***. That means, there would be no rivalry in consumption of public goods. Consumption by one person does not reduce the availability of the goods for another person.
    - It is ***non-excludable***. That means no one can be denied access to public goods, whether one has paid for it or not.
- Examples of public goods are- **free air, public parks, street lights, defense, police services etc.**
- In this context, a difference between ***public provision*** and ***public production*** must be known.
- ***Public provision*** means that they are financed through the budget and can be used without any direct payment. Public goods may be produced by the government or the private sector.
- When goods are produced directly by the government it is called ***public production***.

Redistribution Function of Government Budget

- Government collects taxes and distribute subsidies.
- In this way the budget helps government to influence the personal disposable income of an individual.
- And hence in this way government ensures redistribution of wealth in an economy and hence ensures 'fairness' in the society.

Stabilisation Function of Government Budget

- Any economy is made up of millions of private people doing daily transactions.
- In a free market situation, a general equilibrium of price, wages and employment are established.
- Due to certain reasons, there could be a possibility that this equilibrium gets disturbed.
- Because of this there can be problems like, **price volatility, wage volatility, unemployment etc.**
- To deal with such situation and to intervene in market when a disequilibrium in market hurts poor people, government provides corrective measures.
- These measures are provided using provision of grants and regulations in budget.

Classification of Receipts

Revenue Receipts

- Revenue receipts are those receipts that **do not lead to a claim on government.**
- They are therefore termed as ***non-redeemable***.
- They are divided into tax and non-tax receipts.
- **Tax revenue** consists of direct and indirect tax revenue.
- **Direct taxes** are imposed on people's income directly. Direct tax could be tax on personal income and corporate tax. Security transaction tax is also a type of direct tax.
- Other taxes like wealth tax, gift tax and estate tax were paper taxes and hence abolished by government.
- **Excise taxes** are levied on commodities produced within the nation. **Customs charges** are collected on items imported into and exported from India. These, along with **service taxes** are examples of **indirect taxes.**
- The primary sources of **non-tax revenue** for the central government include interest payments from loans it has made, profits and dividends from investments it has made, and fees and other payments received in exchange for services provided.
- International organisations and foreign governments also provide **cash grants-in-aid.**
- The Finance Bill's tax proposals' effects are factored into the revenue receipt forecasts.

Capital Receipts

- All those receipts of the government which **create liability or reduce financial assets** are termed as **capital receipts.**
- The government also receives money by way of loans or from the sale of its assets.
- Loans will have to be returned to the agencies from which they have been borrowed. Thus, they create liability.
- Sale of government assets, like sale of shares in Public Sector Undertakings (PSUs) which is referred to as **PSU disinvestment**, reduce the total amount of financial assets of the government.
- When government **takes fresh loans**, it will mean that in future these loans will have to be returned and interest will have to be paid on these loans.
- Similarly, when government sells an asset, then it means that in future its earnings from that asset, will disappear. Thus, these receipts can be debt creating or non-debt creating.

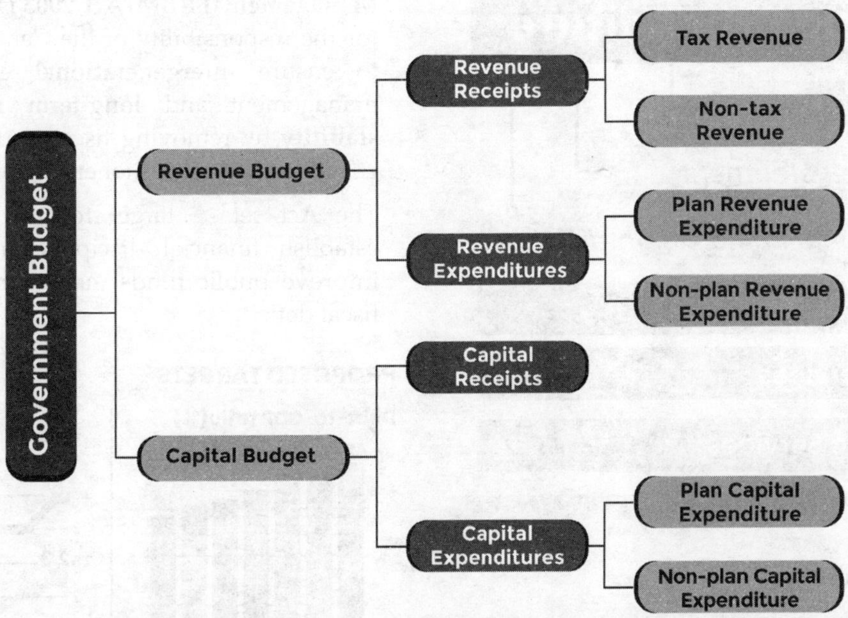

Budget

Classification of Expenditure

Revenue Expenditure

- Expenditure incurred for purposes other than the creation of financial or physical assets for the central government is referred to as revenue expenditure.
- It has to do with costs associated with government departments operating normally and providing various services, interest payments on government debt, and grants to state governments and other parties (even though some of the grants might be intended for asset development).
- Budget documents classify total expenditure into **plan and non-plan expenditure.**
- According to this classification, **plan revenue expenditure** relates to central Plans (the Five-Year Plans) and central assistance for State and Union Territory plans.
- **Non-plan expenditure,** the more important component of revenue expenditure, covers a vast range of general, economic and social services of the government.
- The main items of non-plan expenditure are interest payments, defence services, subsidies, salaries and pensions.
- Interest payments on market loans, external loans and from various reserve funds constitute the single largest component of non-plan revenue expenditure.

- Defence expenditure, is committed expenditure in the sense that given the national security concerns, there exists little scope for drastic reduction.
- Subsidies are an important policy instrument which aim at increasing welfare.
- Apart from providing implicit subsidies through under-pricing of public goods and services like education and health, the government also extends subsidies explicitly on items such as exports, interest on loans, food and fertilizers.

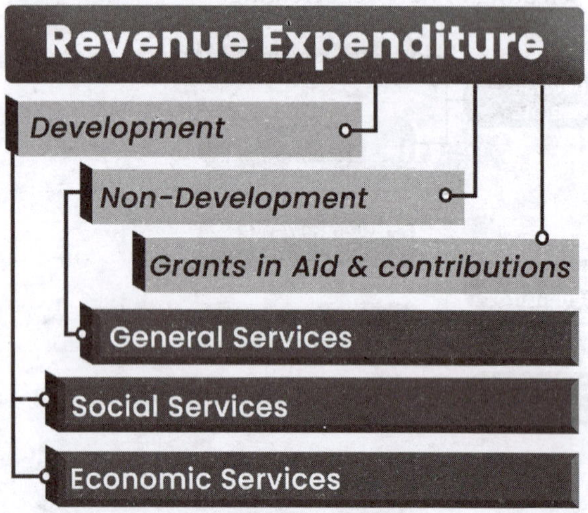

Revenue Expenditure

Capital Expenditure

- There are expenditures of the government which result in creation of physical or financial assets or reduction in financial liabilities.
- This includes expenditure on the **acquisition of land, building, machinery, equipment, investment in shares, and loans and advances by the central government to state and union territory governments, PSUs and other parties.**
- Capital expenditure is also categorised as plan and non-plan in the budget documents.
- **Plan capital expenditure,** like its revenue counterpart, relates to central plan and central assistance for state and union territory plans.
- **Non-plan capital expenditure** covers various general, social and economic services provided by the government.

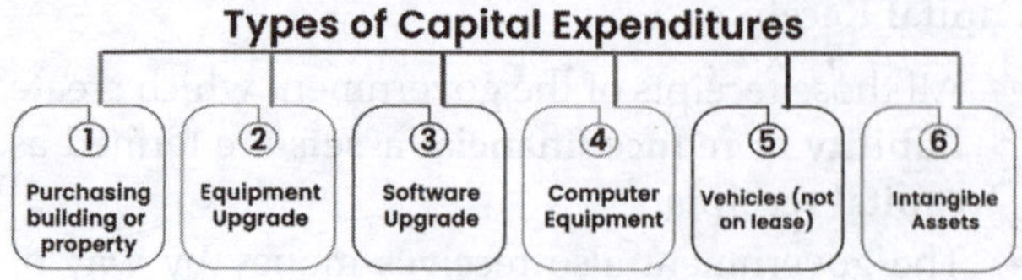

Types of Capital Expenditures

Fiscal Responsibility and Budget Management Act, 2003 (FRBMA)

- **The Fiscal Responsibility and Budget Management (FRBM) Act, 2003** is an act to provide for the responsibility of the Central Government to ensure **intergenerational equity** in fiscal management and **long-term macro-economic stability** by removing fiscal impediments in the effective conduct of monetary policy.
- The Act sets a target for the government to establish financial discipline in the economy, improve public funds management and reduce fiscal deficit.

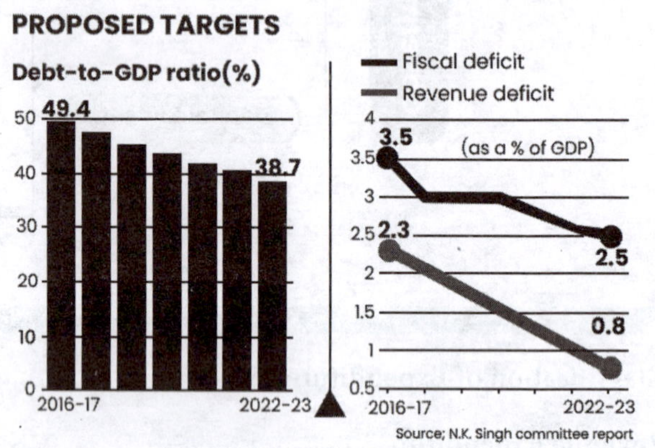

Debt to GDP ratio, Fiscal Deficit and Revenue Deficit

Policy Statements under the FRBM Act, 2003

- The budget both shapes and reflects the economic life of the nation.
- In addition to the budget, the Fiscal Responsibility and Budget Management Act, 2003 (FRBMA) requires the creation of three policy statements.
    - ➢ The **Medium-Term Fiscal Policy Statement** assesses whether revenue expenditures can be sustainably covered by revenue receipts and how effectively capital receipts, including market borrowings, are being utilised. It also

sets a **three-year rolling objective** for key fiscal metrics.

➢ The government's fiscal priorities are outlined in **the Fiscal Policy Strategy Statement**, which also evaluates and defends any changes to significant budgetary initiatives.

➢ The **Macroeconomic Framework Statement** evaluates the state of the economy in terms of GDP growth rate, the central government's fiscal balance, and the external balance.

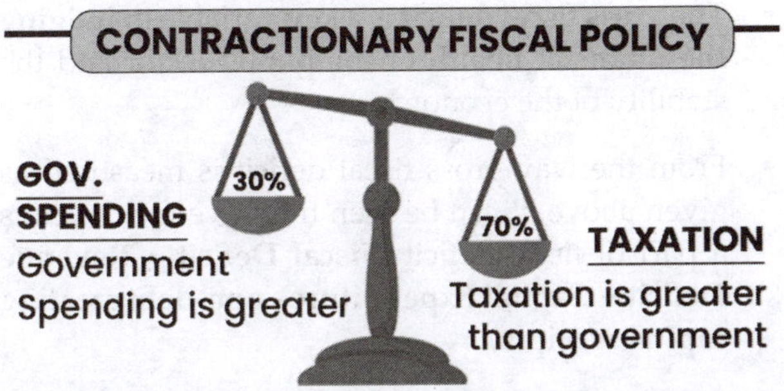

Contractionary Fiscal Policy

Initial FRBM Targets

- These targets were scheduled to be met by 2008-09.
- **Revenue Deficit (RD):** RD should be completely eliminated by 2009. The minimum annual reduction target was 0.5% of GDP.
- **Fiscal Deficit (FD):** FD should be reduced to 3% of GDP by 2009. The minimum annual reduction target was 0.3% of GDP.
- **Contingent Liabilities:** The Central Government shall not give incremental guarantees aggregating an amount exceeding 0.5% of GDP in any financial year beginning 2004-05.
- **Additional Liabilities:** Additional liabilities should be reduced to 9% of the GDP by 2004-05. The minimum annual reduction target in each subsequent year to be 1% of GDP.
- **RBI purchase of government bonds – to cease from 1 April 2006.** This indicates the government not to borrow directly from the RBI.
- The targets were not achieved. So, the **Act was amended first in 2012 and then in 2015 to relax the realisation of fiscal targets.**

Balanced, Surplus and Deficit Budget

- The government may spend an amount equal to the revenue it collects. This is known as a **balanced budget.**
- If it needs to incur higher expenditure, it will have to raise the amount through taxes in order to keep the budget balanced. When tax collection exceeds the required expenditure, the budget is said to be in **surplus.**
- However, the most common feature is the situation when expenditure exceeds revenue. This is when the government runs a **budget deficit.**

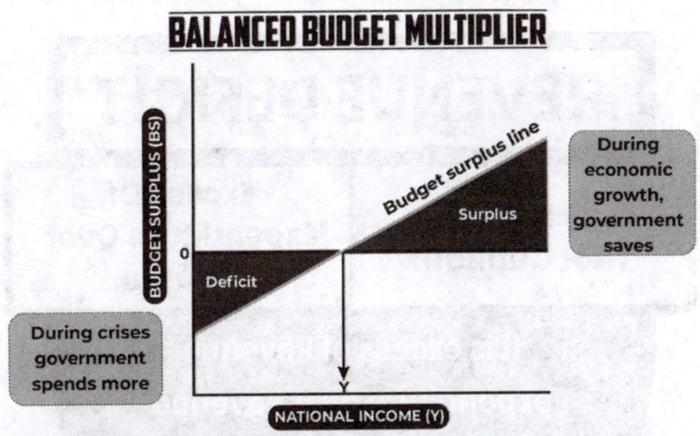

Balanced Budget Multiplier

Measures of Government Deficit

- A government faces a budget deficit when its outlays exceed its revenue collection.
- The government deficit can be measured in a number of ways, and each has an impact on the economy.

Revenue Deficit: The revenue deficit refers to the excess of government's revenue expenditure over revenue receipts.

Revenue deficit = Revenue expenditure – Revenue receipts

- The revenue deficit includes **only such transactions that affect the current income and expenditure of the government.**
- When the government incurs a revenue deficit, it implies that the government is dissaving and is using up the savings of the other sectors of the economy to finance a part of its consumption expenditure.

- This situation means that the government will have to borrow not only to finance its investment but also its consumption requirements.
- This will lead to a buildup of stock of debt and interest liabilities and force the government, eventually, to cut expenditure.
- Since a major part of revenue expenditure is committed expenditure, it cannot be reduced.
- Often the government reduces productive capital expenditure or welfare expenditure.
- This would mean lower growth and adverse welfare implications.

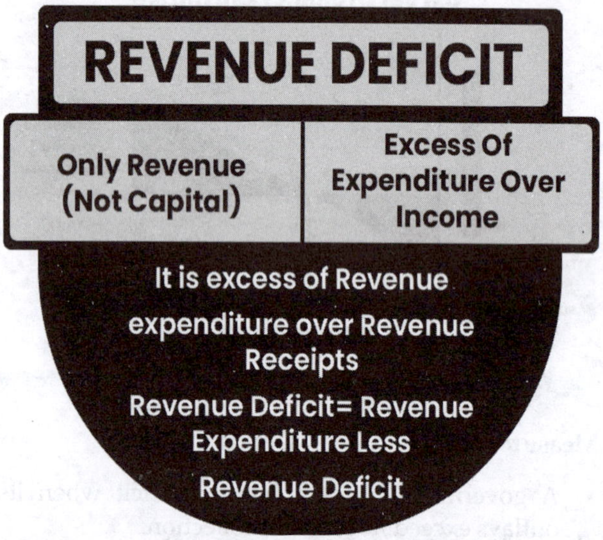

Revenue Deficit

Fiscal Deficit: Fiscal deficit is the difference between the government's total expenditure and its total receipts excluding borrowing.

Gross fiscal deficit = Total expenditure – (Revenue receipts + non-debt creating capital receipts)

- **Non-debt creating capital receipts** are those receipts which are not borrowings and, therefore, do not give rise to debt. Examples are recovery of loans and the proceeds from the **sale of PSUs**.
- The fiscal deficit will have to be financed through borrowing.
- Thus, it indicates the total borrowing requirements of the government from all sources.
- From the financing side gross fiscal deficit can be described as follows:

Gross fiscal deficit = Net borrowing at home + Borrowing from RBI + Borrowing from abroad

- **Net borrowing at home** includes that **directly borrowed** from the public through debt instruments (for example, the various small savings schemes) and **indirectly** from commercial banks through Statutory Liquidity Ratio (SLR).
- The **gross fiscal deficit** is a key variable in **judging the financial health** of the public sector and the stability of the economy.
- From the way gross fiscal deficit is measured as given above, it can be seen that revenue deficit is a part of fiscal deficit (**Fiscal Deficit = Revenue Deficit + Capital Expenditure - non-debt creating capital receipts**).
- A large share of revenue deficit in fiscal deficit indicated that a large part of borrowing is being used to meet its consumption expenditure needs rather than investment.

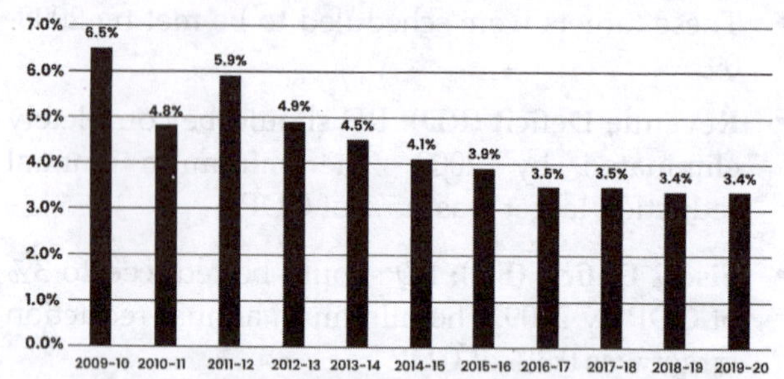

India's Fiscal Deficit

Primary Deficit

- The major part of union budget's fiscal deficit goes to interest payments of previous loans.
- To get a clear view of revenue and expenditure of current year a new concept, that is **primary deficit** is introduced. It is simply the fiscal deficit minus the interest payments.

Gross primary deficit = Gross fiscal deficit – Net interest liabilities

- **Net interest liabilities** consist of interest payments minus interest receipts by the government on net domestic lending.

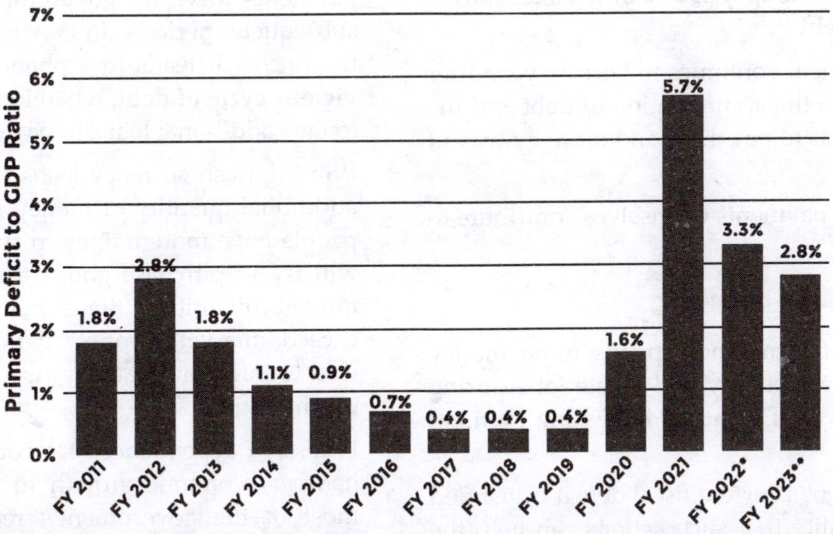

Primary Deficit

Sr.no.	Entity	(As per cent of GDP)
1.	Revenue Receipts (a + b)	9.0
	(a) Tax revenue (net of states' share)	7.3
	(b) Non-tax revenue	1.6
2.	Revenue Expenditure of which	10.9
	(a) Interest Payments	3.1
	(b) Major subsidies	1.4
	(c) Defense expenditure	1.0
3.	Revenue Deficit (2 - 1)	1.9
4.	Capital receipts (a + b + c) of which	3.7
	(a) Recovery of loans	0.1
	(b) Other receipts (mainly PSU disinvestment)	0.4
	(c) Borrowings and other liabilities	3.2
5.	Capital Expenditure	1.8
6.	Total Expenditure [2 + 5 = 6(a) + 6(b)]	12.7
	(a) Plan expenditure	-
	(b) Non-plan expenditure	-
7.	Fiscal deficit [6 – 1 – 4(b)] or [3 + 5 – 4(a) – 4(b)]	3.2
8.	Primary Deficit [7 – 2(a)]	0.1

Receipts and Expenditures of the Central Government, 2017-18

Debt

- Budgetary deficits must be financed by either taxation, borrowing or printing money.
- Governments have mostly relied on borrowing, giving rise to what is called government debt.
- The concepts of deficits and debt are closely related.

- **Deficits can be thought of as a flow** which add to the **stock of debt**.
- If the government continues to borrow year after year, it leads to the accumulation of debt and the government has to pay more and more by way of interest.
- These interest payments themselves contribute to the debt.

Advantages of Deficit Budgeting

- A government sometimes spends more money to develop the economy and create jobs during a recession, even if it means increasing its **fiscal deficit.**
- The government's current fiscal deficit is justified by the possibility that such actions can help the country recover from the recession in the near future.
- Sometime, there is excessive liquidity (cash) available in the market. In such a scenario, the **external debt becomes cheaper.** Hence government may tend to deliver a deficit budget to garner the benefit of reduced cost of capital.
- Country like India, where there is tax to GDP ratio is less compared to its peers, deficit budgeting becomes only way through which government can fund its development initiatives.

Disadvantages of Deficit Budgeting

- When governments borrow, they need to pay additional interest on such loans. Interest payments drive up government expenditure in subsequent periods and increase the deficit in the future. It leads to a phenomenon called the **vicious cycle of debt,** wherein governments have to take additional loans to pay off past debts.
- Printing fresh currency leads to the inflow of an additional quantity of money in the economy. If people have more money to spend, more people will try to purchase goods that are available in limited quantities. Since market demand will exceed market supply, deficit financing can lead to inflation, that is, a rise in the prices of all commodities.
- Excessive dependence of a country on debt can hamper economic growth in the long term. If most of the government's revenues are spent to settle past loans, there will be less money to invest in development and job creation, leading to economic growth.
- The deficit budgeting and hence internal borrowing leads to **"crowding out effect"** for private sector borrowers. Hence cost of capital increases for corporate sector and hence doing business becomes costly.
- The deficit budgeting looks like a lazy method to finance growth. It makes governments complacent to even try out new methods to finance its development initiatives.

Deficit Reduction in India

- One way to minimise the government deficit is to **either raise taxes or cut spending.**

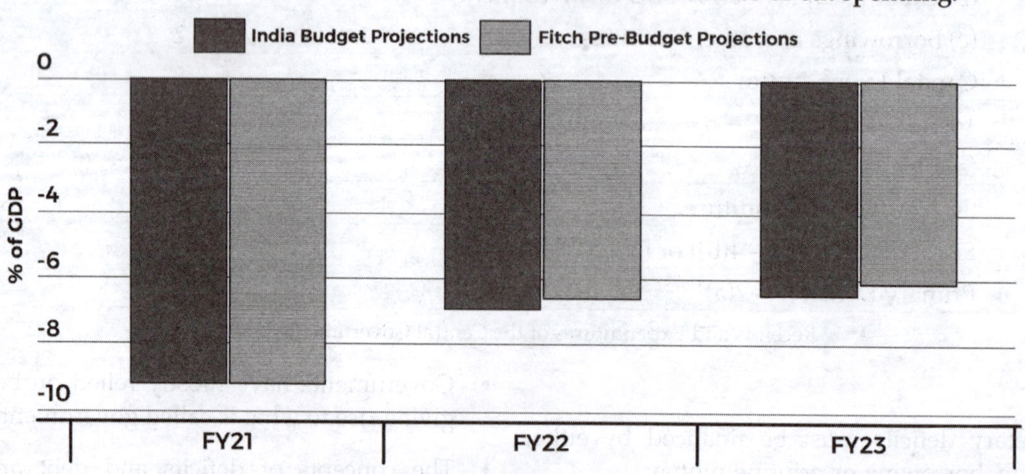

India Central Government Deficit Projections

- The government of India has been attempting to raise tax collection by using more direct taxes (because indirect taxes are regressive and affect all income categories equally).
- Additionally, there has been an endeavour to increase revenue by selling PSU shares.
- Nonetheless, the primary focus has been on cutting back on government spending.
- This could be accomplished by improving programme planning and administration to increase the efficiency of government operations.
- Government has eventually put in place self-imposed constraints of not increasing expenditure over pre-determined levels e.g. FRBM Act.

TEST YOURSELF

Multiple Choice Questions

Q1. What is a government budget?

(a) A plan for managing personal finances.

(b) A plan for managing the country's finances for a specific period.

(c) A plan for managing a company's finances.

(d) A plan for managing the finances of a non-profit organisation.

Q2. What is a revenue budget?

(a) The budget that includes the government's capital expenditure.

(b) The budget that includes the government's revenue expenditure.

(c) The budget that includes the government's borrowings and repayments.

(d) The budget that includes the government's tax revenues only.

Q3. What is a fiscal deficit?

(a) The difference between the government's revenue and expenditure.

(b) The difference between the government's total receipts and total expenditure.

(c) The difference between the government's capital receipts and capital expenditure.

(d) The difference between the government's revenue receipts and revenue expenditure.

Q4. What is the primary deficit?

(a) The difference between the government's total receipts and total expenditure.

(b) The difference between the government's revenue receipts and revenue expenditure.

(c) The difference between the government's capital receipts and capital expenditure.

(d) The difference between the government's fiscal deficit and interest payments.

Q5. What is the capital budget?

(a) The budget that includes the government's revenue receipts and revenue expenditure.

(b) The budget that includes the government's capital receipts and capital expenditure.

(c) The budget that includes the government's borrowings and repayments.

(d) The budget that includes the government's tax revenues only.

Q6. What is a balanced budget?

(a) A budget in which the government's total receipts are equal to total expenditure

(b) A budget in which the government's revenue receipts are equal to revenue expenditure

(c) A budget in which the government's capital receipts are equal to capital expenditure

(d) A budget in which government's borrowings are equal to repayments

Q7. What is a deficit budget?

(a) A budget in which the government's total receipts are greater than total expenditure.

(b) A budget in which the government's revenue receipts are greater than revenue expenditure.

(c) A budget in which the government's capital receipts are greater than capital expenditure.

(d) A budget in which government's total receipts are less than total expenditure.

Q8. What is the purpose of a revenue budget?

(a) To plan the government's borrowing and repayment activities.

(b) To allocate resources for productive activities and infrastructure development.

(c) To meet the regular expenses of the government.

(d) To promote economic growth through tax incentives.

Q9. What is deficit financing?

(a) The process of managing the government's revenue and expenditure.

(b) The process of borrowing to meet the fiscal deficit.

(c) The process of reducing the government's expenditure to match the revenue.

(d) The process of increasing taxes to cover the fiscal deficit.

Q10. What is the purpose of a capital budget?

(a) To meet the regular expenses of the government.

(b) To allocate resources for productive activities and infrastructure development.

(c) To promote economic growth through tax incentives.

(d) To plan the government's borrowing and repayment activities.

Q11. Which of the following statements is/are correct about the 'Government Budget'?

1. There is a Constitutional requirement in India to present before the Parliament a statement of estimated receipts and expenditures of the government.

2. The 'Annual Financial Statement' constitutes the main budget document of the government.

Select the correct answer using the code given below:

(a) 1 only (b) 2 only

(c) Both 1 and 2 (d) Neither 1 nor 2

Q12. Which of the following statements is/are correct about the Capital Expenditure of the Government of India?

(a) These are expenditures incurred for purposes other than the creation of physical or financial assets of the central government.

(b) Expenditures such as interest payments on debt incurred by the government, and grants given to state governments and other parties are some examples of Capital Expenditure.

(c) Capital Expenditures either results in the creation of physical or financial assets or reduction in financial liabilities.

(d) All of the above

Q13. The difference between the government's total expenditure and its total receipts excluding borrowing is known as:

(a) Fiscal Deficit (b) Budget Deficit

(c) Primary Deficit (d) Revenue Deficit

Q14. Which of the following statements is/are Incorrect about the Revenue Receipts of the Government Budget?

1. Revenue receipts are those receipts that do not lead to a claim on the government.
2. Revenue receipts are termed as non-redeemable.
3. The loan received by the government forms a part of the Non-Tax Revenue Receipt.

Select the correct answer using the code given below:

(a) 2 only (b) 3 only

(c) 2 and 3 only (d) None of the above

Q15. Who among the following economists proposed the idea of government intervention in the economy to stabilise the level of output and employment through Fiscal Policy?

(a) Adams Smith (b) J.M Keynes

(c) Karl Marx (d) Friedrich Hayek

Q16. Directions: Given below are two statements labelled as Assertion (A) and Reason (R). In the context of the two statements, which of the following is correct?

Assertion (A): By borrowing, the government transfers the burden of reduced consumption on future generations.

Reason (R): Government usually borrows by issuing bonds to the people living at present and pays it off many years later most often from the income realised from raising taxes.

Select the Correct answer using the codes given below:

(a) Both A and R are true and R is the correct explanation of A.

(b) Both A and Rare true but R is not the correct explanation of A.

(c) A is true but R is false.

(d) A is false but R is true

Q17. Which of the following statements is/are correct about Revenue Deficit?

1. The revenue deficit refers to the excess of the government's revenue expenditure over revenue receipts
2. The growth of revenue deficit as a percentage of fiscal deficit points to a deterioration in the quality of government expenditure involving lower capital formation.

Select the correct answer using the code given below:

(a) 1 only (b) 2 only

(c) Both 1 and 2 (d) Neither 1 nor 2

Q18. Statement 1: Share of the household financial savings goes towards government borrowings. (UPSC 2022)

Statement 2: Dated securities issued at marked-related rates in auctions form a large component of internal debt.

Which of the above statements is/are correct?

(a) 1 only (b) 2 only

(c) Both 1 and 2 (d) Neither 1 nor 2

Q19. With reference to India, consider the following statements: (UPSC -2021)

1. Retail investors through demat account can invest in 'Treasury Bills' and 'Government of India Debt Bonds' in primary market.
2. The 'Negotiated Dealing System-Order Matching' is a government securities trading platform of the Reserve Bank of India.
3. The 'Central Depository Services Ltd.' is jointly promoted by the Reserve Bank of India and the Bombay Stock Exchange.

Which of the statements given above is/are correct?

(a) 1 only (b) 1 and 2 only

(c) 3 only (d) 2 and 3 only

Q20. Consider the following statements: (UPSC-2018)

1. The Fiscal Responsibility and Budget Management (FRBM) Review Committee Report has recommended a debt to GDP ratio of 60% for the general (combined) government by 2023, comprising 40% for the Central Government and 20% for the State Governments.
2. The Central Government has domestic liabilities of 21% of GDP as compared to that of 49% of GDP of the State Governments.
3. As per the Constitution of India, it is mandatory for a State to take the Central Government's consent for raising any loan if the former owes any outstanding liabilities to the latter.

Which of the statements given above is/are correct?

(a) 1 only (b) 2 and 3 only

(c) 1 and 3 only (d) 1, 2 and 3

Q21. Which of the following is/are included in the capital budget of the Government of India? (UPSC-2016)

1. Expenditure on acquisition of assets like roads, buildings, machinery, etc,
2. Loans received from foreign governments
3. Loans and advances granted to the States and Union Territories

Select the correct answer using the code given below.

(a) 1 only (b) 2 and 3 only

(c) 1 and 3 only (d) 1, 2 and 3

Q22. There has been a persistent deficit budget year after year. Which action/actions of the following can be taken by the Government to reduce the deficit? (UPSC-2016)

1. Reducing revenue expenditure.
2. Introducing new welfare schemes.
3. Rationalizing subsidies.
4. Reducing import duty.

Select the correct answer using the code given below.

(a) 1 only (b) 2 and 3 only

(c) 1 and 3 only (d) 1, 2, 3 and 4

Q23. There has been a persistent deficit budget year after year. Which of the following actions can be taken by the government to reduce the deficit? (UPSC-2015)

1. Reducing revenue expenditure.
2. Introducing new welfare schemes.
3. Rationalizing subsidies.
4. Expanding industries.

Select the correct answer using the code given below:

(a) 1 and 3 only (b) 2 and 3 only

(c) 1 only (d) 1, 2, 3 and 4

Q24. In India, deficit financing is used for raising resources for (UPSC -2013)

(a) Economic development.

(b) Redemption of public debt.

(c) Adjusting the balance of payments.

(d) Reducing the foreign debt.

Answer Key

Q1.	b	Q2.	b	Q3.	b
Q4.	d	Q5.	b	Q6.	a
Q7.	d	Q8.	c	Q9.	b
Q10.	b	Q11.	c	Q12.	c
Q13.	a	Q14.	b	Q15.	b
Q16.	a	Q17.	c	Q18.	c
Q19.	b	Q20.	c	Q21.	d
Q22.	c	Q23.	a	Q24.	a

Model Questions for Main Examination

Q1. How can government budget help in reducing inequalities of income?

Q2. Write the differences between revenue and capital receipts?

UNIT 14 Open Economy Macroeconomics

In This Unit

Comprehensive and profound coverage of the following NCERT's chapter:

✓ NCERT Class- 11th (Introductory Macroeconomics), Chapter- 6

Introduction

- An open economy is one which **interacts with other countries**. Up till now, the circular flow of income in simple economy model has not considered the prospect of an economy to trade with other country. A country interacts with others in one of the following three ways:
  - **Through output market** i.e. the output of one country is traded with other country and vice-versa.
  - **Through financial market**, that is the country buys the financial instruments and assets of foreign country and let the foreign nationals buy its own financial instruments.
  - Through **labour market**, that is the labour from the country can work in other country and vice-versa.
- In this international trade, countries make payments using a currency which remains stable and the said currency is used by a number of nations.
- In this context **USA's Dollar** is used by many countries, followed by **Euro, Japanese Yen, Pound etc.**
- Any nation, which wants to use these currencies in international transaction, has to first convert its domestic currency into said currencies. The price of one currency in terms of another currency is known as the *foreign exchange rate* or *simply the exchange rate*.

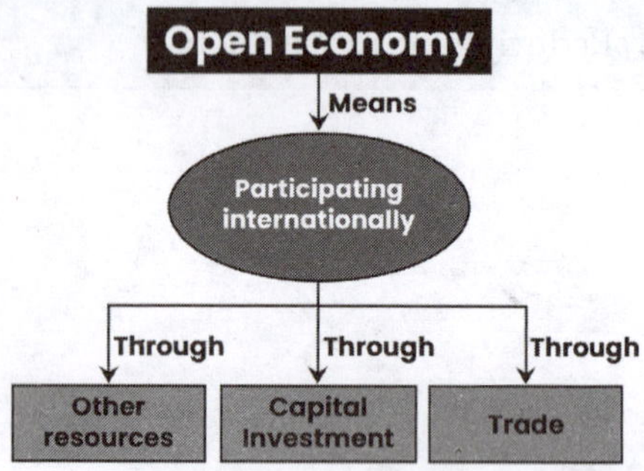

Open Economy

Balance of Payments

- **The balance of payments (BoP)** documents the exchanges of assets, commodities, and services between citizens of a nation and the rest of the globe during a given period of time, usually a year.
- The BoP consists of two primary accounts: the **capital account and the current account.**

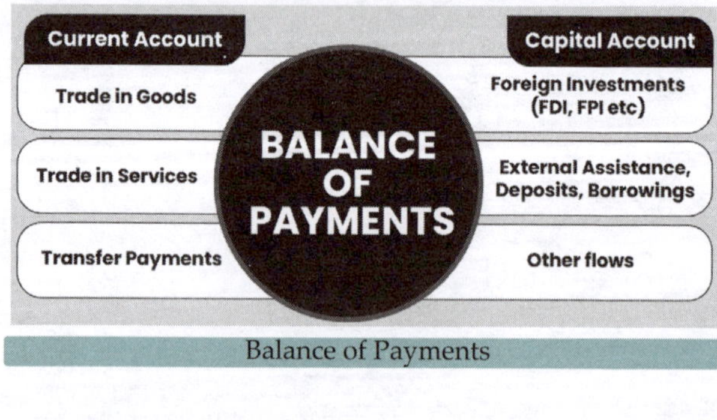

Balance of Payments

Current Account

- Current Account is the record of trade in goods and services and transfer payments.

- **Trade in goods includes exports and imports of goods.**
- **Trade in services includes factor income and non-factor income transactions.**
- Transfer payments are the receipts which the residents of a country get for 'free', without having to provide any goods or services in return.
- They consist of gifts, remittances and grants.
- They could be given by the government or by private citizens living abroad.
- Buying foreign goods is expenditure from our country and it becomes the income of that foreign country.
- Hence, the purchase of foreign goods or imports decreases the domestic demand for goods and services in our country.
- Similarly, selling of foreign goods or exports brings income to our country and adds to the aggregate domestic demand for goods and services in our country.

Components of Current Account

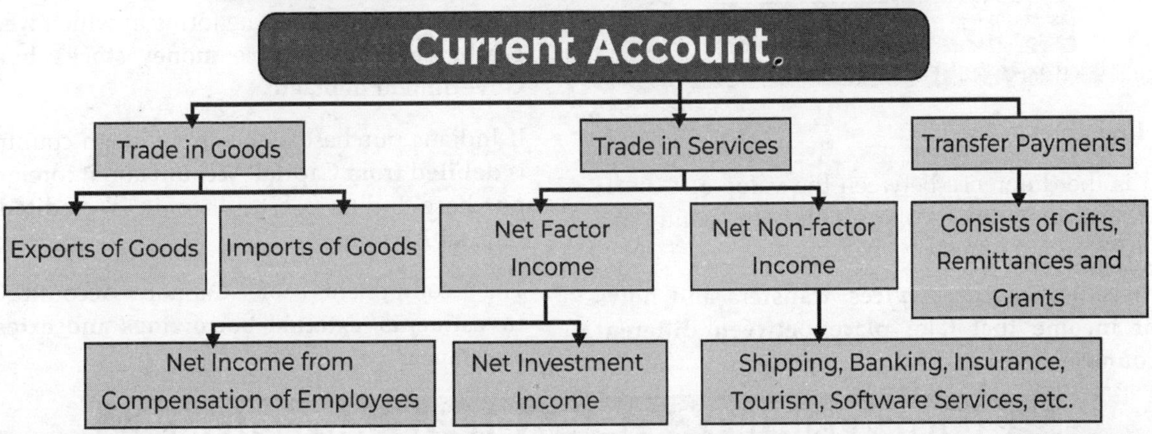

Components of Current Account

Balanced Current Account

- Current Account is in balance when receipts on current account are equal to the payments on the current account.
- A surplus current account means that the nation is a lender to other countries and a deficit current account means that the nation is a borrower from other countries.

Current Account Surplus	Balanced Current Account	Current Account Deficit
Receipts > Payments	Receipts = Payments	Receipts < payments

- A balanced Current Account has two components:
  - ➢ Balance of Trade or Trade Balance
  - ➢ Balance on Invisibles

Balance of Trade (BOT)

- It is the **difference between the value of exports and value of imports** of goods of a country in a given period of time.
- Export of goods is entered as a **credit item** in BOT, whereas import of goods is entered as a **debit item** in BOT.
- It is also known as **Trade Balance.**
- BOT is said to be in balance when **exports of goods are equal to the imports of goods.**
- Surplus BOT or Trade surplus will arise if country exports more goods than what it imports.
- Whereas, Deficit BOT or Trade deficit will arise if a country imports more goods than what it exports.

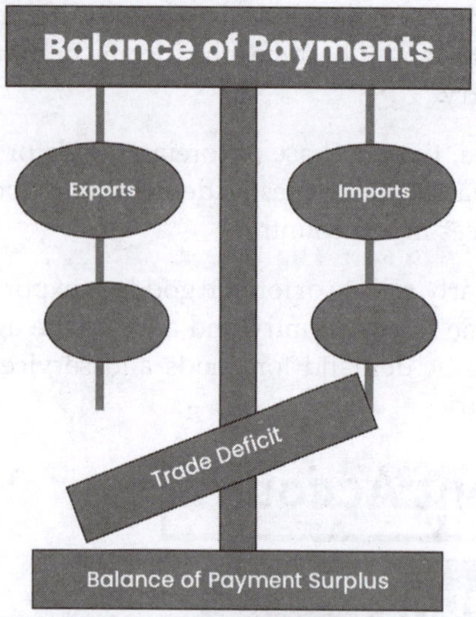

Balance of Payments (Trade Deficit)

Net Invisibles

- It is the difference between the value of exports and value of imports of invisibles of a country in a given period of time.
- Invisibles include **services, transfers and flows of income that take place between different countries.**
- Services trade includes both **factor and non-factor income.**
- **Factor income** includes net international earnings on factors of production like labour, land and capital.
- **Non-factor income** is net sale of service products like **shipping, banking, tourism, software services, etc.**

Capital Account

- Capital accounts record all international transactions of assets.
- An **asset** is any one of the forms in which **wealth can be held**, for example: **money, stocks, bonds, Government debt, etc.**
- If Indians purchase assets in a foreign country it is **debited from Capital Account** and if foreigners purchase Indian assets, then it is **credited in Capital Account.**
- The components of Capital Account are **Investments, external borrowings and external assistance.**

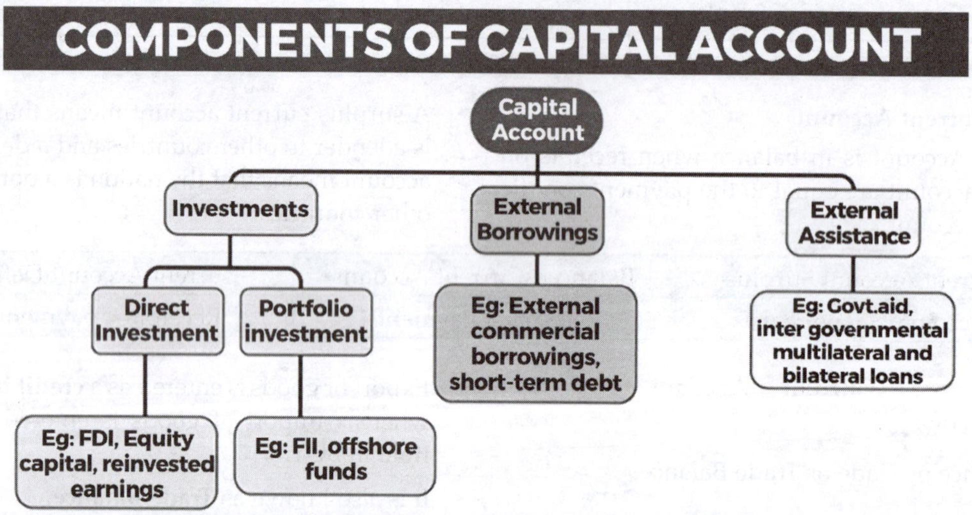

Components of Capital Account

Balance on Capital Account

- Capital account is in balance when capital inflows (like receipt of loans from abroad, sale of assets or shares in foreign companies) are equal to capital outflows (like repayment of loans, purchase of assets or shares in foreign countries).
- Surplus in capital account arises when capital inflows are greater than capital outflows, whereas deficit in capital account arises when capital inflows are lesser than capital outflows.

Balance of Payments Surplus and Deficit

- Just like in domestic sphere, where expenditure more than revenue leads to fiscal deficit, in international trade also, if the **nation's export is less than its import**, the nation is in **a current account deficit.**
- Like domestic economy, nations rely on borrowing or sale of assets, in international sphere also, to fund the current account deficit, nations rely on external borrowings or sale of assets like equity, shares in companies to the foreign players etc. Hence,

  Current Account + Capital Account = 0
- In case when current account deficit cannot be financed from capital account, **nations have to rely on their reserve currency.**
- And when this reserve currency becomes unable to fund the gap of current account deficit, then the nation is likely to be under **balance of payment crisis.**

Difference between Balance of Payment Surplus, Deficit & Equilibrium

BOP Surplus	BOP Deficit	BOP Equilibrium
Sum total of Capital & Current Account is Positive	Sum total of Capital & Current Account is Negative	Sum total of Capital & Current Account is 0
it leads to Increase in Forex Reserves	it leads to decrease in Forex Reserves	There is no change in Forex Reserves

Difference between Balance of Payment Surplus, Deficit and Equilibrium

Autonomous and Accommodating Transactions

- International economic transactions are called **autonomous** when transactions are made due to some reason other than to bridge the gap in the balance of payments, that is, when they are independent of the state of BoP. One reason could be to earn **profit.**
- These items are called **'above the line' items** in the BoP.
- The balance of payments is said to be in surplus (deficit) if **autonomous receipts are greater (less) than autonomous payments.**
- **Accommodating transactions** (termed 'below the line' items), on the other hand, are determined by the gap in the balance of payments, that is, whether there is a deficit or surplus in the balance of payments.
- In other words, they are determined by the net consequences of the autonomous transactions.
- Since the **official reserve transactions** are made to bridge the gap in the BoP, they are **seen as the accommodating item** in the BoP (all others being autonomous).

DIFFERENCE BETWEEN AUTONOMOUS AND ACCOMODATING TRANSACTIONS

AUTONOMOUS TRANSACTION	ACCOMODATING TRANSACTIONS
They are international transactions which are undertaken for profit motive	They are international transactions which are undertaken to cover BOP surplus/deficit
They are undertaken by private sector	They are undertaken by monetary authority (central bank, RBI)
They are undertaken irresperctive of effect on balance of payment	They are undertaken after seeing status of balance of payment surplus/ deficit

Difference between Autonomous and Accommodating Transactions

Errors and Omissions

- It is difficult to record all international transactions accurately.
- Thus, we have a third element of BoP (apart from the current and capital accounts) called **errors and omissions** which reflects this.

IMF's New Accounting System for Balance of Payments

- The balance of payments accounts presented above divide the transactions into two accounts, current account and capital account.
- However, following the new accounting standards introduced by the International Monetary Fund in the sixth edition of the Balance of Payments and International Investment Position Manual (BPM6) the Reserve Bank of India also made changes in the structure of balance of payments accounts.
- According to the new classification, the transactions are divided into three accounts: **current account, financial account and capital account.**
- The most important change is that almost all the transactions arising on account of trade in financial assets such as bonds and equity shares are now placed in the financial account.
- However, RBI continues to publish the balance of payments accounts as per the old system also.
- The details are given in the Balance of Payments Manual for India published by the Reserve Bank of India in September 2010.

The Foreign Exchange Market

- Consider a single person making transaction in international market.
- To buy any product in foreign market, one has to convert his/her domestic currency into foreign currency.
- The rate at which this conversion of domestic currency with foreign currency happens is known as *currency exchange rate*.
- The market in which national currencies are traded for one another is known as the *foreign exchange market*.
- The major **participants** in the foreign exchange market are **commercial banks, foreign exchange brokers and other authorised dealers** and monetary authorities.
- It is important to note that although participants themselves may have their own trading centres, the market itself is world-wide.
- There is a close and continuous contact between the trading centres and the participants deal in more than one market.

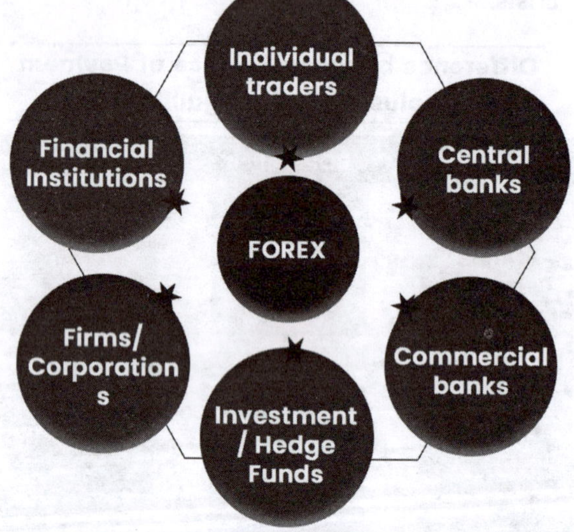

Actors in the Forex Market

Supply of Foreign Exchange

- Supply of foreign exchange happens in the country when export of domestic products rises in the country.
- Foreign nationals buy the domestic currency, hence the availability of domestic currency become scarce in international market and the rate of domestic currency rises in foreign exchange.

- Opposite happens, when the demand of foreign currency rises in international market. The rate of foreign currency rises and price of domestic currency drops with respect to foreign currency.
- **This situation becomes lucrative to foreign consumers to buy domestic goods.** As the drop in domestic currency makes the prices of domestic products look attractive to foreign consumers.
- Hence export from domestic countries may go up.

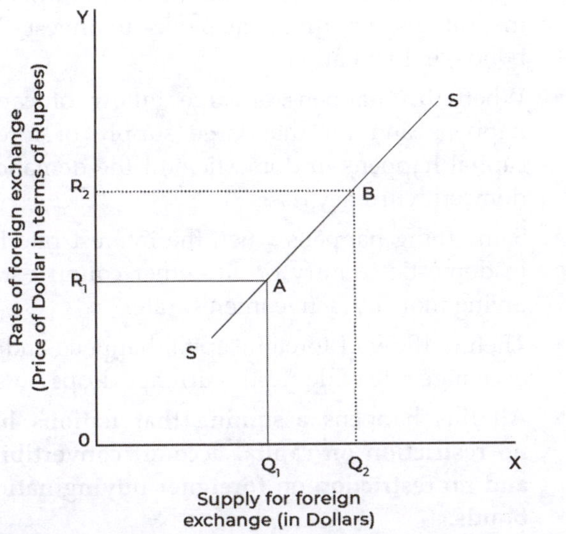

Foreign Exchange

Determination of Exchange Rate

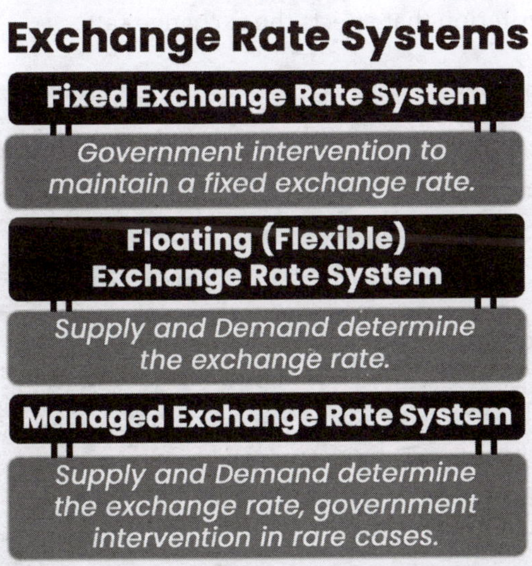

Exchange Rate Systems

Different countries follow different methods of determining their currency's exchange rate. The methods can be **Flexible Exchange Rate, Fixed Exchange Rate or Managed Floating Exchange Rate.**

Flexible Exchange Rate

- This exchange rate is **determined by market forces.**
- The rate or price of exchange is determined by supply and demand of currencies in international currency market.

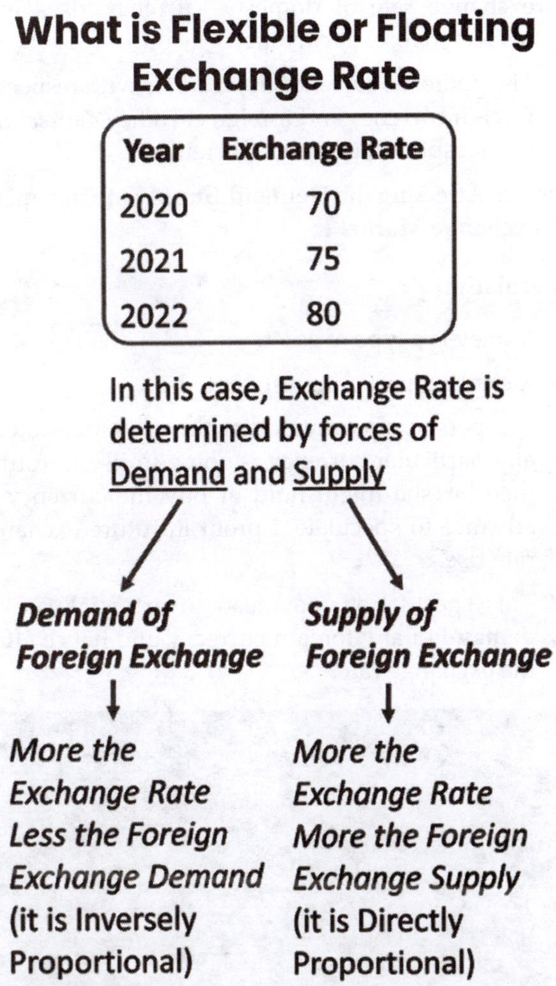

Flexible Exchange Rate

- As per demand-supply equilibrium of currency, when demand of any currency is equal to supply of that currency, then a certain exchange rate is established.
- If for some reason, the demand of foreign currency **increases** in international market, then

this equilibrium price shifts to upward to a new equilibrium point.

- The foreign currency in this sense is said to be *appreciated* with respect to domestic currency and domestic currency is said to be *depreciated* with respect to foreign currency.
- **Vice-versa** can also be said, when the demand of domestic currency rises or supply of foreign currency rises with respect to demand. Then exchange rate of domestic currency rises with respect to foreign currency.
- The domestic currency ***appreciates*** with respect to foreign currency and foreign currency ***depreciates*** with respect to domestic currency.

Factors Affecting the Demand-Supply of Currencies In Exchange Market

Speculation

- Money is a type of asset.
- It can be a part of investment also.
- If a person **speculates** that the exchange rate of any particular currency is going to rise in future, then he/she might hold or buy the currency in advance to speculate a profit in future exchange rate rise.
- This speculation may lead to **artificial rise in demand** of any foreign currency and hence effect the exchange rate.
- Similar can be said about speculation of a future drop in price of any currency.

Interest Rate and Exchange Rate

- Any individual does not want to hold money idly.
- One always wants to get extra return on his/her investment.
- In this context the interest rate given by any nation to money investment attracts the high wealth individuals, sovereign governments, multilateral institutions, international banks to invest (buy bonds) in that nation.
- When this happens, a large inflow of capital happens and for that large supply of foreign capital happens in domestic and the demand of domestic currency rises.
- Same thing happens when the interest rate falls in domestic country or any other country starts giving more attractive interest rate.
- Then outflow of foreign capital happens and the exchange rate of domestic currency drops.
- All this happens **assuming that nations have no restriction on capital account convertibility and no restriction on foreigner buying nations' bonds.**

Income and the Exchange rate

- The rise or drop of per capita income is also a criterion that affects the exchange rate.

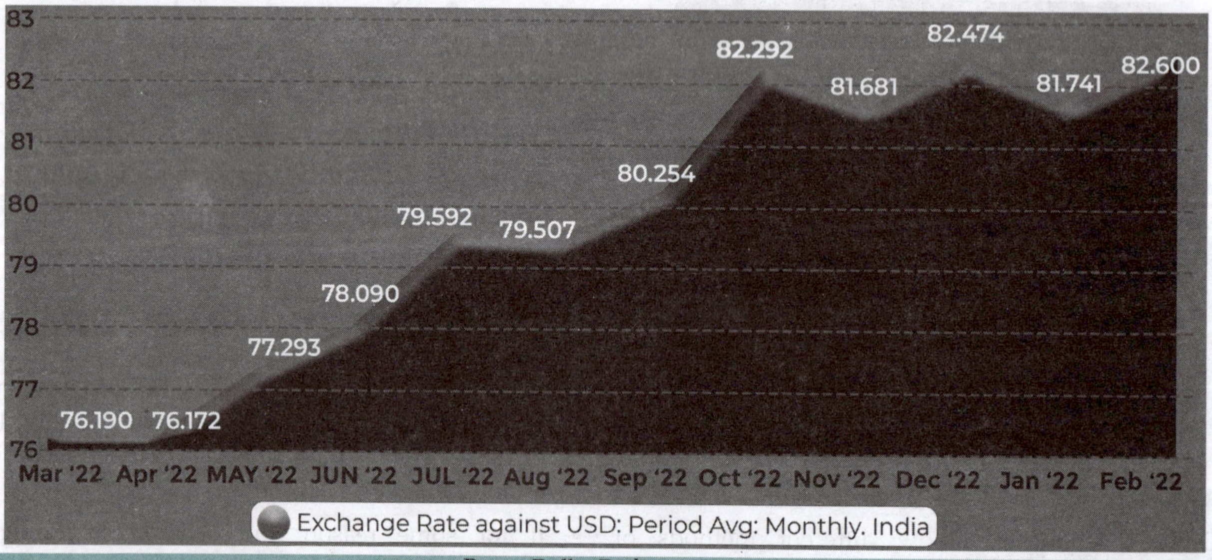

Rupee-Dollar Exchange Rate

- If the per capita income of any nation increases so does the **capacity to consume of the population.**
- Hence, the population starts buying foreign products more. Hence demand of foreign currency rises and depreciation in domestic currency may happen.
- If **depreciation of domestic currency happens** with respect to foreign currency, then a rise in export may follow, as the domestic products would look cheap to foreigners.
- This leads to rise in demand of domestic currency and hence appreciation of domestic currency afterwards.
- The net result of rise in per capita income on exchange rate depends on, whether imports grow faster or exports grow faster.

Exchange Rates In The Long Run

- The Purchasing Power (PPP) theory is used to make long-run predictions about exchange rates in a flexible exchange rate system.
- According to the theory, **as long as there are no barriers to trade** like tariffs (taxes on trade) and quotas (quantitative limits on imports), **exchange rates should eventually adjust so that the same product costs the same** whether measured in rupees in India, or dollars in the US, yen in Japan and so on, except for differences in transportation costs.
- Over the long run, therefore, exchange rates between any two national currencies adjust to reflect differences in the price levels in the two countries.

Example:

If a shirt costs $8 in the US and Rs 400 in India, the rupee-dollar exchange rate should be Rs 50. To see why, at any rate higher than Rs 50, say Rs 60, it costs Rs 480 per shirt in the US but only Rs 400 in India. In that case, all foreign customers would buy shirts from India. Similarly, any exchange rate below Rs 50 per dollar will send all the shirt business to the US. Next, we suppose that prices in India rise by 20 per cent while prices in the US rise by 50 per cent. Indian shirts would now cost Rs 480 per shirt while American shirts cost $12 per shirt. For these two prices to be equivalent, $12 must be worth Rs 480, or one dollar must be worth Rs 40. The dollar, therefore, has *depreciated.*

Fixed Exchange Rate System

- In a fixed exchange rate regime, **governments fixes a particular exchange rate** for its domestic currency.
- When government wants to increase the export, it fixes the exchange rate higher than the current one.
- This process of increasing the exchange rate by governments is known as **devaluation of domestic currency with respect to foreign currency.**
- And if government drops the exchange rate, then the process is known as **revaluation of domestic currency with respect to foreign currency.**
- Absorption of excess of foreign currency supply in market due to devaluation of domestic currency is done by central bank of that country using its foreign currency reserves.

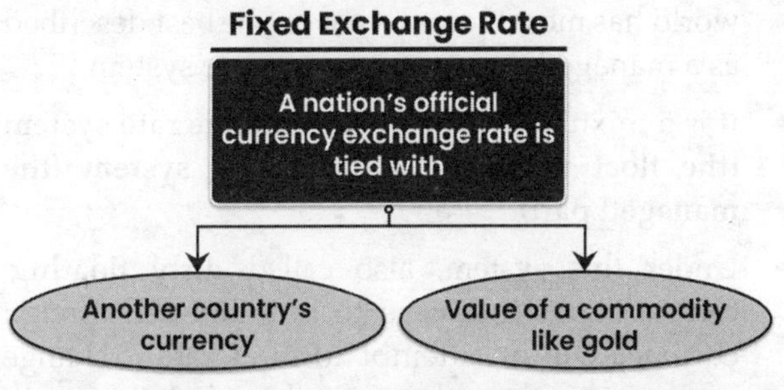

Fixed Exchange Rate

Merits and Demerits of Flexible and Fixed Exchange Rate Systems

- The main feature of the fixed exchange rate system is that there must be **credibility that the government will be able to maintain** the exchange rate at the level specified.
- Often, **if there is a deficit in the BoP, in a fixed exchange rate system, governments will have to intervene** to take care of the gap by use of its official reserves.
- If people know that the amount of reserves is inadequate, they would begin to doubt the ability of the government to maintain the fixed rate.

- **This may give rise to speculation of devaluation.**
- When this belief translates into aggressive buying of one currency thereby forcing the government to devalue, it is said to constitute a speculative attack on a currency.
- Fixed exchange rates are prone to these kinds of attacks, **as has been witnessed in the period before the collapse of the Bretton Woods System.**
- The flexible exchange rate system gives the government more flexibility and they do not need to maintain large stocks of foreign exchange reserves.
- The **major advantage** of flexible exchange rates is that movements in the exchange rate automatically take care of the surpluses and deficits in the BoP.
- Also, countries gain independence in conducting their monetary policies, since they do not have to intervene to maintain exchange rate which are automatically taken care of by the market.

Managed Floating Exchange Rate System

- Without any formal international agreement, the world has moved on to what can be best described as a managed floating exchange rate system.
- It is a mixture of a **flexible exchange rate system (the float part) and a fixed rate system (the managed part).**
- Under this system, also called **dirty floating**, central banks intervene to buy and sell foreign currencies in an attempt to moderate exchange rate movements whenever they feel that such actions are appropriate.
- Official reserve transactions are, therefore, not equal to zero.

Types of Exchange Rates: Primarily three types exist which are, Effective Exchange Rate (EER), Nominal Effective Exchange Rate (NEER) and Real Effective Exchange Rate (REER)

Effective Exchange Rate (EER)

- **Effective Exchange Rate (EER)** is a summary indicator of movements of the home currency against a **basket of currencies of trading partners**.
- Effective exchange rates (EERs) serve as a gauge for assessing the fair value of a currency and the external competitiveness of an economy.
- It also serves as a guidepost for setting monetary and financial conditions.
- There are of two types of EERs: **Nominal effective exchange rate (NEER) and Real effective exchange rate (REER).**

Nominal Effective Exchange Rate (NEER)

- The **Nominal Effective Exchange Rate (NEER)** is an **index of the weighted average of bilateral exchange rates of home currency with respect to a basket of currencies of trading partners.**
- It is also known as the **trade-weighted currency index.**
- The important aspect of NEER is that it is **not adjusted for inflation**. Thus, it does not say anything about the real strength of a currency; it is just a relative value.
- However, it can be used to measure the relative strength of different currencies.
- An **increase in NEER** indicates that the **domestic currency has appreciated** against the basket of currencies whereas a decrease indicates a relative depreciation.
- There is no fixed standard used to determine the basket of currencies. The OECD basket is different from that of the IMF or that of the US Federal Reserve. Most of the institutions rely on the IMF's basket of currencies.

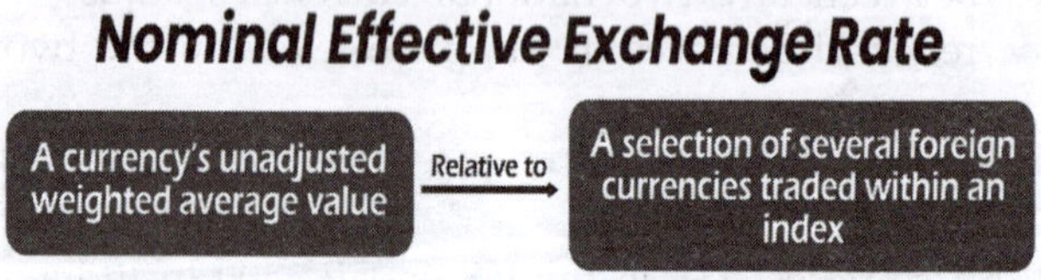

Nominal Effective Exchange Rate

Nominal Effective Exchange Rate (REER)

- The Nominal Effective Exchange Rate **(REER)** is the NEER adjusted by inflation differentials between the domestic currency and that of the trading partners.
- Thus, it speaks about the real strength of a domestic currency against a basket of currencies, unlike NEER.

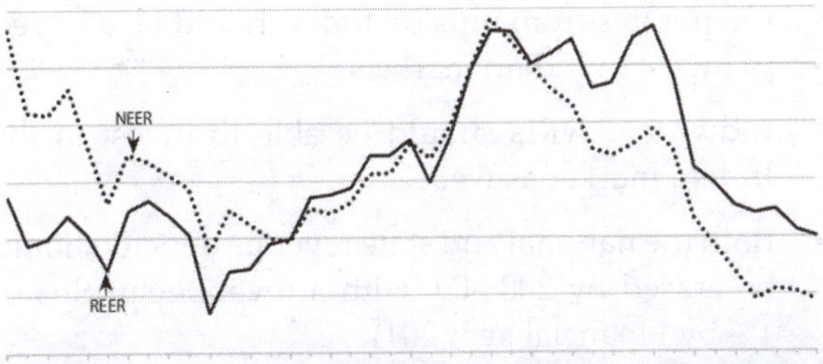

REER v/s NEER

Exchange Rate Management: The Indian Experience

- India's exchange rate policy has evolved in line with international and domestic developments.
- Post-independence, in view of the prevailing **Bretton Woods system**, the Indian rupee was **pegged** to the ***pound sterling*** due to its historic links with Britain.
- A major development was the devaluation of the rupee by 36.5 per cent in June, 1966.
- With the breakdown of the ***Bretton Woods system***, and also the declining share of UK in India's trade, the **rupee was delinked from the pound sterling** in September 1975.
- During the period between 1975 to 1992, the exchange rate of the rupee was officially determined by the Reserve Bank within a nominal band of plus or minus 5 per cent of the weighted basket of currencies of India's major trading partners.
- The Reserve Bank intervened on a day-to-day basis which resulted in wide changes in the size of reserves.
- The exchange rate regime of this period can be described as an **adjustable nominal peg with a band**.
- The beginning of 1990s saw significant rise in oil prices and suspension of remittances from the Gulf region in the wake of the *Gulf crisis*.
- This, and other domestic and international developments, led to severe ***balance of payments*** problems in India.
- The drying up of access to commercial banks and short-term credit made financing the current account deficit difficult.
- India's foreign currency reserves fell rapidly from US $ 3.1 billion in August to US $ 975 million on July 12, 1991.
- Apart from measures like sending gold abroad, curtailing non-essential imports, approaching the IMF and multilateral and bilateral sources, introducing stabilisation and structural reforms, there was a two-step devaluation of 18 –19 per cent of the rupee on July 1 and 3, 1991.
- In March 1992, the ***Liberalised Exchange Rate Management System (LERMS)*** involving dual exchange rates was introduced.
- Under this system, 40 per cent of exchange earnings had to be surrendered at an official rate determined by the Reserve Bank and 60 per cent was to be converted at the market-determined rates.
- The dual rates were converted into one from March 1, 1993; this was an **important step towards current account convertibility, which was finally achieved in August 1994** by accepting ***Article VIII*** of the ***Articles of Agreement of the IMF***.
- The **exchange rate** of the rupee thus became ***market determined***, with the Reserve Bank ensuring orderly conditions in the foreign exchange market through its sales and purchases.

Quest for Capital Account Convertibility in India

Capital Account Convertibility (CAC)

- The **ability to convert domestic financial assets into international financial assets** and vice versa is referred to as **CAC.**
- It represents the development and liquidation of claims on, or by, the rest of the world, and is related to changes in ownership of foreign/domestic financial assets and liabilities.
- Other than limits on external payments, CAC can and does coexist.

S. S Tarapore Committee

- The Reserve Bank of India established the Committee on **Capital Account Convertibility**

(CAC) or **S.S Tarapore Committee** to propose a **roadmap for full convertibility** of the rupee on the capital account.

- **In May 1997, the committee submitted its report.**
- There is **no clear definition of CAC, according to the committee.**
- According to industry standards, the CAC refers to the **ability to convert local financial assets into international financial assets** or vice versa at market-determined exchange rates.

Recommendations of S.S Tarapore Committee

- NRI tax benefits are being cut down.
- RBI will have more power.
- Allowing investment channels to pass through a specific country (such as Mauritius).
- Reduction of the government's interest in banks from 51% to 33%.
- Allowing industrial houses to take a stake in existing banks or start new ones.
- Allowing international banks to have a stronger footprint.
- The 10% voting cap on bank investments should be abolished.
- Corporates from outside India should be allowed to invest in Indian markets.
- Individual NRIs should be able to invest in the Indian market as well.
- Both the national and state revenue deficits should be erased by 2008-09, with a revenue surplus of 1% by Financial Year 2011.
- Raising the limit on commercial borrowing from outside the U.S. under the External Commercial Borrowing (ECB) mechanism.
- Participatory Notes (PNs) will be banned, and current PNs will be phased out over the next year.
- Raising the government debt ceiling from $2 billion to 10% of new issuance and $1-5 billion to 25% of new corporate debt issuances in a year.
- Building sufficient reserves and keeping the current account deficit below 3% of GDP.
- The Companies Act should be applied to all banks.
- All three essential stakeholders in this process, residents, domestic enterprises, and foreign investors, should have more financial flexibility, according to the committee.

Proposed Changes by Tarapore Committee

Investment Relaxation	Phase-I 2006-07	Phase-II 2007-09	Phase-II 2009-11
External commercial borrowing	Status quo on ECB limit of $18 billion	Gradual increase, but automatic limit to be raised from $500 million to $750 million	Gradual increase, but limit to be raised to $1 billion per financial year
Resident individual's overseas investment	$25,000 limit should be hiked to $50,000 per calendar year	Raised to $1,00,000	Raised to $2,00,000
MFs overseas investment	$2 billion investment limit to be raised to $3 billion	Further raised to $4 billion	Further raised to $5 billion
FII investment	Fresh participatory notes should be banned	Ban to continue	Ban to continue
FIIs' debt investment	G-Sec investment limit of $2 billion to be modified as 6 per cent of gross borrowing	8 per cent of total gross borrowing	10 per cent of gross borrowing
JVs/Wholly-owned subsidiary abroad investment	200 per cent of net worth limit should be raised to 250 percent	Further raised to 300 per cent of net	Further raised to 400 per cent

Proposed changes by Tarapore Committee

Advantages and Disadvantages of Fully Capital Account Convertibility

Advantages

- Availability of more funds due to improved access to international financial markets.
- Reduction in cost of capital.
- The incentive for Indians to acquire and hold international securities and assets.
- Greater financial competitiveness.
- Will help Indian corporates to use External commercial borrowing route without RBI or Government approval.
- Indian residents can hold and transact foreign currency denominated deposits with Indian banks.
- A Certain class of financial institutions and later NBFCs can access global financial markets.
- Banks and financial institutions can trade in Gold globally and issue loans.

Disadvantages

- Market determined exchange rates being higher than officially fixed exchange rates can raise import prices and cause Cost-push inflation.
- Improper management of CAC can lead to currency depreciation and affect trade and capital flows.
- The advantages have been found to be short lived as per studies, and also International financial institutions are sceptical about CAC post-2008 crisis.
- **Speculative activity can lead to capital flight** from the country as in case of some South East Asian economies during 1997-98.
- Imposing control would become difficult in a globalised environment once CAC is introduced.

TEST YOURSELF

Multiple Choice Questions

Q1. What is the balance of payments?

(a) The difference between a country's exports and imports.

(b) The difference between a country's total receipts and total payments with the rest of the world.

(c) The difference between a country's savings and investment.

(d) The difference between a country's government revenue and expenditure.

Q2. What are the components of the balance of payments?

(a) Current account and capital account.

(b) Export account and import account.

(c) Investment account and savings account.

(d) Revenue account and expenditure account.

Q3. What does the current account of the balance of payments measure?

(a) The flow of goods and services between a country and the rest of the world.

(b) The flow of capital between a country and the rest of the world.

(c) The flow of income between a country and the rest of the world.

(d) The flow of loans and borrowings between a country and the rest of the world.

Q4. What does the capital account of the balance of payments measure?

(a) The flow of goods and services between a country and the rest of the world.

(b) The flow of capital between a country and the rest of the world.

(c) The flow of income between a country and the rest of the world.

(d) The flow of loans and borrowings between a country and the rest of the world.

Q5. What is a trade surplus?

(a) When a country's exports exceed its imports.

(b) When a country's imports exceed its exports.

(c) When a country's savings exceed its investment.

(d) When a country's investment exceeds its savings.

Q6. What is foreign exchange?

(a) The exchange of goods and services between countries.

(b) The exchange of currencies between countries.

(c) The exchange of capital between countries.

(d) The exchange of information between countries.

Q7. What is the foreign exchange market?

(a) The market where goods and services are traded between countries.

(b) The market where currencies are bought and sold.

(c) The market where stocks and bonds are traded internationally.

(d) The market where governments borrow money from foreign entities.

Q8. What is the exchange rate?

(a) The rate at which goods and services are exchanged between countries.

(b) The rate at which one currency can be exchanged for another.

(c) The rate at which stocks and bonds are traded internationally.

(d) The rate at which interest is charged on foreign loans.

Q9. What is a floating exchange rate?

(a) An exchange rate that is fixed by the government.

(b) An exchange rate that is determined by market forces.

(c) An exchange rate that is used for international trade only.

(d) An exchange rate that is determined by the World Bank.

Q10. What is a fixed exchange rate?

(a) An exchange rate that is determined by market forces.

(b) An exchange rate that is used for international trade only.

(c) An exchange rate that is fixed by the government.

(d) An exchange rate that is determined by the World Bank.

Q11. What is devaluation?

(a) A decrease in the value of a country's currency relative to other currencies.

(b) An increase in the value of a country's currency relative to other currencies.

(c) The removal of currency exchange restrictions.

(d) The imposition of currency exchange restrictions.

Q12. The Bretton Woods Conference held in 1944 set up which of the following International Institutions?

1. International Monetary Fund (IMF)
2. World Bank
3. World Trade Organisation
4. World Economic Forum

Select the correct answer using the code given below:

(a) 1 only (b) 1 and 2 only

(c) 1, 2 and 3 only (d) 1, 2, 3 and 4

Q13. Which of the following statements is/are correct about World Trade Organisation (WTO)?

(a) The WTO was founded in 1995 as the successor organisation to the General Agreement on Trade and Tariff (GATT).

(b) WTO is expected to establish a rule-based trading regime in which nations cannot place arbitrary restrictions on trade.

(c) The WTO agreements facilitate international trade through removal of tariff as well as non-tariff barriers and providing greater market access to all member countries.

(d) All of the above

Q14. With reference to the Indian economy, consider the following statements:(UPSC 2022)

1. An increase in Nominal Effective Exchange Rate (NEER) indicates the appreciation of rupee.
2. An increase in the Real Effective Exchange Rate (REER) indicates an improvement in trade competitiveness.
3. An increasing trend in domestic inflation relative to inflation in other countries is likely to cause an increasing divergence between NEER and REER.

Which of the above statements are correct?

(a) 1 and 2 only (b) 2 and 3 only

(c) 1 and 3 only (d) 1, 2 and 3

Q15. The effect of devaluation of a currency is that it necessarily: (UPSC 2021)

1. Improves the competitiveness of the domestic exports in the foreign markets.
2. Increases the foreign value of domestic currency.
3. Improves the trade balance.

Which of the above statements is/are correct?

(a) 1 only (b) 1 and 2 only

(c) 3 only (d) 2 and 3 only

Q16. In the context of India, which of the following factors is/are contributor/contributors to reducing the risk of a currency crisis? (UPSC 2019)

1. The foreign currency earnings of India's IT sector.
2. Increasing the government expenditure.
3. Remittances from Indians abroad.

Select the correct answer using the code given below:

(a) 1 only (b) 1 and 3 only

(c) 2 only (d) 1, 2 and 3

Q17. Which of the following is/are not among the components of Current Account?

1. Portfolio Investments
2. External Borrowings
3. Transfer payments
4. Trade in Services

Select the correct answer using the code given below:

(a) 1 only (b) 1 and 2 only

(c) 1, 2 and 3 only (d) 1, 2, 3 and 4

Q18. Which of the following records all the transactions in goods, services and assets between residents of a country with the rest of the world for a specified time period typically a year?

(a) Current Account

(b) Capital Account

(c) Government Budget

(d) Balance of Payments

Q19. Consider the following statements: (UPSC-2019)

1. Most of India's external debt is owed by governmental entities.
2. All of India's external debt is denominated in US dollars.

Which of the statements given above is/are correct?

(a) 1 only (b) 2 only

(c) Both 1 and 2 (d) Neither 1 nor 2

Answer Key

Q1.	b	Q2.	a	Q3.	a
Q4.	b	Q5.	a	Q6.	b
Q7.	b	Q8.	b	Q9.	b
Q10.	c	Q11.	a	Q12.	b
Q13.	d	Q14.	c	Q15.	a
Q16.	b	Q17.	b	Q18.	d
Q19.	d				

Model Questions for Main Examination

Q1. Write advantages and disadvantages of fixed exchange rate system?

Q2. Are devaluation and depreciation of currency same thing? Discuss.

UNIT 15

Introductory Microeconomics

In This Unit

Comprehensive and profound coverage of the following NCERT's chapter:

✓ NCERT Class- 12th (Introductory Microeconomics), All Chapters

Introduction

Traditionally, the subject matter of economics has been studied under two broad branches:

- Microeconomics
- Macroeconomics

Difference	Microeconomics	Macroeconomics
Meaning	Microeconomics is a branch of Economics **concerned with the study of individual**, household, and corporate behaviour in decision making and resource allocation. It includes **markets for goods and services and addresses economic challenges.**	Macroeconomics is the branch of Economics that **studies the overall behaviour and performance of the economy**. The **most essential parameters** investigated in macroeconomics are **GDP, unemployment, inflation, and growth rate**, among others.
Study Area	It **studies the particular market segment or the individual economic units of the economy**. It addresses a variety of issues including **demand, supply, factor pricing, product pricing, economic welfare, production, consumption** etc.	It **studies the whole economy,** which covers several market segments. It deals with various issues **like national income, distribution, employment, general price level, money** etc.
Significance	It is **useful in regulating the prices of a product** alongside the prices of factors of production (labour, land, entrepreneur, capital etc.) within the economy. It helps in business decision making, production planning etc.	It **helps to evaluate the resources and capabilities of an economy**, churn out ways to **increase the national income, boost productivity, and create job opportunities to upscale an economy** and **solve** the **major issues** of the economy **like deflation, inflation, unemployment, and poverty** as a whole.

Central Problems of an Economy

The **problem of resource allocation** arises from the fact that resources are limited and demands are infinite. Among the most fundamental economic activities of life are the production, trade, and consumption of goods and services. During these fundamental economic operations, any community must deal with:

A. **Scarcity of resources**

B. **Problem of choice**

The problems of an economy are very often summarised as follows:

1. What is produced and in what quantities?

   Every society has to choose how much of each of the countless products and services it will manufacture.

2. How are these goods produced?

   Each community must determine how much of each resource to employ in order to produce the various goods and services.

3. For whom are these goods produced?

   Therefore, dividing the created products and services among the persons within the economy and allocating limited resources to the creation of various conceivable commodities and services are problems that every economy must deal with.

Production Possibility Frontier

An allocation of the scarce resource of the economy gives rise to a particular combination of different goods and services. Given the total amount of resources, it is possible to allocate the resources in many different ways and, thereby achieving different mixes of all possible goods and services. The collection of all possible combinations of the goods and services that can be produced from a given amount of resources and a given stock of technological knowledge is called the **production possibility set** of the economy.

Opportunity Cost: We will have less of the other good if we desire more of one of the items. Therefore, having a little bit more of one good always comes at a cost in terms of the quantity of the other good that must be given up. It's referred to as the opportunity cost of purchasing one more unit of the items.

Theory of Consumer Behaviour

The consumer has to decide how to spend his income on different goods. Economists call this **the problem of choice**. Most naturally, any consumer will want to get a combination of goods that gives him maximum satisfaction. This depends on the **likes of the consumer** and what the consumer can afford to buy. The 'likes' of the consumer are also called **'preferences'**. And what the consumer can afford to buy, depends on prices of the goods and the income of the consumer.

Utility

A consumer usually decides his demand for a commodity on the basis of **utility** (or satisfaction) that he derives from it.

- Utility of a commodity is **its want-satisfying capacity.** The more the need of a commodity or the stronger the desire to have it, the **greater is the utility derived from the commodity.**
- Utility is **subjective.** Different individuals can get **different levels of utility** from the same commodity.

Measures of Utility

1. **Total Utility:** It refers to the **total satisfaction or benefit** that a consumer derives from consuming a certain quantity of a good or service. It represents the **sum of the utility or satisfaction** obtained from each unit of the good or service consumed.
2. **Marginal Utility:** Marginal utility (MU) is the **change in total utility due to consumption of one additional unit** of a commodity. It measures the change in total utility resulting from a small change in the quantity consumed. For example, suppose 4 bananas give us 28 units of total utility and 5 bananas give us 30 units of total utility. Clearly, consumption of the 5th banana has caused total utility to increase by 2 units (30 units minus 28 units). Therefore, the marginal utility of the 5th banana is 2 units.

Law of Diminishing Marginal Utility

It states that marginal utility from consuming each additional unit of a commodity **declines as its consumption increases,** while keeping consumption of other commodities constant. In simpler terms, it means that the more you have of something, the less value or enjoyment you get from each additional unit.

Example: Suppose you're eating ice cream on a hot day. The first scoop brings you immense pleasure and satisfaction. As you continue eating, each subsequent scoop provides less and less additional satisfaction. Eventually, you may even reach a point where you start to feel less enjoyment, and consuming more ice cream may become less desirable or even unpleasant.

Budget Set

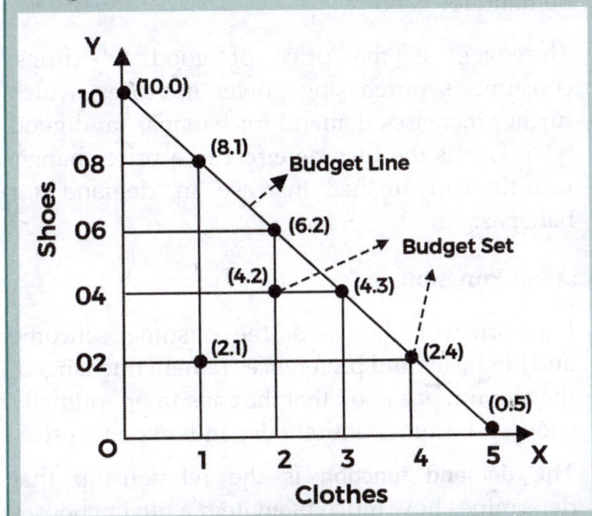

Budget Set

- ✓ In economics, the **budget set** is the **collection of all bundles of goods** that a consumer can buy with her income at the prevailing market prices.
- ✓ The **budget line** represents all bundles which cost the consumer her entire income.
- ✓ The budget line is **negatively sloping.**
- ✓ The budget set changes if either of the two prices or the income changes.

Indifference Curve

An indifference curve is a graphical representation used in microeconomics to depict the **various combinations of two goods or services** that provide **equal levels of satisfaction** or utility to a consumer. It shows **all the possible combinations of goods** among which the consumer is indifferent or has no preference.

A curve joining **all points representing bundles** among which the consumer is indifferent is called an indifference curve. All the points such as A, B, C and D lying on an indifference curve provide the consumer with the same level of satisfaction.

It is clear that when a consumer gets one more banana, he has to forgo some mangoes, so that her total utility level remains the same and she remains on the same indifference curve. Therefore, the indifference curve **slopes downward.**

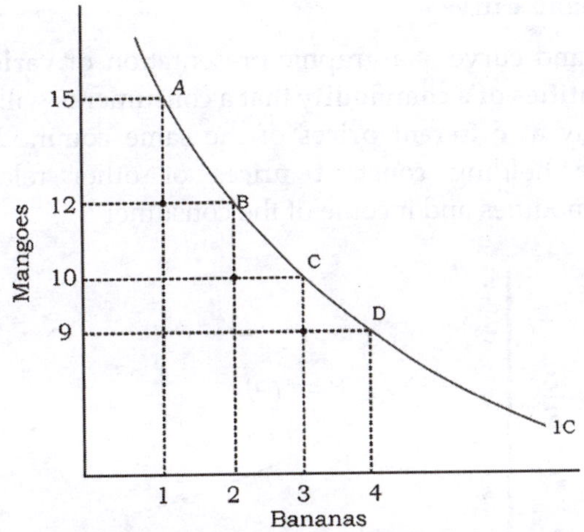

***Indifference curve.** An indifference curve joins all points representing bundles which are considered indifferent by the consumer.*

Indifference Curve

The amount of mangoes that the consumer has to forego, in order to get an additional banana, her total utility level being the same, is called **marginal rate of substitution (MRS).** In other words, MRS is simply the rate at which the consumer will substitute bananas for mangoes, so that her total utility remains constant.

Features of Indifference Curve

- Indifference curve slopes **downwards from left to right.**
- Higher indifference curve gives **greater level of utility.**
- Two indifference curves **never intersect each other.**

Demand

- The quantity of a commodity that a consumer is **willing to buy** and is **able to afford,** given prices of goods and income of the consumer, is called demand for that commodity.
- Demand for a particular commodity, apart from the price of this commodity, depends on factors such as:
  - ➢ Prices of other commodities
  - ➢ Income of the consumer
  - ➢ Tastes and preferences of the consumers

Demand Curve

Demand curve is a graphic presentation of **various quantities of a commodity** that a consumer is willing to buy **at different prices** of the same commodity, while holding **constant prices** of other related commodities and income of the consumer.

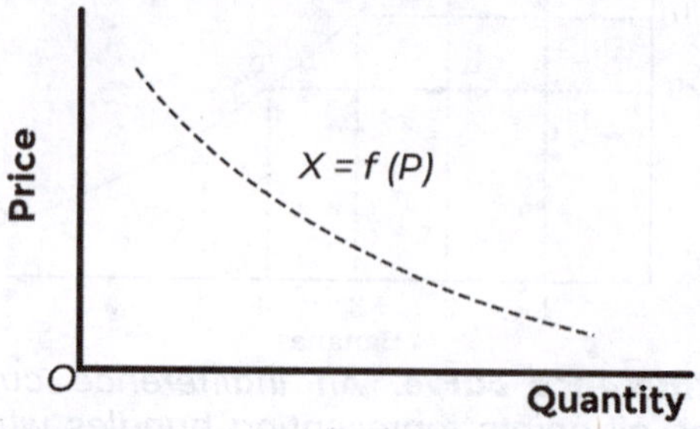

Demand Curve. *The demand curve is a relation between the quantity of the good chosen by a consumer and the price of the good. The independent variable (price) is measured along the vertical axis and dependent variable (quantity) is measured along the horizontal axis. The demand curve gives the quantity demanded by the*

Demand Curve

The **downward sloping demand curve** shows that **at lower prices**, the individual is **willing to buy more** of commodity x; **at higher prices**, she is **willing to buy less** of commodity x.

Therefore, **there is a negative/inverse relationship between price of a commodity and quantity demanded which is referred to as the Law of Demand.**

- **Law of Demand** states that other things being equal, there is a **negative relation between demand for a commodity and its price.** In other words, when price of the commodity increases, demand for it falls and when price of the commodity decreases, demand for it rises, other factors remaining the same.

The negative slope of the demand curve can also be explained in terms of the two effects namely, **substitution effect and income effect** that come into play when the price of a commodity changes.

- When good 'x' becomes cheaper, the consumer maximises his utility by substituting 'x' for good 'y' in order to derive the same level of satisfaction of a price change, resulting in an increase in demand for good 'x'.
- Moreover, as the price of good 'x' drops, consumer's purchasing power increases, which further increases demand for bananas (and good 'y'). This is the **income effect** of a price change, resulting in further increase in demand for bananas.

Demand Function

- If the prices of other goods, the consumer's income and her tastes and preferences remain unchanged, the amount of a good that the consumer optimally chooses, becomes entirely dependent on its price.
- The **demand function** is the relationship that determines how much of an item a buyer chooses to purchase at an optimal price. As a result, while all other factors stay the same, the consumer's demand function for a good indicates how much of the good they prefer at various price points.
- The relationship between a good's price and consumer demand can be expressed as

$$X = f(P)$$

where, X denotes the quantity and P denotes the price of the good.

Goods, Normal and Inferior Goods

- **Goods:** By goods we mean **physical, tangible objects** used to satisfy people's wants and needs. The term 'goods' should be contrasted with the term **'services',** which captures the **intangible** satisfaction of wants and needs.
- As compared to food items and clothes, which are examples of goods, we can think of the tasks that doctors and teachers perform for us as examples of services.
- **Normal Goods:** The quantity of a good that the **consumer demands can increase or decrease** with the rise in income depending on the nature of the good. For most goods, the quantity that a consumer chooses, increases as the consumer's income increases and decreases as the consumer's income decreases. Such goods are called normal goods.
- **Inferior Goods:** There are some goods the **demands** for which **move in the opposite**

direction of the income of the consumer. Such goods are called inferior goods. As the **income** of the consumer **increases**, the **demand** for an **inferior good falls,** and as the **income decreases,** the demand for an **inferior good rises.**

E.g.: Food items like coarse cereals, wheat flour and jowar flour

Giffen goods

- A **rise in the purchasing power** (income) of the consumer can sometimes induce the consumer to reduce the consumption of a good.
- In such a case, the substitution effect and the income effect will work in opposite directions.
- Depending on the relative strength of these two opposing effects, the price of an item might have a positive or negative relationship with its demand.
- The relationship between the price and demand of an item would remain inverse if the substitution effect outweighs the income effect.
- However, if the **income effect is stronger** than the substitution effect, the demand for the good would be positively related to its price. Such a good is called a Giffen good.
- Giffen good is an **inferior non-luxury good** for which **demand increases** as the price of the good rises, **contradicting the law of demand.** Giffen goods are **named after the Scottish economist Sir Robert Giffen,** who suggested their existence.

Substitutes and Complements

The quantity of a good that the consumer chooses can increase or decrease with the rise in the price of a related good depending on whether the two goods are substitutes or complementary to each other.

- Goods which are **consumed together** are called **complementary goods.**
  - ➢ Examples of goods which are complement to each other include tea and sugar, shoes and socks, pen and ink, etc.
  - ➢ Since tea and sugar are used together, an increase in the price of sugar is likely to decrease the demand for tea and a decrease in the price of sugar is likely to increase the demand for tea.
  - ➢ Generally speaking, the price of complementary goods moves in the opposite direction of the demand for a good.
- Goods like tea and coffee are not eaten together, in contrast to complements. As a matter of fact, they are mutually exclusive.
  - ➢ Due to the fact that tea can be used in place of coffee, its use is expected to grow if the price of coffee increases. On the other hand, tea usage is probably going to decline if coffee prices drop.
  - ➢ A good's demand typically follows the price of its alternatives in terms of movement.

Shifts in the Demand Curve

- Given the prices of other goods and the preferences of a consumer, **if the income increases,** the **demand for the good at each price changes,** and **hence, there is a shift in the demand curve.**
  - ➢ For normal goods, the demand curve shifts rightward and for inferior goods, the demand curve shifts leftward.

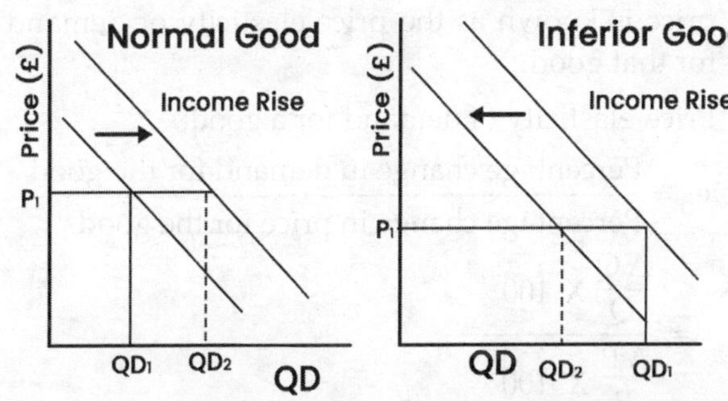

There is a rightward (positive) shift caused by income rising (a non-price factor) thus an increase in demand.

There is a leftward (negative) shift caused by a rise in income thus demand decreasing.

Shift in Demand Curve

- Given the consumer's income and her preferences, **if the price of a related good changes,** the **demand for a good at each level of its price changes,** and **hence, there is a shift in the demand curve.**
  - ➢ **If there is an increase in the price of a substitute good, the demand curve shifts rightward.**

- On the other hand, **if there is an increase in the price of a complementary good, the demand curve shifts leftward.**

- The demand curve can also shift due to a change in the tastes and preferences of the consumer.
  - **If the consumer's preferences change in favour of a good, the demand curve for such a good shifts rightward.**
  - On the other hand, **the demand curve shifts leftward due to an unfavourable change in the preferences of the consumer.**
  - The demand curve for ice-creams, for example, is likely to shift rightward in the summer because preference for ice-creams goes up in summer.
  - Revelation of the fact that cold-drinks might be injurious to health can adversely affect preferences for cold-drinks. This is likely to result in a leftward shift in the demand curve for cold-drinks.

Elasticity of Demand

- Price elasticity of demand refers to how easily a **good's demand can adjust in response to changes in its price**. The percentage change in a good's demand divided by the percentage change in its price is known as the price elasticity of demand for that good.
- Price-elasticity of demand for a good:

$$e_D = \frac{\text{Percentage change in demand for the good}}{\text{Percentage change in price for the good}}$$

$$= \frac{\frac{\Delta Q}{Q} \times 100}{\frac{\Delta P}{P} \times 100}$$

$$= \left(\frac{\Delta Q}{Q}\right) \times \left(\frac{P}{\Delta P}\right)$$

Where, ΔP is the change in price of the good and ΔQ is the change in quantity of the good

- **Elasticity can be described as:**
  - **Elastic or very responsive**: When the percentage change in quantity demanded is more than the percentage change in market price, the demand is said to be highly responsive to changes in market price and the estimated **eD is more than one (eD > 1).** The demand for the good is said to be elastic at that price. E.g., Demand for luxury goods.
  - **Inelastic or not very responsive:** When the percentage change in quantity demanded is less than the percentage change in market price, **eD is estimated to be less than one (eD < 1)** and the demand for the good is said to be inelastic at that price. e.g., Demand for essential goods.
  - **Unitary elastic:** When the percentage change in quantity demanded equals the percentage change in its market price, **eD is** estimated to be **equal to one (eD = 1)** and the demand for the good is said to be Unitary-elastic at that price.

Supply

- A firm's **'supply'** is the quantity that it chooses **to sell at a given price**, given technology, and given the prices of factors of production.
- **Quantity supplied** refers to a specific amount of **commodity offered for sale** at a particular price at a point of time.
- The **supply curve** of a firm shows the **levels of output** that the firm **chooses to produce** corresponding to **different values of the market price,** again keeping technology and prices of factors of production unchanged.

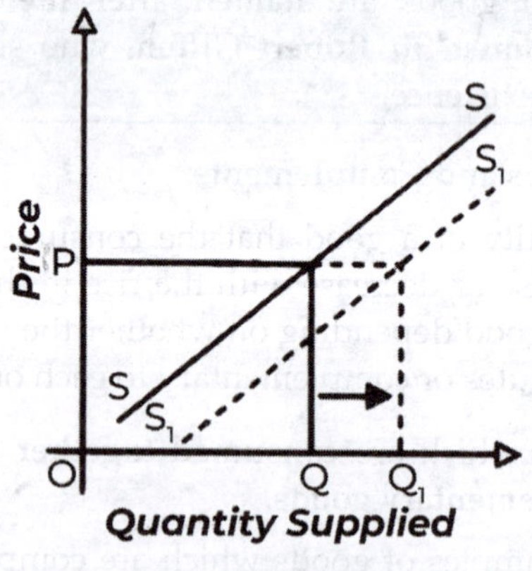

Supply Curve

- The **supply curve is upward sloping** as it follows the law of Supply which states that **there is a direct relationship between the price of the good and quantity supplied of the good.** That is,

as prices go up, quantity supplied increases and **as prices go down, quantity supplied decreases.**

- Law of Supply
  - Law of supply states that there is a **direct and positive relation between price of a good and its quantity supplied**, other things being constant.
  - **As the price of a good rises, the suppliers will supply more of that good and as the price of a good falls, the suppliers will supply less of that good** as the consumers are paying less for that good.
    - E.g., If the price of rice is 10 then the quantity supplied is 100. So, when the price increases to 20, the quantity supplied becomes 200. Similarly, if the price decreases from Rs. 20 to Rs. 10, the quantity supplied decreases from 200 to 100.

Production And Costs

Production

- Production is the process by which **inputs are transformed into 'output'.** Production is carried out by producers or **firms.** A firm acquires different inputs like labour, machines, land, raw materials etc. It uses these inputs to produce output.
  - This output can be consumed by consumers, or used by other firms for further production.
- In order to acquire inputs a firm has to pay for them. This is called the **cost of production**. Once output has been produced, the firm sells it in the market and earns **revenue.** The difference between the revenue and cost is called the firm's **profit**.
- The inputs that a firm uses in the production process are called **factors of production**.

Short Run And The Long Run

- In the near term, capital or labour are the only two factors that are fixed because they are neither changeable. The company can only change the other factor in order to change the output level. The variable factor is the one that the company may change, whereas the fixed element is the one that stays constant.
- In the **long run**, **all factors of production can be varied.** A firm in order to produce different levels of output in the long run may vary both the inputs simultaneously. So, **in the long run, there is no fixed factor.**
- We define a period as long run or short run simply by looking at **whether all the inputs can be varied or not.**

Total Product, Average Product and Marginal Product

- **Total Product:** It refers to the **total quantity or amount of output** produced by a given level of **input**, such as labour. It represents the **cumulative production** resulting from the **combination of inputs.** The relationship between the variable input and output, keeping all other inputs constant, is often referred to as **Total Product (TP)** of the variable input.
- **Average product:** Average product is the **total product** divided by the **quantity of input used.** It represents the average output per unit of input. Average product provides an **indication of the productivity** of each unit of input.
- **Marginal product**: It is defined as the **change in output** per unit of **change in the input** when all other inputs are held constant. It represents the additional output gained by adding an extra unit of input.

Costs

Short Run Costs

- In the short run, some of the factors of production cannot be varied, and therefore, remain fixed. The cost that a firm incurs to employ these fixed inputs is called the **total fixed cost (TFC).**
- Whatever amount of output the firm produces, this **cost remains fixed for the firm**. To produce any required level of output, the firm, in the short run, can adjust only variable inputs. Accordingly, the cost that a firm incurs to employ these variable inputs is called the **total variable cost (TVC).** Adding the fixed and the variable costs, we get the **total cost (TC)** of a firm.
- In order to increase the production of output, the firm must employ more of the variable inputs. As a result, total variable cost and total cost will

increase. Therefore, **as output increases, total variable cost and total cost increase.**

Long Run Costs

- In the long run, **all inputs are variable.** There are **no fixed costs.**
- The total cost and the total variable cost therefore, coincide in the long run.

> ✓ **Shut Down Point**: The last price-output combination at which the firm produces positive output is the **Shut Down Point.**
>
> ✓ **Normal Profit:** The minimum level of profit that is needed to keep a firm in the existing business is defined as normal profit. A firm that does not make normal profits is not going to continue in business. Normal profits are therefore **a part of the firm's total costs.**
>
> ✓ **Super-normal profit:** Super-normal profit is the profit a company makes **over and beyond its average profit.**
>
> ✓ **Break-even point**: The firm's break-even point is the location on the supply curve where it only makes a regular profit.

The Theory of the Firm Under Perfect Competition

- **Perfect Competition** - A perfectly competitive market has the following defining features:

1. The market consists of a **large number of buyers and sellers**. It means that each individual buyer and seller is very small compared to the size of the market. This means that no individual buyer or seller can influence the market by their size.
2. **Each firm produces and sells a homogenous product** i.e., the product of one firm cannot be differentiated from the product of any other firm. It means that the product of each firm is identical. So, a buyer can choose to buy from any firm in the market, and she gets the same product.
3. **Entry into the market as well as exit from the market are free** for firms. This condition is essential for the large numbers of firms to exist. If entry was difficult, or restricted, then the number of firms in the market could be small.
4. **Information is perfect**. It implies that all buyers and all sellers are completely informed about the price, quality and other relevant details about the product, as well as the market.

Market Equilibrium

- The **goal of consumers is to maximise their preferences,** while the **goal of businesses is to maximum their profits.** In the equilibrium, the goals of enterprises and consumers are consistent.
- A state in which all consumers' and enterprises' plans align and the **market clears** is known as an **equilibrium**. When the market is **in equilibrium, supply and demand are equal**; that is, the total amount that all businesses want to sell and the total amount that all customers want to purchase.
- The price at which equilibrium is reached is called **equilibrium price** and the quantity bought and sold at this price is called **equilibrium quantity.**
- **If at a price, market supply is greater than market demand,** we say that **there is an excess supply in the market at that price** and **if market demand exceeds market supply at a price,** it is said that **excess demand exists in the market at that price.**
- Therefore, another way to describe equilibrium in a completely competitive market is as a scenario where there is **zero surplus supply** and **zero excess demand.**
- There is a propensity for prices to fluctuate whenever market supply and demand are out of balance, which results in an unbalanced market.

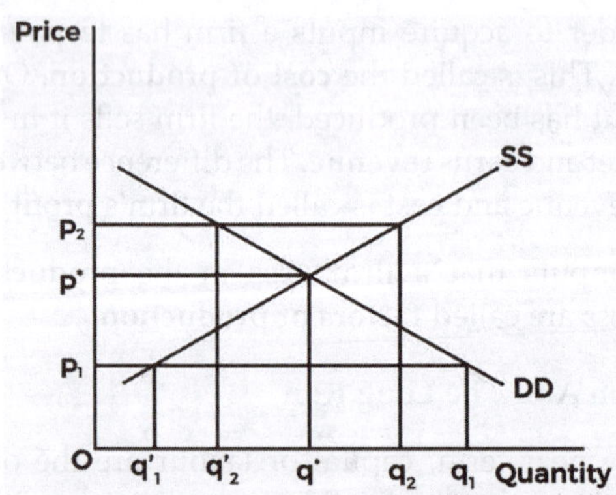

Market Equilibrium with Fixed Number of Firms. *Equilibrium occurs at the intersection of the market demand curve DD and market supply curve SS. The equilibrium quantity is q* and the equilibrium price is p*. At a price greater than p*, there will be excess supply, and at a price below p*, there will be excess demand.*

Equilibrium

Simultaneous Shifts of Demand and Supply

The simultaneous shifts can happen in four possible ways:

(i) Both supply and demand curves shift rightwards.

(ii) Both supply and demand curves shift leftwards.

(iii) Supply curve shifts leftward and demand curve shifts rightward.

(iv) Supply curve shifts rightward and demand curve shifts leftward.

Shift in Demand	Shift in Demand	Quantity	Price
Leftward	Leftward	Decreases	May increase, decrease or remain unchanged
Rightwar	Rightwar	Increases	May increase, decrease or remain unchanged
Leftward	Rightwar	May increase, decrease or remain unchanged	Decreases
Rightwar	Leftward	May increase, decrease or remain unchanged	Increases

Impact of Simultaneous Shifts on Equilibrium

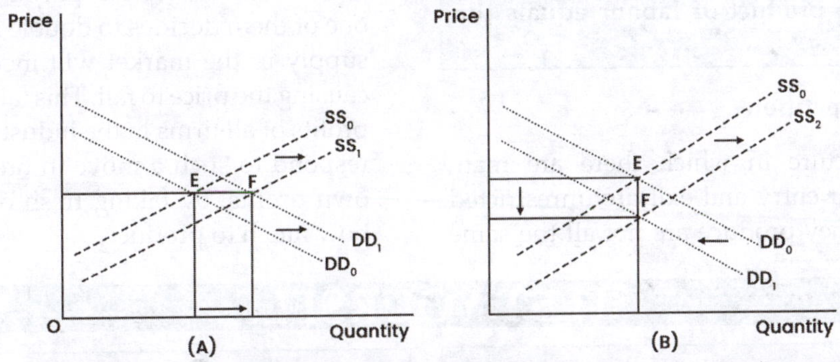

***Simultaneous Shifts in Demand and Supply.** Initially, the equilibrium is at E where the demand curve DD, and supply curve SS, intersect. In panel (a), both the supply and the demand curves shift rightwards leaving price unchanged but quantity getting increased In panel (b), the supply curve shifts rightward and demand curve shifts leftward leaving quantity unchanged but price decreased.*

Simultaneous Shifts in Demand and Supply

Price Floor: The **government establishes** floors or minimum prices for various commodities and services because it is undesirable for their prices to drop below a specific point. Price floors are **lower limits set** by the government on what can be charged for specific goods or services. The most well-known instances of price floors being imposed are **minimum wage laws** and agricultural price support programmes.

- There is surplus demand when a price ceiling (i.e. maximum price at which a good can be sold) is imposed below the equilibrium price.
- An excess supply results from imposing a price floor above the equilibrium price.

Non-Competitive Markets

Monopoly

- A monopoly is a type of market arrangement where there is **only one seller**. A market system with a monopoly demands that -

➢ A specific commodity is produced by a single entity.

➢ This commodity cannot be replaced by any other commodity;

➢ And for this to continue over time, there must be enough barriers in place to stop any other company from joining the market and beginning to sell the commodity.

- **Consumers** are **price takers** in this market.

> **Note**
>
> In general, there is an **inverse relationship between competitive behaviour and competitive market structure:** the more competitive the market structure, the less competitive the company behaviour. Conversely, more firms will behave competitively towards one another under a less competitive market structure. There isn't another company to compete with in a monopoly.
>
> Each firm employs labour upto the point where the **marginal revenue product of labour equals the wage rate.**

Monopolistic Competition

- A market structure in which there are many enterprises, their entry and exit are unrestricted, but the goods they produce are not all the same. We refer to this type of market structure as monopolistic competition.
- Monopolistic competition is commonly found in industries such as **restaurants, clothing, personal care products, and consumer electronics**, where firms try to differentiate their products through branding, design, or other unique features.

Oligopoly

- An oligopoly is a market structure in which there are many vendors in a given commodity market, but the **total number of sellers is small.**
- **Duopoly** is the name given to the unique instance of oligopoly in which there are **precisely two vendors.**
- **Assumption** is that the **products** that both companies sell are **identical** and
- The level of output in the industry, the level of prices, as well as the profits, are outcomes of **how firms are interacting** with each other. For example, if the two firms in a duopoly are equal in size, and one of them decides to double its output, the total supply in the market will increase substantially, causing the price to fall. This fall in price affects the profits of all firms in the industry. Other firms will respond to such a move in order to protect their own profits, by taking fresh decisions regarding how much to produce.

TEST YOURSELF

Multiple Choice Questions

Q1. If a commodity is provided free to the public by the Government, then (UPSC 2018)

(a) The opportunity cost is zero.

(b) The opportunity cost is ignored.

(c) The opportunity cost is transferred from the consumers of the product to the tax-paying public.

(d) The opportunity cost is transferred from the consumers of the product to the Government.

Q2. Which of the following describes Total Utility:

(a) It refers to the total satisfaction or benefit that a consumer derives from consuming a certain quantity of a good or service

(b) It is the change in total utility due to consumption of one additional unit of a commodity.

(c) Total utility from consuming each additional unit of a commodity declines as its consumption increases

(d) Total utility is consumption of all goods and services.

Answer Key	
Q1.	c
Q2.	a

Model Questions for Main Examination

Q1. What is the Indifference Curve and what are its features?

Q2. What are substitutes and complements? How do they impact the demand for goods?